JESUS AND HIS CHURCH

Authors in the Biblical and Theological Classics Library:

JESUS AND HIS CHURCH

A STUDY OF THE IDEA OF THE
ECCLESIA IN THE NEW TESTAMENT

By
R. Newton Flew
M.A., D.D.

paternoster
press

Reprinted in 1998 by Paternoster Publishing
as part of the Biblical and Theological Classics Library series

04 03 02 01 00 99 98   7 6 5 4 3 2 1

Paternoster Publishing is an imprint of Paternoster Publishing,
P.O. Box 300, Carlisle, Cumbria, CA3 0QS, U.K.
http//www.paternoster-publishing.com

British Library Cataloguing in Publication Data
A catalogue record for this book is available from the British Library.

ISBN 0-85364-877-8

Cover Design by Mainstream, Lancaster
Typeset by WestKey Ltd, Falmouth Cornwall
Printed in Great Britain by
Caledonian International Book Manufacturing Ltd., Glasgow

TO MY FIRST TEACHER IN THEOLOGY

Quaerebamus inter nos apud praesentem Veritatem
(St. Augustine, writing of his mother)

Contents

PART THREE

The Unity of the Apostolic Teaching

PART FOUR

Preface

'Sir, you wish to serve God and go to heaven? Remember that you cannot serve Him alone. You must therefore find companions, or make them; the Bible knows nothing of solitary religion.'[1] This advice of an unnamed 'serious man' to John Wesley was influential in the formation of the Holy Club in 1729. The rejection of mere individualism in religion ultimately leads to a doctrine of the nature of the Church. But is the idea of the Ecclesia to be found in the teaching of our Lord? This is the problem handled in the present book, which is therefore offered as a contribution to the study of New Testament theology.

The invitation to deliver the Fernley-Hartley Lecture for 1938 came to me with a request that the subject should be related to the task of the great oecumenical movements which are seeking to bring together the separated communions of Christendom. The trustees thought it fitting that, in a year of world-wide commemoration of the conversion of the Wesleys, the eyes of Methodist students should be turned to the future, and to the relation of Christians to one another. As one of the three representatives of the Methodist Church who had been appointed to attend both the Oxford World Conference on Life and Work, and the Edinburgh World Conference on Faith and Order, I was naturally eager to respond to this request. For some years now, I have been occupied, both in private study and in public lectures,

---

[1] Henry Moore, *Life of John Wesley* (1824), i. 162; *Journal* (Standard ed. 1909), i. 469.

with the subject of 'The Idea of the Ecclesia in Christian Theology'. It had become clear that there was only one great Christian doctrine, that of the nature of the Church, which really divided the different communions from one another. It seemed to be the duty of a theological teacher to prepare for the discussions on that subject, which are likely to take place in the near future between representatives of the various traditions. I believe that it is a mistake to set the divisive subject of the Christian ministry in the central arena of debate, unless the prior question has first been faced: What is the nature of that Body to which the various ministries belong, and which its ministers serve? How is the Ecclesia constituted, and what makes it one, in spite of all severances?

The conviction that Christian people in the last two centuries have given insufficient attention to the doctrine of the Ecclesia was widely shared at the Oxford and Edinburgh World Conferences of 1937. In our own Church, the Methodist Conference of 1935, led by its Secretary, the Reverend Dr. Robert Bond, appointed a Committee to prepare a statement on 'The Nature of the Christian Church according to the Teaching of the Methodists'. This statement was adopted unanimously by the Methodist Conference of 1937, and was immediately published.[2]

Of that Committee I had the honour to be the Convener. I am deeply in debt to all its members, both for the inspiration and the friendliness of the discussions, and for the searching and constructive criticisms which all our varying views encountered; especially I should like to record gratitude to Dr. C. Ryder Smith, and to the Chairman, Dr. W. F. Lofthouse, whose sympathetic guidance made our arduous task easier. Similarly I must acknowledge a debt to the group of Cambridge theological teachers which meets in Professor Raven's rooms, and which for some time has been handling the larger problems of the nature of revelation; and to the company of theologians who met at Gloucester in August, 1936, to produce the report contained in *The Ministry and the Sacraments* (1937, ed. Dunkerley and Headlam).

---

[2]   By the Epworth Press.

As will be seen in the following pages, I am treading in the path made by that great Cambridge theologian, Professor F. J. A. Hort. I can agree whole-heartedly with Professor C. H. Dodd (*Essays Congregational and Catholic*, 1931) in his verdict on the famous Lectures of Hort, *The Christian Ecclesia*: 'the standard work to which we all go back . . . indeed it is so sober and objective that there is little of substance in it which is antiquated.' At the same time Hort does not give much attention to the problem with which the present lecture is concerned. To the writings of Professor Dodd himself, I must acknowledge my especial indebtedness. The sections on the Apostolic *kerygma* (chapter 8, *see* also Part III) presuppose the results demonstrated in his book, *The Apostolic Preaching and its Developments* (1936). I have continually used the magnificent work now being edited by Professor Gerhard Kittel, *Theologisches Wörterbuch zum Neuen Testament* (Kohlhammer, Stuttgart, 1932, and following years), and have availed myself of the surprisingly conservative conclusions to which these philological studies frequently lead. A book which I have found especially valuable is *Die Eschatologie des Reiches Gottes bei Jesus* (1931) by Professor Heinz Dietrich Wendland of the University of Kiel. I am in agreement with his chief conclusions. An interesting English article from his pen will be found in the Oxford World Conference volume on *The Kingdom of God and History* (1938).

It is a genuine pleasure to record my gratitude to my friends who have helped me in bringing out this book; especially to the Reverend Canon J. Martin Creed, D.D., Ely Professor in this University, and to the Reverend Vincent Taylor, D.D., Principal of Wesley College, Headingley, Leeds, both of whom, in their generosity, have placed their exact and profound scholarship at the disposal of a fellow-student; to Mr. C.J. Barker, M.A., of Preston, formerly Scholar of Christ Church, Oxford, and to my colleague in Wesley House, the Reverend William F. Flemington, M.A., both of whom have read the book again and again, with sympathetic vigilance; to the Reverend W. Harold Beales, M.A., who has helped me to guard against probable misunderstandings in the exposition of the teaching of our Lord on the Kingdom of

God; to the Reverend Philip S. Watson, M.A., lately Fellow of the University of Durham, and Mr. Kenneth Grayston, B.A., two members of this College, who have given most valuable help in the reading of the proofs; and to my wife, for help in the preparation of the indices. Of the one to whom the book is dedicated, I can say with Hort (*Life*, ii. 66): 'All men's debts to their mothers are great, and it is folly to imagine comparisons with the world of sons; but few, I think, can owe what I do.' I am daring enough to hope that others who were taught by their mothers and fathers to love the company of the people of God, will be helped by this book to help others also to understand the 'mystery' of the love which Christ has for His Church.

'"You shall understand that I am a Christian," said Victorinus. And Simplicianus answered: "I will not believe it, and I will not count you among the Christians, unless I see you in the Church of Christ." So Victorinus smiled on him, and said: "Is it then the walls that make Christians?"'(Augustine, *Confessions*, viii. 2). The old story has many modern parallels. Men have a quarrel with the Church which is not quite the same thing as their estrangement from Christ; and often when they think themselves privately reconciled to Him, they regard the Church as mere 'walls'. But such individualism falls short of Christianity. To belong to the people of Christ is to confess Him before men. It is deliverance, as Victorinus found, from 'being ashamed of the sacraments of the humility of God's Word'.

R. NEWTON FLEW.

WESLEY HOUSE,
CAMBRIDGE.
June 23, 1938.

Introduction

The world is living to-day in the shadow of a great fear. The conflict which threatens is due, at least in part, to a clash of doctrines. On the one side there is the principle of dictatorship, the 'Leader Principle'; on the other the principle of communism, or sharing. The first is conjoined with a political Messianism, the other with the dialectic materialism of Karl Marx. Both in their present expression are hostile to the principle of individual liberty. The proclamation of an all-embracing community life which claims to be the source and goal of every human activity is a challenge to the freedom, and ultimately to the existence, of the Christian Church.

But the Church is essentially the embodiment of an idea based on God's final revelation of His purpose for mankind, an idea which combines the principle of leadership and the principle of sharing, the idea of a divine authority and the idea of freedom for the individual to do the will of God in the service of all mankind. The conviction is growing[1] that the need of Christian people is a fresh vision of the Church of Christ as God meant it to be, His own creation, the instrument of His agelong purpose, the reconciling Body in which all mankind might meet in a worship and service which would extend to the farthest boundaries of human life.

---

[1] See the Report of the Oxford Conference on Life and Work, *The Churches Survey their Task* (1937), 29–34; and the Edinburgh *Report of the Second World Conference on Faith and Order* (1937), 8–13.

The present essay is intended as a contribution, however imperfect, towards the elucidation of the essential idea of the Ecclesia. Though in form it deals only with the New Testament, and even within that field of study makes no claim to display the riches of the New Testament doctrine of the Ecclesia, it arises out of practical needs. Christians generally have little understanding either of the place of the Ecclesia in the Christian revelation or of its oecumenical nature. It seems to the present writer that the first task is to break down the widespread doubt whether there is room for the idea of the Ecclesia in the teaching of our Lord. The major part of this book is therefore devoted to this question. The saying on which the foundation of the Church by our Lord has traditionally rested is insufficient ground on which to build the great edifice. Although following Karl Ludwig Schmidt, Kattenbusch, and others, in believing that saying to be substantially genuine, I cannot but think that the rest of His teaching, and the concurrent witness of the life of the primitive Church, afford a surer basis for the conviction that He was working with an Ecclesia in view.

The argument of Part One is divided into three unequal chapters. In the first place, the idea of the Kingdom of God is examined. The conviction underlying this section is shared by many modern scholars, that the phrase primarily denotes the Reign or Sovereignty or Kingly Rule of God, and as a second or derivative meaning, the sphere in which the rule is exercised, the realm or 'domain' of God. But the Rule is never to be equated or identified with those who enter it. These are the subjects of the Rule, who enter it, live under it, and are governed by it. It is a profound mistake to infer that the rejection of the medieval view, that the Ecclesia equals the Kingdom of God on earth, implies that the Ecclesia is being dismissed from the teaching of Jesus. The Ecclesia is indeed the necessary correlative to the *Basileia*, or Kingly Rule. It is destined to be the instrument of the divine purpose revealed in the preaching and activity of Jesus, who Himself manifests the Kingly Rule of God. Similarly, it is a mistake to suppose that those who reject the modern view of the Kingdom of God as merely equivalent to the organization of a world brotherhood believe that the Kingdom is only a spiritual relation between the individual and his God, and are therefore minimizing the Christian motive for the transformation of society.[2] The Kingdom of God is God Himself in His kingly activity. The Lord's Prayer is for the new era to come on earth as it already is in heaven. This eschatological prayer is directed towards the final consummation of the era which has already been inaugurated by the work of Jesus. The whole activity of Jesus, therefore, is the warrant for those who believe that part of the mission of the Ecclesia is to transform the relationships of men with one another, as a necessary result of the message that God's reign is already here. It is in His teaching that we may see portrayed that care for the whole area of human life and suffering which should distinguish His Church.

Chapter 2 deals with the objection that in view of the expected end of human history, Jesus could not have contemplated the gathering of a new community. The answer is that there was an interval in time between the first announcement of the Reign of God as present, and the final consummation. The recorded prophecies of Jesus contemplate a series of events in time, and Jesus did not know how long that interval would be.

The third and longest chapter contains a fivefold argument:

(1) The preaching of Jesus is directed to the re-constitution of Israel in view of the advent of God's Rule. The little flock to which He speaks is the true Israel.

(2) The ethical teaching of Jesus can only be understood aright as directed to this nucleus of the New Israel, and as involving a promise of God's power to enable the disciples to translate the teaching into life. Thus the ethical teaching points forward to the gift of the Spirit promised for the Last Days.

(3) The conception of Messiahship, especially in the form in which Jesus uses it, inevitably implies the gathering of a new community.

(4) The conception of the 'Word' or 'Gospel', or 'Mystery', which Jesus proclaims, is regarded as constitutive of the new

---

[2] R. J. Barker in a fine and moving book, *It Began in Galilee (1938),* 33–6, *has taken this view.*

community. Those who receive the divine 'Word' know that it is 'good news'. To those who reject the Gospel it is a 'Mystery' not yet revealed. The Gospel includes the idea of a new covenant to be established with the newly constituted People of God.

(5) The Mission of the New Community is declared when Jesus sends forth disciples.

Underlying these five arguments there is a conviction that three decisive moments may be discerned in the action of Jesus in constituting the Ecclesia. First He 'called' disciples and taught them. Second, He sent them forth to proclaim the good news that the new era had dawned, and their proclamation was both by word and in deed. Third, at the Last Supper He instituted the new covenant with them as representing the new people of God.

In Part Two, on the life of the Primitive Church, these five arguments reappear as five marks characterizing the early community, and this may be taken as additional evidence that the first disciples already had been made familiar with these ideas through the teaching and actions of our Lord. In Part Three the essential unity of the apostolic teaching is demonstrated by appeal to five writers of the New Testament, and in a final chapter certain conclusions are drawn as to the principle of authority to be deduced from this consensus.

The result of the argument may seem surprisingly conservative to those who are acquainted with the criticism of the fifty years since Hort wrote his famous lectures on *The Christian Ecclesia*. But the conservative result has not been reached by the traditional route. If the reader is inclined to feel impatient with the attention given to questions of the authenticity of the Sayings of Jesus, I would remind him that these doubts of the lecture room have a way of reappearing at meetings in the open air. It is true that they usually appear years after they have been answered by scholars. But that does not absolve students of the Gospels from studying them, especially as they involve the problem of the preservation of the tradition between A.D. 30 and A.D. 65. In the discussion of the present subject the question of authenticity is unusually important, inasmuch as many conservative scholars have abandoned the belief that the words in Matthew xvi. 18–19 were actually spoken by Jesus.[3] It will be noticed that these words are only reviewed and interpreted at the end of Part One (123–35) after the main argument for the presence of the Ecclesia in the teaching of Jesus has been developed.

But if the substance of that argument be accepted on the ground of other sayings which are hardly ever disputed, the doctrine of the nature of the Christian Ecclesia which we find in St. Paul and St. John is seen in a fresh light. The universal conviction of the early Christians that the Church was the true Israel is thus traced to Jesus Himself. The consciousness of severance from the worship and ritual of the historical Israel is not an essential element in this conviction. Jesus continued His appeals to Israel till His death. His disciples after His resurrection immediately renewed those appeals to the very people who had murdered Him. The rule of preaching of the Apostle of the Gentiles was always: To the Jew first! But every act of rejection was accentuating the separation between the new Israel and those who, in the Christian view, were forfeiting the promises made of old.

I have not thought it necessary in the following chapters to include a detailed survey of the actual uses of the word Ecclesia in the New Testament.[4] Here it is enough to note that the two chief uses of the word as applied to the Church are: (1) the whole company of believers in some particular place; (2) the universal Church on earth, to which all Christians belong. These two meanings are probably derived from the fact that in the Septuagint, *Ecclesia* is the common translation of the Hebrew *qāhāl*, the holy congregation of Israel. The local community is a microcosm

---

[3] An interesting recent discussion is in *Romanism and the Gospel* (1937), by Dr. C. A. Anderson Scott, 212–18.

[4] Hort's account is still valuable, *The Christian Ecclesia*, 3–16; see also Burton, *Galatians*, 417–20, W. K. Lowther Clarke, *Divine Humanity*, 151–60; Cadbury in *Beginnings of Christianity* (1933), v. 387–9; P. G. S. Hopwood, *Religious Experience of the Primitive Church* (1936), 227–30. But the chief discussions are in Kittel's *Theologisches Wörterbuch*, iii. 502 ff., and *Die Kirche im Neuen Testament* in the *Festgabe für Deissmann* (1932, 2nd ed. 1932), both by K. L. Schmidt.

of the whole Church. Here then we have a word which could cover both meanings, and convey the idea that each local community was linked inseparably with the one universal community of Christians throughout the world. A great claim was involved in the choice of the word. 'The new religion did not start as a group of conventicle cult-communities.'[5] The primary meaning is that of the whole assembly of the faithful gathered together in worship before God, in whatever local community they might actually be found. They were heirs of a great tradition, stretching far back to the call of Abraham, but they were also actually entering into the promised inheritance. They were seeing with their own eyes the fulfilment of the final purpose of God.

---

[5] J. Weiss, *History of Primitive Christianity* (E. tr. 1937), ii. 617.

Part One

The Teaching of Jesus

Chapter One

The *Basileia* and the *Ecclesia*

In this world of space and time Christianity must always take form as a visible community, and therefore the idea of the Church is essential to Christian theology. 'Just as you cannot say "citizen" without implying the State, so, the New Testament teaches, you cannot say "Christian" without in turn implying the Church.'[1] But in the course of the nineteenth century this truth was often neglected or obscured. Even Christian thinkers did not always find it necessary to expound the nature of the Church as one of the essential doctrines of the Faith. Indeed the doubt was entertained whether the Church could be regarded in any sense as a deliberate and direct foundation of Christ.

Thus the master among the historians of primitive Christianity, Adolf Harnack himself, declared that both the Catholic view and the Protestant view of the foundation of the Church by Christ 'have the whole historical development of the apostolic and post-apostolic age against them'. Besides, 'they stand or fall with the question of the authenticity of a few New Testament passages, especially in the Gospel of Matthew'. If these were put aside, then every direct external bond between Jesus and the 'Church' would be severed, but there would remain the inner spiritual bond, 'even if Jesus neither founded nor even intended the Church'. So Harnack concludes that the Church was a 'tortuous double development'. Those early disciples had a spiritual experience of God, but

---

[1]   H. R. Mackintosh, *The Divine Initiaive* (1921), 89.

they were members of a definite historical organization, the Jewish theocracy. The Catholic Church was the inevitable result of the attempt to unite the spiritual with the institutional, and this union was outside the intention of Jesus Christ.[2]

There is a strange dualism lurking behind these views, and it is still not without influence to-day. But the study of early Christianity has led the successors of Harnack far away from the views of their master. At first the rise and progress of that school of interpretation which placed the teaching of Jesus within an eschatological framework did nothing to encourage a return to traditional views. If the present age was about to end and the Son of Man was expected to return on the clouds in glory, what place is left for the Church and its institutional life in the mind of our Lord? So a modern expositor can ask: 'Could Jesus speak of an organized earthly institution between the Jewish national fellowship and the future Kingdom of God?'[3] He expects the answer, 'No'.

Another influential writer declares that Jesus 'had not consciously formed a society', though the Church was 'the inevitable outcome of His work'.[4] Troeltsch assumes that the first outstanding characteristic of the ethics of Jesus is an unlimited, unqualified individualism, and then asserts that during the time of Jesus' life on earth there was no sign of an organized community,[5] 'Jesus founded no Church'[6] – this statement has become almost a dogma of critical orthodoxy.[7]

There is probably some confusion in the meaning assigned to the word Church. The word is being used in a modern sense. If by the statement, 'Jesus did not organize a Church', Troeltsch means that Jesus did not lay down a constitution or ordain a graduated hierarchy of officials who were to govern the community, we may all agree. Similarly, we may agree that He did not

---

[2]   Harnack, *The Constitution and Law of the Church* (E. tr. 1910), 3–5, 257–8.

[3]   Klostemann, *Das Matthäusevangelium* (1927), 140.

[4]   E. F. Scott, *The Gospel and its Tributaries* (1928), 78, 79.

[5]   *Social Teaching of the Christian Churches*, 55, 62.

[6]   Michaelis, *Täufer, Jesus, Urgemeinde* (1928), 105.

[7]   Linton, *Das Problem der Urkirche* (1932), 179.

deliberately plan for a community which should be immediately separated from Judaism, as the Christian Church became in the course of a few decades separate from the Jews. But if 'Church' means a new religious community, with a new way of life, a fresh and startling message, and an unparalleled consciousness of inheriting the divine promises made to Israel of old, then Jesus did most certainly, as I hope to show, take action with such a community in view. Indeed, He gathered such a community when He chose His disciples and when He sent them forth to preach. Perhaps we shall be compelled to penetrate farther back to the very message which He proclaimed as involving essentially the gathering of a new community. If the phrase 'organizing a Church' may include the idea of taking action in this world of space and time whereby a new confraternity should be created to be an instrument of God's final purpose for human history, then in that sense Jesus 'organized a Church'.

It would seem therefore that for the sake of clarity we should abandon the particular form in which the problem has been posed. Instead of asking, 'Did Jesus found the Church?' or 'Did Jesus organize a Church?' we should ask whether Jesus directed His teaching to a particular community, and whether His ministry had in view the formation of a community as one of His dominant aims. If we are driven by the facts to an affirmative answer, we should also inquire whether His teaching enables us to describe the community which He has in view with any degree of definiteness, so as to determine its characteristic marks, its essence, and abiding idea. The question whether such a community could be contained in the Judaism of the first century, or whether a decisive break would be necessary, need not have been answered by Him, or even raised in His mind. The outward structure and organization of such a community – the officials required, the particular forms which its assemblies might assume when His followers joined in worship or prayer or deliberation, the construction of formulae in which the distinctive beliefs of such a community might be marked off from the beliefs of other Jews – all such questions, which were doubtless inevitable at a later stage, would hardly have been asked. Some outward structure is required by any confraternity, however loosely organized. Before the end of His life there were two simple rites which in different ways He sanctioned. The choice of twelve men in itself implies the beginning of an organization. The teaching of a particular prayer is the beginning of a distinctive worship. But in His earthly life a community of followers is already gathered around Him, and in that community later generations have recognized the prototype and essential embodiment of the idea of the Ecclesia. We may, for example, still be able to claim Hort's sentence[8] as historically accurate, when he says of the disciples at the Last Supper: 'The Twelve sat that evening as representatives of the Ecclesia at large.'

An answer to the question which has thus been raised must depend on a more thorough investigation than was possible at the beginning of this century, as to the meaning of 'the Kingdom of God' for the mind of our Lord. What is the relation of the Kingdom to the Ecclesia?

At this point the modern student encounters two types of explanation which do not meet the facts, but which are widely current to-day. According to the first, the Kingdom may mean the Utopia which some day is to be established on earth by human progress or by human effort. It may mean 'the organization of humanity through action inspired by love' (Ritschl), or 'the universal moral community, the aspect under which humanity is included in God's purpose for Himself' (Herrmann). This is a modern view. According to the second and older explanation, the Kingdom of God on earth is identified with the Church. The equation is made by Roman Catholics[9] who appeal to a passage of St. Augustine where he apparently makes the identification. Through Luther and Bucer and Calvin this view has passed into the traditional Protestant exegesis. Thus the Dragnet (Matt. xiii. 47–50) is identified with the Church in Calvin's commentary on the Gospels.[10] The 'field' in the Parable of the Tares is allegorized as the Church.[11] This exegesis is reproduced in the twentieth

---

[8] *The Christian Ecclesia*, 30.

[9] e.g. Karl Adam, *Spirit of Catholicim* (E. tr. 1929), 14.

[10] E. tr. (Calvin Translation Society), ii. 133.

[11] Op. Cit., ii. 119.

century by Swete[12] and others, and the resultant doctrine is woven into systematic form by Fairbairn: 'The Kingdom is the immanent Church, and the Church is the explicated Kingdom, and nothing alien to either can be in the other . . . the Church is the Kingdom done into living souls and the society they constitute.'[13] The student of to-day has no easy task if he dares to withstand an interpretation which has held sway for many centuries.

But there is now a widespread agreement that the primary meaning of the word *Basileia* is 'kingly rule', or 'kingship',[14] or 'sovereignty'. Other meanings are secondary and derivative. There are several converging lines of evidence whereby this conclusion may be established.

(1) The Hebrew word *Malkuth* when applied to God means the 'kingly rule', never the 'kingdom', as if it were meant to suggest the territory governed by Him.[15] Naturally the kingly rule of God does not operate in the void. God rules over the world of nature; He has subjects who are governed by Him. But these subjects could not be spoken of as constituting the Malkuth. Indeed, according to Hebrew thought, the omnipotent rule of God was an eternal reality even if all men rebelled against Him, even if the kings of the earth set themselves in array and sought to break His bands asunder, God will have the last word. His almighty power 'was not in Judaism a theological attribute of omnipotence which belongs in idea to the perfection of God; it was as in the prophets, the assurance that nothing can withstand his judgement or thwart his purpose' (see especially Isaiah x ff.). 'The omnipotence of God

---

[12] *The Parables of the Kingdom* (1920), 28–31, 56. For a more accurate exegesis see C. H. Dodd, *Parables of the Kingdom* (1935), 183–8; B. T. D. Smith, *The Parables of the Synoptic Gospels* (1937), 196–201.

[13] *Christ in Modern Theology* (4th ed. 1893), 529; see also James Denney, *Studies in Theology* (1906), 184. I owe these two references to the Rev. E. C. Blackman, *Expository Times* (May 1936), 370.

[14] K. L. Schmidt, in *Theologisches Wörterbuch*, i. 582; Rawlinson, *St. Mark* (1925), liii; V. Taylor, *Jesus and His Sacrifice* (1937), 8–11; I may refer to an extended exposition in my book, *The Idea of Perfection* (1934), 8–40.

[15] Dalman, *The Words of Jesus* (E. tr. 1902), 94.

is thus interlocked with the teleology of history. . . . His plan includes a golden age for his people.'[16] Hardly ever in the Old Testament do we encounter the phrase 'in the Kingdom of God'. In I Chron. xvii. 14 'the word of God' to Nathan includes the prophecy for the seed of David: 'I will settle him in mine house and in my kingdom for ever: and his throne shall be established for ever.' Even here the word translated kingdom means kingly rule. It is God who gives to the descendants of David their kingly rule. So, too, the famous passage in Daniel vii contains the promise of the kingdom given 'to the people of the saints of the Most High'. Here the Aramaic word *Malku* is used of the rule given to the pre-eminently righteous in Israel over all the surviving nations. It does not mean that the saints of the Most High constitute a community among themselves; they exercise a sovereignty delegated to them by God Himself.[17]

(2) In the Rabbinic literature the Kingdom of God again means His kingship, 'never the sphere which is governed by Him'.[18] The frequent phrase: 'to take the yoke of the kingdom of God on oneself' means to acknowledge God as King and Lord.[19] Thus in the Tractate Berakhoth, R. Joshua ben Karha (c. A.D. 130–160) speaks of 'accepting the yoke of the kingdom of Heaven' as referring to the recitation of the Shema, the acknowledgement of the unity of God.[20] Earlier still, R. Jochanan ben Zakkai (*c*. A.D. 80) makes mention of the yoke of the kingdom of heaven alongside of the yoke of flesh and blood, thereby bringing God into contrast with men.[21] The value of this evidence is not dependent on the date of the instances quoted. They bear their testimony to the strong reluctance of Hebrew teachers to confuse

---

[16] G. F. Moore, *Judiasm*, i. 375.

[17] Von Rad in *Theol. Wörterbuch*, i. 569; Montgomery, *Daniel* (I.C.C., 1927), 178, 315; Charles, *Book of Daniel* (1929), cxii–cxiii. 187, where Charles infers that the faithful remnant of Israel are to be transformed into heavenly or supernatural beings as in 1 Enoch xc. 38.

[18] Kuhn, in *Theol. Wörterbuch*, i. 570.

[19] Examples in Skack-Billerbeck i. 173 ff. *passim*.

[20] Danby, *The Mishna* (1933), 3; *Berakhoth*, 2, 2.

[21] Dalman, *The Words Of Jesus*, 92.

the rule of God with the human beings over whom that rule is exercised. But they held to the hope that a time would come when all men would own and serve the one true God. 'The Lord shall be King over all the earth; in that day shall the Lord be one, and his name one' (Zech. xiv. 9). 'For this supremacy of God the familiar Jewish name is Malkut Shamaim, the kingdom of heaven, by which is to be understood not the realm over which God rules, but His *kingship*, His character of king.'[22]

(3) It is remarkable that in the first four centuries of the Christian era the identification of the Church with the kingdom of God on earth is nowhere made. Usually in the patristic literature the kingdom is regarded as future; in Clement of Alexandria and Origen, and in those who follow in their steps, it is also the inward and spiritual reign of God in the soul. Even in St. Ambrose, whose reverence for the Church is manifest, I have not discovered any passage where the kingdom is regarded as a society. The earliest readers of the Gospels did not interpret the kingdom as meaning the Church. It has recently been urged by Professor Lake on the strength of some passages in the Gospels (Matt. xiii. 52, Matt. xi. 7 ff. = Luke vii. 24 ff.) which will be discussed later, that 'it is tolerably certain that some Christians, possibly in Antioch, thought of the kingdom of God as the Church'.[23] It is certainly a difficulty for such a view that those Christians left no successors for three centuries.

(4) The evidence of the words of Jesus as recorded in the Synoptic Gospels must provide the final arbitrament on this question. Principal Vincent Taylor, in his recent work *Jesus and His Sacrifice*, has pointed out that if we exclude parallel versions of the same saying, there are sixty sayings and parables in which Jesus speaks of the Basileia. Only in nine of these sixty 'is the thought of a community prominent or distinctive. . . . In the overwhelming majority the thought is that of the Reign or Rule of God'.[24]

---

[22] G. F. Moore, *Judaism*, ii. 371–2
[23] *Beginnnings of Christianity* (1920), i. 331; cf. iv. 4, 239.
[24] pp. 8–9.

(*a*) This Kingly Rule is to be consummated in the future, when it may be said to have 'come'. Jesus taught His disciples to pray:

> Thy Kingdom come:
> Thy will be done,
>> As in heaven,
>> So on earth.

But the coming of the Rule is nevertheless anticipated in the activity of Jesus. 'If I by the finger of God cast out devils, then the kingdom of God has come upon you.'[25] This may be described as 'realized eschatology', if we allow that the full realization of God's Rule is still reserved by Jesus for the future. It is Jesus Himself who represents in His own preaching, teaching, and redemptive activities the final establishment of God's kingly Rule on earth. This Rule is dynamic; God is always active.[26] When Jesus does His mighty deeds, He does them 'by the finger of God'. There is essentially no difference in meaning between this phrase and the parallel phrase in Matthew, 'by the Spirit of God'. In Hebrew thought the Spirit is God Himself, active in the world of men. But it is noticeable that the only references to 'the finger of God' in the Old Testament are to certain epochal events, which to the Hebrew mind lit up the meaning of history. Thus in Psalm viii. 3 the heavens are the work of the finger of God. This is a reference to the creation. In Exodus viii. 19, 'the magicians said unto Pharaoh, This is the finger of God'. God's activity is marked at the time of the signal deliverance of the nation from Egypt. In Exodus xxxi. 18, we read:

'And he gave unto Moses, when he had made an end of communing with him upon Mount Sinai, the two tables of the testimony, tables of stone, written with the finger of God.'

Here are three notable evidences of God's activity in the world, first at the creation, then in the redemption of His people from the house of bondage, and finally in the giving of His law.

---

[25] (Luke xi. 20).
[26] cf. A. E. Garvie, *The Christian Ideal* (1930), 444, with references to Gloege.

So Jesus ascribes His own activity to the same power. He delivers human beings from the thrall of evil spirits, He moves among the outcasts of society, seeking and saving the lost, He mediates God's forgiveness to the sinful woman, He teaches a new way of life, and announces that all things are possible to faith. He goes on saving men, though He be rejected by the nation, and He gives His life as a ransom for many. In all these activities of Jesus, God's sole saving sovereignty was being exercised. This conclusion is a legitimate deduction from His own words about God's kingly rule, which, when it shall have come, will manifest the final victory of sovereign love. 'The attitude, the action, the demands, the judgements, the assurances of Jesus in His earthly ministry, justify such an identification of Him as agent with this sole, sovereign, saving activity of God.'[27]

This interpretation of the phrase 'the kingdom of God' will enable us to understand the place of the Church in relation to the kingdom. The Church is not to be identified with God's Kingly Rule. Neither is it a conception substituted for that of the kingdom in the later writings of the New Testament. The Church is in the first place the object of the divine activity, and then the organ or instrument of God's saving purpose for mankind. If in the activity of Jesus in His earthly life the sovereignty of God is being exercised, that same sovereignty is apparent in the gathering of disciples and the choosing of the Twelve, the mission of the Twelve and the Seventy, and the institution of the new Covenant at the Last Supper. In the light of this principle we may proceed to discuss some of the chief passages dealing with the Kingdom of God where a community is envisaged or implied.

(*b*) We have begun with the primary meaning of *Basileia* in the teaching of our Lord as God's sovereignty. But the sovereignty does not operate in a vacuum. We are led to a secondary sense of the word, to describe the sphere in which the Kingly Rule is exercised. The word realm is almost as ambiguous as is the word kingdom, because it contains both the idea of a domain and the idea of a community. I venture to suggest the word 'domain' as

---

[27] Garvie in *Essays Congregational and Catholic* (1931), 182.

accurately translating this sense of the word *Basileia*. By its etymology and ultimate connexion with the Latin 'dominus' 'Lord', the word preserves the sense of the sphere in which a Lord exercises his dominion rather than the actual people who live in the domain. There are a number of passages which call for such a word. Jesus speaks of some one as 'going into' or 'entering' the Basileia.

> It is good for thee to enter into the kingdom of God with one eye, rather than having two eyes to be cast into hell. MARK ix. 47.
> Not every one that says to me Lord, Lord, shall enter into the kingdom of heaven. MATT. vii. 21.
> Woe unto you . . . because ye shut the kingdom of heaven against men. MATT. xxiii. 13: cf. LUKE xi. 52.

With this should be classed:

> I will give unto thee the keys of the kingdom of heaven. MATT. xvi. 19.
> From that time the gospel of the kingdom of God is preached, and every man entereth violently into it. LUKE xvi. 16.
> Of such is the kingdom of God. Verily I say unto you, Whosoever shall not receive the kingdom of God as a little child, he shall in no wise enter therein. MARK x. 14–15.

This last passage is particularly interesting, because it combines several characteristics of the Basileia. It may be spoken of as 'belonging to' such as are like little children. It may be 'received' as a gift. It may be 'entered'. Thus the Basileia is the whole new activity of God which is proceeding in the life and work of Jesus. To receive it is to accept the gift, a new personal relationship with God; to belong to it is to live like a little child, to live a new life of dependence. To enter it is to gain admittance to a new domain where God's will may be done on earth.

> Verily I say unto you, that the publicans and the harlots go into the kingdom of God before you. MATT. xxi. 31.

Even Bultmann[28] does not question the authenticity of this saying. It is notable among the sayings of the First Gospel as containing the phrase 'the kingdom of God' instead of the more usual 'kingdom of heaven' (cf. Matt. xxi. 43 and Matt. xii. 28, the only other instances, with the doubtful exception of xix. 24). Perhaps the Basileia is here thought of as present, though the future sense is not impossible. For our purpose the saying is interesting and unusual in specifying two classes of those who are in the new community of the new age. The only name which according to our sources is given to them is the Elect (Matt. xxii. 14; also in Mark xiii, three times and in Matthaean parallels; Luke xviii. 7).

In all these passages the 'domain' which is entered can only be described with reference to the One whose will is to be done, whose sovereignty is to be accepted, whose completed reign is close at hand. The meaning of God's sovereignty is primary, in the term *Basileia*; the meaning of domain, though inevitably following after it, is secondary and derivative.

(c) In the third place we find certain sayings about the *Basileia* where the idea of a community is implied. But this again follows on the idea of entering into a 'domain'. Those who are in it are naturally together and there are also distinctions among them. First, we may notice the saying in Matthew xi. 11:

> Verily I say unto you, among them that are born of women there hath not arisen a greater than John the Baptist: yet he that is but little in the kingdom of heaven is greater than he.

On the usual translation, 'He that is least in the kingdom of God is greater than he', the *Basileia* would be a present reality.[29]

---

[28] *Geschicte d. Syn. Tradition*, 192.

[29] cf. T. W. Manson, in *The Mission and Message of Jesus* (1937), 362. The second part of the verse may be interpreted in another way. If the comparative μικρότερος is to be taken literally, the verse might possibly be translated: 'He that is less (than John the Baptist) is in the kingdom of God greater than he.' This interpretation of J. Weiss, *Die Predigt Jesu* (1900), 81–2, is adopted by Hauck, *Das Evangelium des Lukas* (1934), 99, who further believes that μικρότερος refers to Jesus Himself. On this

It is incredible that Jesus meant to exclude John the Baptist from the final consummation of the *Basileia* in the future, when men 'shall come from the east and west and from the north and south, and shall sit down in the kingdom of God' (Luke xiii. 29).

If the *Basileia* is now manifested, there are, according to this saying (Matt. xi. 11), some who have received the good news, have believed it, and now are in the domain of God's kingly rule. These would be from among the 'poor' who have had the good news preached to them (Matt. xi. 5). Among these there are gradations, as there will be gradations in the new age when the Kingdom has fully come (cf. Matt. v.19; xix. 28; Luke xxii. 30).

The Parable of the Mustard Seed also implies the idea of a community:

> And He said, How shall we liken the kingdom of God? or in what parable shall we set it forth? It is like a grain of mustard seed, which, when it is sown upon the earth, though it be less than all the seeds that are upon the earth, yet when it is sown, groweth up, and becometh greater than all the herbs, and putteth out great branches; so that the birds of the heaven can lodge under the shadow thereof. MARK iv. 30–2, and parallels.

This parable is misread if it is interpreted as referring directly to the growth of the Church. It was early interpreted as an allegory. A fragment of Irenaeus[30] has been preserved in which he expounds the seed as the heavenly doctrine; the field is this world; Christ, the judge of the whole world, is planted in the earth for three days, and thence blossoms forth as a great tree, of which the twelve apostles are the branches; on these the Gentiles take shelter like the birds. We do not know when this allegorizing process

---

view the Basileia is spoken of as still in the future, and refers to the final consummation. Against this, we may place the undoubted fact that the comparative is often used as a superlative in Hellenistic Greek (Moulton, *Prolegomena*, 78). Further, the preceding pericope (Luke vii. 18–23) contains one of the chief passages where the Basileia is regarded by Jesus as present.

[30]   Ed. Harvey, ii. 494 Fragm. xxix.

began. It may go back to the days of the formation of the Gospel
tradition. Certainly the central meaning of the parable is to be
found in the contrast between the proverbially tiny mustard-seed
and the large bush which grows from it.[31] We may infer that Jesus
was illustrating the immeasurable results which would follow the
preaching of the Kingdom. Or perhaps we are penetrating farther
into the mind of our Lord if we connect the saying with the whole
activity of Jesus,[32] just as His healing the sick and casting out
demons were intended to convey to John the Baptist the first
evidence that the Kingdom had arrived, that the supreme manifestation of God's Rule was not only close at hand but actually
beginning (Luke vii. 21–3 =Matt. xi. 4–6), so from this humble
beginning of God's working in the life of Jesus His disciples were
to infer the splendour of the future results of this ministry. This
suggestion has at least the merit of interpreting the parable in the
light of another logion of Jesus, which again is in harmony with
what we know of His ministry. So, after all, Clement of Alexandria was not far from the truth when he said[33] in speaking of the
love of Christ:

'He Himself declaring Himself very beautifully, likened Himself to a grain of mustard-seed.'

But when such a parable is spoken, an active human mind will
inevitably go on thinking. What are to be the magnificent results
of the planting of the tiny seed? There are two passages in the Old
Testament which would be recalled by such a similitude. In Daniel
iv. 12 the greatness of Nebuchadnezzar is described by the picture
of a tree:

The beasts of the field had shadow under it, And the fowls of the
heaven dwelt in the branches thereof.

These lines are distinctive, and easily remembered because they
form part of a poem of two strophes. But this poem in turn
borrows from the imagery of Ezekiel xxxi. 3, 6.

---

[31] So Jülicher, *Gleichnisreden* ii. 576, 580 f.
[32] cf. B. T. D. Smith, *The Parables of the Synoptic Gospels* (1937), 120.
[33] *Paed.*, I. xi.

> Behold, the Assyrian was a cedar in Lebanon with fair branches,
>   And with a shadowing shroud of a high stature; . . . And all the
> fowls of heaven made their nests in his boughs, and under his
> branches did all the beasts of the field bring forth their young, and
> under his shadow dwelt all great nations.

Here the birds signify dependent peoples (see verse 12).

Was it Jesus Himself who added this touch of poetry about the birds, with its reminiscence of Daniel and Ezekiel? It is not of course impossible that the words may have become attached to the parable in the period of oral tradition.[34] At this time the early Church was preoccupied with the problems raised by the admission of the Gentiles; to the early missionaries the birds would naturally signify the Gentiles; and this interpretation became part of the inheritance of Irenaeus. But there is a restraint and delicacy about the closing of the parable which are not unworthy of a great artist. Surely it would be like Jesus to remember the birds. And if great results are to follow from the preaching of the word, or from the things He began to do and to teach, what could those results be but the adding of men and women to the company of His disciples? If the final words of the parable are the words of Jesus Himself, we may say that without any laboured allegory, but with a reminiscence of the familiar imagery, He shows that He has the gathering of a community in view.

There is a group of passages in which reference is made to the fellowship of believers with one another, and with their Lord, in the future *Basileia*.

(See especially Matt. xxv. 10, 21, 23, 34; Matt. xxvi. 29 = Mark xiv. 25.) These sayings do not necessarily imply the formation of a community in the interval before the kingdom is consummated. But one passage is important, as containing the idea of a new dispensation.

> I appoint unto you a kingdom even as my Father appointed unto me,
> that ye may eat and drink at my table in my kingdom. LUKE xxii.
> 29–30.

---

[34] So B. T. D. Smith, op. cit., 121.

Luke adds here the saying: 'and ye shall sit on thrones judging the twelve tribes of Israel', which Matthew xix. 28, sets in another context.

Two translations are possible here. It is probable that the less familiar is to be preferred.[35] 'Even as my Father covenanted unto me lordship (the kingdom, or kingly rule), I covenant unto you that ye shall eat and drink at my table in my kingly rule.' 'The idea is that, in virtue of the royal power which he has received from His Father, Jesus can guarantee their participation in the Joy of the perfected rule of God.'[36]

Two points are noticeable here. First, the disciples (like the publicans and harlots of Matt. xxi. 31) are expressly mentioned as sharing in the bliss of the new age. They are among those who were called and who have responded, and are therefore among the 'Elect'. Second, the verb used twice is διατίθεμαι, διέθετο. It is difficult to resist the conclusion that the conception of the New Covenant lies behind this word. The disciples are partakers in a new dispensation. This is surely one of the roots of the idea of the Ecclesia.[37]

So far we have discovered that the sayings and parables of Jesus with regard to the *Basileia* have not furnished us with more than a few slight indications that He had a community in view. The fewness of these at first sight is baffling. Nowhere does Jesus speak of members of the Kingdom.[38] The only descriptions of those who have been gathered into His company are 'disciples', 'the elect'. Only once is He reported to have used the word 'ecclesia' of the community of those who had believed in His message, and that passage has unusual difficulties. I have deliberately left any discussion of it until the full argument can be developed that the idea of the Ecclesia can be traced in the life and teaching of our Lord.

---

[35] J. M. Creed, *Gospel according to St. Luke*, ad. loc.

[36] V Taylor, *Jesus and His Sacrifice*, 189.

[37] See extended treatment of this, *infra*, pp. 99–106.

[38] cf. Johannes Weiss, *Die Predigt Jesu vom Reiche Gottes* (1900), 78–9.

Chapter Two

The Community of the Interval

Another difficulty has first to be faced. Is it possible that the very conception of the *Basileia* which Jesus preached precludes the conception of any kind of new community, because He thought that the end of human history was at hand?

The answer to this difficulty lies in the fact that, according to our sources, Jesus anticipated a certain sequence of events in history, and that therefore He allowed for a future in time and on this earth in which His followers would have to live and work. Further, He expressly declared that He did not know how long this interval would endure.

The teaching of Jesus was set in the frame of the thought-forms of the contemporary Apocalyptic. This is the stone of stumbling, the rock of offence for the humanism of to-day. At the centre of Apocalyptic lies the distinction between two ages or aeons, the present age and the age to come. Jesus reaffirmed this distinction. He began His public ministry with the proclamation that the new age was at hand. He declared that the supreme moment of history was upon the world, that the fulfilment of all the hopes and dreams of the seers of Israel was even now in sight. As a sign of it, witness His own activity, His works, His words, His death. John the Baptist was greater than any prophet because to John was given the privilege of heralding the coming age. Jesus Himself believed that He was the Messiah through whom the Rule of God should take actuality and win the supreme victory, because to Him had been granted a unique consciousness of sonship. But while

His words testify that the Kingdom had already dawned, He was aware that the full consummation of it was in the future. He prescribed no time. But the early tradition is built on the assumption that the transformation of human life as hitherto lived, and the coming of the Son of Man were not to be long delayed. This assumption is traced back to Jesus Himself.

To an historian who approaches the first century with our modern presuppositions as to the continuity of history, the probability of further millennia for the human race on this planet, and the disinclination to believe in the possibility of any radical transformation of human nature, there are elements in this message which seem fantastic and mistaken. The chequered history of the Christian Church, the chasm between the teaching of Jesus and the lives of many of His followers, and above all the fact that contrary to the expectation of the early Christians the Son of Man has not yet come in power and glory – all those interpose barriers in the way of our literal acceptance of this message of Jesus. But if our examination of it is based on the presupposition that Jesus actually did bring to this earth the supreme revelation of the nature of God, we may be granted a new respect for the central idea of Apocalyptic. Let us then make an attempt to penetrate to the meaning of the concept of 'revelation' and see how in the time of Jesus a new revelation could best be brought home to mankind.

A new revelation of God, a fresh divine Word for men who live in the flux of history must come from outside history, from beyond human life, and yet it must impinge upon history, make contact with the lives of men, and claim some foothold, some ground on which to move amongst us. Dibelius has distinguished between that element in each of the great historical religions which is original and creative, and the particular forms which that creative fact has fashioned in the world. 'Religion in its deepest sense has no relationship to the world.'[1] This saying overstates the profound truth that all religion which has left a lasting mark on history has drawn its life and victory from a source beyond

[1] *Geschichtliche und übergeschichtliche Religion im Christentum* (1925), 20.

history. It has been to men the revelation of a higher world. That higher world is of an order contrasted with, and even opposed to, that of the present world, although reaching into it and demanding passionate allegiance to itself.

In the central idea of Apocalyptic this contrast between two worlds is found in a temporal form. It is a contrast between present and future. In Platonism there is another determining mode of contrast, between the seen and the unseen, between the lower and the higher, between the shadows of the phenomenal world and the realities of the heavenly. The time-factor is essential in Judaism's view of the world which Jesus shared. When the Psalmist says (Ps. xc. 4) that 'A thousand years in thy sight are but as yesterday', he does not declare that God is beyond time. Or when the author of 2 Peter (iii. 8) declares that 'In the Lord's sight one day is as a thousand years, and a thousand years as one day', he is not asserting that God's eternity means God's simultaneity, or non-successiveness, as Philo did. But Jesus speaks of God's Rule as the characteristic and determining mark of the coming age. It is to be finally and supremely manifested in that age, and yet it reaches into the present age. The new order is being 'anticipated' in the activity of Jesus. The new powers of the age to come are invading the present era, in which evil holds its precarious rule.

To such a statement of His message we are forced by the apparently conflicting sayings which speak of the Kingdom of God now as present, now as future. On this view it may be argued, I think, that the sharp distinction between this age and that which is to come is already breaking down. This is due, first, to the conception that in His own activity the Reign of God is present; second, to the stress laid on faith as enabling men to appropriate the distinctive blessings which in prophetic expectation were attached to the Messianic Age. The kingdom has come, in the person of Jesus. Its blessings can be enjoyed now, through faith. But it has not fully come. The final consummation is delayed.

If we apply these considerations to the view of the future which Jesus held we shall find that His 'prophecies', as recorded in the earliest sources, form an intelligible sequence, even if they have been obscured in the course of the oral or written tradition. First, Jesus anticipates His own resurrection following on His passion and death. Second, He anticipates the early destruction of the Temple. Third, He proclaims the end of history, with the Son of Man coming on the clouds of heaven for the final judgement. This Coming of the Son of Man is not to be identified with the 'coming' of the Kingdom, but only with the last act of God's Kingly Rule in history, the final consummation of the Kingdom, the supreme end of God's purpose for mankind.[2]

---

[2] For this reason it is, I believe, a mistake to speak of the Kingly Rule of God on earth as being 'timeless', as Gloege does, *Reich Gottes und Kirche* (1929), 66–85, in his justifiable protest against reading modern evolutionary ideas into the Gospels. Compare the criticism of such a term as 'Die Überseitlichke des königlichen Wirkens Gottes' by K. L. Schmidt in *Theol. Wörterbuch*, i. 579, note. An attempt has been made in a most valuable and influential book (C. H. Dodd, *The Parables of the Kingdom*, 1935) to identify the reference of Jesus to the day of the Son of Man with the Resurrection, as expressing a timeless fact, and to explain several of the sayings about the future Kingdom (Mark xiv. 62; Matt. x. 32–3 = Luke xii. 8–9; Matt. xix. 28; Luke xxii. 28–30), as symbolic in character, and as referring to events which are eternal, beyond time. 'These future lenses are only an accommodation of language. There is no coming of the Son of Man "after" His coming in Galilee and Jerusalem, whether soon or late, for there is no before and after in the eternal order. The Kingdom of God in its full reality is not something which will happen after other things have happened. It is that to which men awake when this order of time and space no longer limits their vision, when they "sit at meat in the Kingdom of God" with all the blessed dead, and drink with Christ the "new wine" of eternal felicity. "The Day of the Son of Man" stands for the timeless fact. . . . That which cannot be experienced in history is symbolized by the picture of a coming event, and its timeless quality is expressed as pure simultaneity in time – "as the lightning flashes"' (108).

This interpretation is attractive. But it introduces into the mind of our Lord an assumption which would be only partially valid for Philo (see *Quod Deus immut.*, 6; Drummond, *Philo Judaeus*, i. 291–5). We have no other evidence that any of the sayings of Jesus implied that God's

These forecasts of the future imply that there is a future in time, whether a long or a short period. All the New Testament writers expected the period to be short, and it is probable that Jesus shared their views. A logion embedded in the Apocalyptic discourse (Mark xiii. 32) represents Jesus as saying of the day when the Son of Man shall be seen coming in the clouds:

> Of that day or that hour knoweth no one, not even the angels in heaven, neither the Son, but the Father.

This logion was once regarded as a foundation-pillar of the Gospel tradition, a saying that was indubitably authentic because none of the followers of Jesus would have placed a confession of ignorance on His lips. Recent critics have not been so respectful. Bultmann dismisses it, without discussion, as unauthentic. But it is surely sound to conclude that if Jesus had not given such an intimation that He did not know the time of His Parousia, no such tradition as this would ever have been formed.[3] According to this logion Jesus is anticipating an interval of time, it may even be a long interval, between His earthly life and the final consummation.

The ethical teaching of Jesus is meant for His followers in this interval. In another sense than that of Schweitzer we may use the phrase *Interimsethik*. All Christian ethics are 'ethics of the interim'. Whether the days be swifter than a weaver's shuttle or prolonged through immense vistas of time, the obligation of the Christian to live every moment in the perfect love of God is categorical. The words of Milton's Archangel:

---

eternal order was beyond time. The logia about the future Coming of the Son of Man, so deeply rooted in the Synoptic tradition and in the subsequent faith of the New Testament, are too much coloured by eschatology to be interpreted in a Platonic rather than a Hebraic way; and New Testament 'eschatology' does not merely mean what happens after death, but assumes that men and women are living in the last age of human history.

[3]   Branscomb, *The Gospel of Mark* (1937), 240.

> What thou liv'st
> Live well; how long or short permit to heaven.

are as valid for the community as for the individual life.[4]

We may conclude, therefore, that the length of the interval before Jesus returns is really irrelevant to the question whether He 'founded' a Church. He regarded life in the community which He was gathering as the true way for those who were expecting the full consummation of the Kingdom, an acclimatization to the perfect life of the future. His eschatology represented the Kingdom as the fulfilment of the final purpose of God, and all history as part of that purpose. His endorsement of the highest prophetic teaching of the past implies that the new Israel will honour and observe the ethical and social principles of mercy, righteousness, humility, service, and love. For Him, as for the prophets and for us, the way of life to which He called His followers did not depend primarily on the conviction that the present era would disappear within a fixed period of time, but rather on the consciousness of living in a new era which had already begun, in which God's supreme purpose was already being manifested. This consciousness was immediately translated into a new acceptance of God's rule, a new attitude to others, a new standard of life in a newly constituted community.

---

[4] See the excellent remarks of H.D. Wendland, *Die Eschatologie des Reiches Gottes bei Jesus* (1931), 102 ff.

Chapter Three

The Idea of the Ecclesia in the Mind of Our Lord

It is not only to the teaching of Jesus but to His acts during His earthly life that we must turn, if we are to describe the idea of the community which He had in view. I propose to assemble under five main headings the evidence that He had in view a community of a new kind.

First, there is the conception of a new Israel which appeared in His teaching and actions.

Second, the fact that He taught His disciples, as the nucleus of the new Israel; the ethical teaching of Jesus presupposed a new community, and the power to fulfil the new demands.

Third, His conception of Messiahship.

Fourth, the conception of 'the Word of God' or 'Gospel' as constituting the new community; the fact that He preached and that His message was of a certain kind, inevitably marked off those who accepted it from those who did not.

Fifth, the fact that He sent out His disciples on a certain mission. That mission governed His conception of apostleship.

1. The Nucleus of the New Israel

The roots of the conception of the Ecclesia lie deep in the religion of Israel. First, there is the dominant conviction that Yahweh, the God of Israel, is a redeeming God, whose activity is manifested on the plane of history. Second, there is the conception of Israel as the 'people of God'. Within these two main dogmas, and issuing out of them, there are other convictions, each one of which has its own influence in the formation of the Christian community, and is apparent in the teaching or action of Jesus Himself. Of these we may mention as the third conviction, the idea that Israel will be saved through the Remnant. Fourth, an attempt is made to form this Remnant by the calling and instruction of disciples. 'Bind up God's testimony, seal the revelation among my disciples. And I will wait for Yahweh that hideth His face from the house of Jacob, and I will look for Him' (Isaiah viii. 16 ff.). Robertson Smith has described[1] the formation of this little community gathered round Isaiah, treasuring the word of revelation, and waiting for Yahweh, as a new thing in the history of religion. They were 'signs and tokens in Israel from Jehovah of Hosts that dwelleth in Mount Zion'. It was 'the birth of a new era in the Old Testament religion for it was the birth of the conception of the Church'.

Fifth, there is the conception of the universal mission of Israel, especially as expressed through the figure of the Servant of Yahweh in the oracles of Deutero-Isaiah. Last in point of time comes the apocalyptic vision of the saints of the Most High, vanquishing by God's act and intervention the successive empires of the four Beasts, and symbolized by the figure of 'one like unto a son of man'. his last vision has been called the spring from which arises the idea of the Ecclesia.[2] It is probably truer to say that the idea of the Ecclesia is like a river issuing forth purified from a great lake into which many tributary streams have flowed.

Jesus nowhere speaks of the disciples whom He is gathering as the nucleus for a new Israel. But His actions speak more clearly than any words. In one sense, for Him, as for all the New Testament writers, the Church was already in existence before He came. The Jewish Church was the people of God. His main

---

[1] *The Prophets of Israel* (new ed. 1919), 274–5.
[2] F. Kattenbusch, in *Harnack-Festgabe* (1921), 143–72: Der Quellort der Kirchenidee; Daniel vii.

mission was to the lost sheep of the house of Israel. But His actions indicate His conviction that the old Israel was to be purged and reconstituted in view of the nearness of the Kingdom of God.

Jesus was baptized by John the Baptist. This fact caused difficulty to the author of the First Gospel (Matt. iii. 14–15), who evidently thought that it needed to be explained. The fact may be assumed as indisputable,[3] whatever debate may proceed on the details and the meaning of the various traditions. By accepting Baptism Jesus accepted an eschatological sacrament. Both terms demand closer definition. It is unlikely that John's baptism was believed to effect a miraculous operation in the cleansing of the sinner, like baptism in a later sense within the Christian Church. It was a sacrament in so far as it was an outward rite with a divine meaning in it. But the meaning was a declaration, a Word of God like that which came to the old prophets, that the divine Judgement was at hand; on the part of the recipient it was an acceptance of this message, a repentance in the Hebraic sense of turning to God, rather than in the Hellenic sense of a change of mind;[4] an awaiting of the coming of the Messiah who would baptize with spirit and with fire. It was eschatological in view of this expectation.

It is tempting to infer that all who received baptism at the hands of John were thereby banded together in a new brotherhood. There are two highly original characteristics in the teaching of John the Baptist; first is the insistence on this new kind of baptism, which cannot be explained merely by Jewish lustral rites, nor by the proselyte-baptism by which Gentiles entered Judaism;[5] second, the insistence of John that in the coming Judgement the privilege of belonging to the chosen people will play no part at

---

[3]　cf. Dibelius, *Die urchristl. Überlieferung von Joh. dem Täufer* (1911), 59.

[4]　I accept the argument of J. Kosnetter, *Die Taufe Jesu* (Vienna, 1936), that though the word 'metanoein' is usually a translation in the LXX of 'nicham' the sense of 'shub' better suits the N.T. passages. cf. A. H. Dirksen, *Metanoia* (Washington, 1932), 205. Malachi iii. I–3, 7, is the true explanation of Matt. iii. 2, 7 ff.

[5]　Kosnetter, op. cit., 41–69.

all. 'Think not to say within yourselves, We have Abraham to our father: for I say unto you, that God is able of these stones to raise up children unto Abraham'[6] (Matt. iii. 9 = Luke iii. 8). The Baptist was deliberately defying the current nationalism in religion. Was he seeking to bind together by this sacrament a new confraternity of penitents, to await the coming Judgement?[7] There is a curious phrase in Josephus, where he describes John the Baptist, as 'commanding the Jews . . . to come together in Baptism' (βαπτισμῷ συνίεναι). The scanty evidence in the New Testament (Luke xi. I; Acts xix. 2–7) for the later history of the followers of John the Baptist shows that they were such a confraternity. It is difficult to see how all the multitudes who were baptized by John could be bound together in any effective brotherhood when they returned home.[8] Nevertheless, by the solemn baptism beneath the waters of the Jordan, by the acceptance of a new way of life, by embracing a new message as to the imminence of judgement, they were in some sense separated from the rest of the nation. The rite of waterbaptism pointed forward to the spirit-baptism of the future to be administered by the Messiah Himself.

Jesus entered on His public ministry after John had been imprisoned. According to one tradition (Matt. iii. 2) the Baptist had proclaimed the imminence of the Kingdom as Jesus did Himself. Whether this be accurate or not, John had emphasized judgement, and the terrors of the coming Messiah, while Jesus poured the conception of mercy and self-sacrificing love into the idea of the Kingly Rule of God. John said 'Soon', Jesus said 'Now', even though the Kingdom were hidden, even though His forerunner himself might not recognize the tokens of the coming. John had gathered a circle of disciples round himself. So did Jesus, but with a deliberateness and sense of purpose which have left an ineffaceable impression on all the various strata of the Synoptic

---

[6] Bultmann, *Gesch. Syn. Trad.*, 263, 123, ascribes these words to Christian tradition. If they were thus made up, at the time of the controversy over the admission of the Gentiles into the Church, it is strange that they were not put into the mouth of Jesus.

[7] So Goguel, *Life of Jesus* (E. tr. 1933), 268.

[8] Kosnetter, op. cit., 14.

tradition.[9] There is evidence of a campaign of evangelism for the renewal of Israel under the Kingly Rule of God. The number 'twelve' in His choice of the inner circle is deliberate.[10] His conception of the community to be gathered was that of a new Israel.

There are hints of a similar kind in the parable of the vineyard (Mark xii. 1–9) and in the strange story of the cursing of the fig-tree (Mark xi. 13, 14, 20 ff.), which is perhaps an early misreading of an original parable; and in the parable of the fig-tree (Luke xiii. 6 ff.). Fig-trees were quite commonly planted in vineyards; both fig-tree and vineyard are used to suggest Israel. The preaching is directed to the renewal of Israel. The meaning of all three passages is that the final opportunity for Israel has dawned, and may be lost. Indeed, Jesus is faced with the probability that it will be lost. What then? We cannot appeal with any great confidence to the phrase: 'the lord of the vineyard will give the vineyard to others' as proving that Jesus had in mind the new Israel which He was gathering together by His preaching, though certainly the early Christians and Mark himself interpreted the parable in this sense. But a more secure foundation is found in the saying:

> Fear not, little flock; for it is your Father's good pleasure to give you the kingdom. LUKE xii. 32.

There is no reason to suspect the authenticity of this logion.[11]

The imagery goes back to Micah (v. 4) and Deutero-Isaiah (xl. II), and is found elaborated in Ezekiel (xxxiv. 12–24). In the Psalms of Solomon (xvii. 45) the same picture is found of the Messianic king tending the flock of Yahweh. But in the Old Testament passages the flock is not the whole of Israel. In Micah (iv. 4–7) the idea of the Remnant is found determining the nature

---

[9] For Mark, see i. 16–20, ii. 14; iii. 13–19; for Q, the Mission charge Luke x. 1–12, Matt. ix. 35–x. 16; for Luke, vi. 12–13; for Matt., v. I; x. I; x.40–xi. I.

[10] See especially the saying, Matt. xix. 28.

[11] As Bultmann does, *Geschichted. Syn. Trad.*, 116, 134.

of the flock. It is in Isaiah that the influential doctrine of the Remnant comes first to magnificent expression. It is a Remnant of the people that will return and enjoy the redeeming grace of God (Isa. vii. 3). 'In the main this is an eschatological idea. The Remnant is what is left when the judgement is overpast. . . . In the two prophecies of the Exile (Ezekiel and Deutero-Isaiah) the Remnant doctrine bifurcates: and in all later religious teaching, where it is present, it takes the form either of a saved Remnant or a *saving* Remnant.'[12]

'The little flock' of Jesus is the saved Remnant which as we shall see is also commissioned to save. Jesus is sent to the lost sheep of the house of Israel. He speaks of His work as seeking and saving the one lost sheep. By these passages this logion is placed in its true context in His mind, and demonstrates what all our evidence hitherto has made increasingly probable, that the community which Jesus is gathering is living in the hope of the final manifestation of the sovereignty of God. The little flock is regarded as the true Israel, inheriting the promises made to Israel of old.

It has been suggested by Professor Burkitt[13] that behind the story of the Triumphal Entry we may trace the desire of Jesus for a renewal of the true worship of Israel's God in the national shrine. The use of green branches and the cry 'Hosanna' are appropriate to the Maccabean Feast of the Rededication of the Temple. This was itself the celebration of a great national deliverance from false worship as well as from alien rule, and would therefore carry with it Messianic associations akin to those of Zechariah ix. 9–11. The attractiveness of this suggestion is that it provides a link between the Entry into Jerusalem and the Cleansing of the Temple. 'A new Dedication' – that is the underlying *motif* of both. The purpose of Jesus is to reconstitute the Israel of God on the basis of a

---

[12]   T. W. Manson, *the teaching of Jesus* (1931), 176, 181; cf. the valuable chapter on 'Judgement and Salvation' in Köhler, *Theologie des Alten Testaments* (1936), esp. 222–7.

[13]   *Journal of Theological Studies*, xvii. (1916), 142–5; see also Montefiore, Synoptic Gospels i. 259–61; J. V. Bartlet, *St. Mark* (1922), 314–15; Branscomb, St. Mark (1937), 198–200.

purified worship. Whether this suggestion be accepted or not, the Cleansing of the Temple is a Messianic act, proclaiming that the original purpose of God in ordaining worship in His house is to be honoured, and that the people of God is to be prepared for His coming reign.

The idea of the destruction of the old Israel and the rebuilding of the new appears through a saying which except in the Fourth Gospel has only been preserved in the accusation brought against Jesus at His trial:

> We heard him say, I will destroy this temple that is made with hands, and in three days I will build another made without hands. MARK xiv. 58.
> But afterward came two, and said, This man said, I am able to destroy the temple of God, and to build it in three days. MATT. xxvi. 60[b]–I.

The Markan version is ascribed to false witnesses. But in the Fourth Gospel we find the saying in another form and regarded as authentic, but allegorized, as referring to the resurrection of the body of Jesus:

> Destroy this temple, and in three days I will raise it up. JOHN ii. 19.

In the Apocalyptic chapter (Mark xiii. 2 and parallels) the saying in another form is expressed and ascribed to Jesus; as He looks at the Temple:

> Seest thou these great buildings?
> There shall not be left here one stone upon another, which shall note thrown down.

In Acts vi. 14 there is another echo of the saying in the accusation brought against Stephen:

> We have heard him say, that this Jesus of Nazareth shall destroy this place, and shall change the customs which Moses delivered unto us.

This accusation is practically admitted by Stephen[14] (vii. 47–8):

> But Solomon built him a house. Howbeit the Most High dwelleth not
> in houses made with hands.

It is highly probable that there is a genuine saying of Jesus behind
these various versions. Even Bultmann admits this,[15] though he does
not venture to guess at its original form. We may agree with him
that we can lay no stress on the contrast in the Markan version (xiv.
58) between 'made with hands' (τόν χειροποίητον) and 'made
without hands' (ἀχειροποίητον), though in view of the prayer of
Solomon (I Kings viii. 27) we are surely allowed to assume that the
contrast was as possible for Jesus as for His later followers such as
Stephen and Paul (Acts xvii. 24). The idea of a new and more glorious
Temple to be erected in the Messianic age was current in Jewish
eschatology, long before the catastrophe of A.D. 70, as Bousset has
proved.[16] There is a striking passage in Enoch xc. 28, 29:

> And I stood up to see till they folded up that old house; . . . And I saw
> till the Lord of the sheep brought a new house, greater and loftier
> than that first, and set it up in the place of the first which had been
> folded up . . . and all the sheep were within it.

So in liii. 6, 'the Righteous and Elect One shall cause the house of
his congregation to appear.'

In the Book of Jubilees (i. 17, 27; iv. 26) there are similar
prophecies:

> I shall build my sanctuary in their midst, and I shall dwell with them
> and I shall be their God and they will be my people in truth and
> righteousness. i.17.

The saying in Mark xiv. 58 goes beyond these prophecies of
the Apocalyptic literature, in ascribing the destruction of the old

---

[14] So Lake, in *Beginnings of Christianity*, iv. 69.
[15] *Gesch. Syn. Trad.* (2nd ed. 1931), 126–7.
[16] *Religion des Judentums* (3rd ed. 1926), 239; cf. 115.

Temple and the building of the new to the personal act of the Messiah himself. But it is not incredible that Jesus at the end of His ministry saw the inevitable result of the Messianic judgement on the old Israel. Only a Remnant had accepted His message and discerned in His life the signs of the Rule of God. A new building was being erected through His own work, with living men and women as its stones. 'The stone which the builders rejected has become the headstone of the corner.' The logion looks forward to a time when there will be a new shrine 'made without hands' for the worship and service of the congregation of Christ's flock.[17]

It is unlikely that the early Christians, at a time when they adhered devoutly to the temple cultus, would have given currency to a saying such as this; their perplexity as to its meaning has left its traces in the various ways in which the saying has come down to us.[18]

There is surely no reason for doubting (1) that Jesus declared that by His own activity, in which the Rule of God was manifest, the Temple and its worship would be superseded, and that a new spiritual edifice would be erected speedily wherein the new Israel would worship an ever-present God; (2) that this logion was easily

---

[17] This conclusion is not quite the same as that of Otto, *Kingdom of God and Son of Man*, 62, but is closely allied to it, and is, I venture to think, more firmly based on the evidence, especially the parallels in the Apocalyptic literature.

[18] Bertram, *Die Leidensgeschichte Jesu* (1922), 56–7; Dodd, *Parables of the Kingdom*, 61. The logion is accepted as authentic by Goguel, *Life of Jesus*, 507–9, following Johannes Weiss, *Das älteste Evangelium* (1903), 313–14, *Die Schriften des N.T.* (1907), 214, without χειροποίητον and its opposite; Joachim Jeremias, *Jesus als Weltvollender* (1930), 39–40; Bertram, op. cit.; Wellhausen, *Evangelium Marci* (2nd ed.), 124; V. Taylor, *Jesus and His Sacrfice* (1937), 144. The objection of Lietzmann, *Der Prozess Jesu, Sitzungsberichte der preuss. Akad.* (1931), that the cleansing of the Temple proves that Jesus could not have uttered this prophecy is surely groundless. The additional, or alternative, explanation on which Bultmann falls back (*Gesch. Syn. Trad.*, 127), that the prophecy of Jesus depends on a myth which may underlie certain sayings in the Mandaean literature, is too fantastic for discussion here.

misunderstood; (3) that it was regarded as a chief count in the indictment of Jesus at His trial.

2.   The Ethical Teaching of Jesus and the Power of the Spirit

Our first conclusion is that Jesus gathered together a band of disciples, as the Remnant, the little flock which was to be the nucleus of the new Israel, to live as God's children under His kingly rule, to serve Him in expectation of the final consummation. What manner or life were they meant to live? The answer is given mainly in the three chapters in which the author of the First Gospel has arranged with a rare artistry the various ethical sayings of Jesus which he has collected. He follows a tradition which asserts that Jesus called His disciples on a mountain (Mark iii. 1 3), and declares that Jesus gave this teaching there. He is doubtless interested in the parallel between Moses, the lawgiver on Mount Sinai, and Jesus, the giver of a new and final law on another mysterious mountain-top. To-day it is almost a fashion to ascribe all these connecting links between the various sections within any Gospel to the fancy or unfettered discretion of the evangelist.[19] But if Jesus was a teacher, He would desire a place free from distraction. In the densely populated Galilee of that time, it would be to the mountains that He would naturally turn for quietness. Is it really incredible that Mark (iii. 13–14[a]) gives us a sober record of fact?

> And he goeth up into the mountain, and calleth unto him whom he himself would: and they went unto him. And he appointed twelve, that they might be with him.

A distinction is made here between an outer and an inner circle of disciples. The Twelve are chosen out of a wider company. The Synoptic testimony to the choice of Twelve is supported by the

[19]   K. L. Schmidt, *Der Rahmen der Geschichte Jesu* (1919), 70; cf. 109–10. Rawlinson, *St. Mark* (1925), 39, 'the *mise-en-scéne* . . . due to the Evangelist'.

reference to them in St. Paul.[20] If there is any choosing of Twelve at all – if the whole story is not merely an imaginative 'delineation of a dogmatic idea',[21] if it is not 'beyond the realm of history',[22] they may very well have been chosen out of a larger band as close companions for the wandering Prophet. It may have been in a secluded place among the mountains that the teaching to the 'little flock' was given. Such teaching was given and was remembered by human beings. It is to that company of human beings that we must look for the nucleus of the coming Christian ecclesia. From the fact that such teaching was given to the disciples for their daily life, we infer that they were expected to live at that lofty level. This is a second argument for the distinctive character of the new community.

Of the ethical teaching of Jesus three assertions may be set down for our present purpose; first, that the teaching is set within the framework of eschatology; second, that the demands are given to be met and fulfilled; third, that with the demands goes a promise of the power whereby they may be fulfilled.

(1) The Eschatological Framework. The theory that the ethics of Jesus laid no claim to absolute validity has met with little favour. For Schweitzer the spirit of Jesus is a world-negating spirit.[23] 'The whole of ethics lies under the concept of repentance – penitence for the past and the determination to live hence-forward liberated from everything earthly, in expectation of the Messianic kingdom.'[24] In this sense, the phrase 'Interimsethik' meant an ethic entirely uninterested in the normal concerns of ordinary life, in work and civil order and marriage and festal joy. So Johannes Weiss regarded the ethical teaching of Jesus as 'exceptional laws'[25] analogous to the regulations issued in time of war, which cannot be carried through in time of peace. But the

---

[20] I Cor. xv. 5

[21] J. Weiss, *Das älteste Evangelium* (1903), 165.

[22] K. L. Schmidt, op. cit., 110.

[23] *Quest of the Historical Jesus* (E. tr. 2nd ed. 1922), 400.

[24] *Mysticism of Paul*, 293.

[25] 'Ausnahmegesetze': *Die Predigt Jesu vom Reiche Gottes* (1900), 139.

teaching of Jesus is founded on the will of God. The parables prove that Jesus Himself is interested in the normal work of mankind. The world is to be redeemed ad not merely renounced. There is good in the present order as well as evil, and that good is to be fulfilled and not destroyed.

There are two types of sayings in the ethical teaching of Jesus, just as there are two ways of speaking of the Kingdom. Some writers have labelled them as 'eschatological' and 'non-eschatological'.[26] But that distinction only begs the question at issue. Let us rather say that there are sayings which bear stamped on them the impress of the coming Judgement and the end of this age; and there are sayings which at first sight do not seem to bear that stamp. On the one hand there are the Beatitudes which point forward to the future age; there are explicit references to the coming Rule in Matt. v. 19–20. The sayings in Matt. v. 25–6 are in the Matthaean setting an illustration of the wisdom of casting out anger. But in the Lukan setting (xii. 58–9), which is probably more original,[27] Jesus says: 'Make amends to your brother before the case comes before the Judge.' Luke has linked this eschatological parable with the saying about those who are wise in discerning the signs of the weather, but blind to the signs of the coming age.

In Matt. v. 29–30 the 'occasions of stumbling' are set in the awful shadow of the future judgement. The Lord's Prayer looks forward to the coming Kingdom. In the sayings about the soul's treasure (vi. 19–21), judging (vii. 1–2), and the two ways (vii. 13–14), in the warning about those who say 'Lord, Lord', and in the final parable of the two houses, the eschatological background is unmistakable.

But there are other sayings in this collection where the eschatological colouring does not appear. The disciples are called 'salt' and 'light' in the present age. There is an explicit direction to be reconciled before offering a gift at the Temple altar. There is a

---

[26] Windisch, *Der Sinn der Bergpredigt*, 21; cf. the criticisms of H. D. Wendland, *Die Eschatologie des Reiches Gottes*, 10.

[27] cf. B. T. D. Smith, *Parables of the Synoptic Gospels*, 113–14.

deepening of the meaning of the old commands as to adultery, oaths, and anger. There is even a saying about divorce. Revenge is forbidden; enemies are to be loved with a love like that of God Himself. And there are no more appealing or sympathetic sayings in all literature than those at the end of the sixth chapter where Jesus shows His insight into 'care', the anxiety of common folk about the common necessaries of life, and reveals the love of a heavenly Father who feeds the birds and clothes with beauty the lilies of the field.

Here again we must apply to the ethical sayings the three canons of interpretation already laid down in the discussion of the *Basileia*. (1) Some sayings imply that the Kingdom is still in the future, and that all life must be lived in the shadow of that coming crisis. (2) Some sayings of Jesus imply that the ideal life can be lived now, without strain, amid the normal activities of the present age. (3) Both these aspects of the ethical teaching must be held together. 'We should naturally expect that a passionate expectation of a tremendous change should disturb and destroy the interest of the present. But the real problem of Christian eschatology is that it does not.'[28] The solution of this problem is that Christian ethics rest on one vital conviction: in order to determine your conduct here on earth you must first have secured a pivot in the coming age. All the ethical teaching of Jesus is set in the light of eschatology. Jesus is portraying human life as it is meant to be, as seen from God's side. The two assumptions of the theory of *Interimsethik* as set forth by Schweitzer are (i) that the Apocalyptic outlook, even for Jesus, involved a profound pessimism as to the present age, and therefore a world-negating ethic, and (ii) that the Apocalyptic outlook, even for Jesus, involved an essential discontinuity between the present age and the age to come. Both these assumptions are false. The distinction of the teaching of Jesus is that it spans both ages. The eschatological outlook is permanently necessary to the ordinary life in the present world.

---

[28] H. Scott Holland, *The Real Problem of Eschatology* (1916), 16.

For our present purpose, the conclusion must be that to a selected company of His followers Jesus gave memorable teaching about the life to be lived in the present age, and in outline determined the moral standards of the new Israel. For Him all ethics were Interim-ethics, in a profounder sense, since human life in this age was but an interval, whether long or short, between creation and the final consummation, and was meant to be lived by those who had to give account before the judgement seat of God.[29]

(2) How could this teaching, so apparently impossible, be carried into life? The very sayings in the Sermon on the Mount which are free from eschatological colouring are precisely those which seem to heighten the moral demand to an impossible plane.[30] 'The ethical teaching of Jesus is an ethical teaching for heroes.'[31] As Brünner has stated the dilemma: 'Only the impossible is the Will of God.'[32]

There can be no doubt that the ethical teaching of Jesus is grounded in His conception of the will of God. Brünner sees this. But he declares that the Sermon on the Mount is concerned with the absolute good, the final Kingdom as it ought to be, the impossible. This is to give up the problem, to cut the knot with a dangerous two-edged sword, to declare that the Will of God cannot be done in the present world.

Against this conclusion, we may state, first, that the Jews were familiar with a Law which was given to be obeyed. After a discussion of the fundamental passages, Deut. xi. 26–8, and xxx. 15–20, G. F. Moore declares: 'that man is capable of choosing between right and wrong and of carrying the decision into action was not questioned.'[33] So Montefiore says: 'it was doubtless supposed that there were a few superlatively righteous people who really did observe the law from A to Z.'[34] This conviction may very

[29] cf. H. D. Wendland, *Die Eschatologie des Reiches Gottes bei Jesus* (1931), 106–7.
[30] cf. *The Idea of Perfection* (1934), 18–21
[31] C. G. Montefiore *The Old Testament and After* (1923), 241.
[32] The Mediator (E. tr. 1934) 419.
[33] *Judaism*, i. 454; cf. 227.
[34] *Rabbinic Literature and Gospel Teachings* (1930), 169.

well go side by side with what Montefiore describes[35] as the usual
Jewish idea, 'that no man is free of sin, that all men . . . need the
grace of the forgiveness of God'. In the second place, Jesus recognized that His teaching went far beyond the claims of the Jewish
law, and yet said that they must exceed the righteousness of Scribes
and Pharisees,[36] and must indeed become as little children,[37] if they
were to enter the new order at all. But He expected these demands
to be fulfilled.[38] This was the will of God. In the third place, He
promised God's aid in face of apparent impossibilities.

> With men it is impossible, but not with God: for all things are possible
> with God. MARK x. 27 and parallels.
>
> Whosoever shall say unto this mountain, Be thou taken up and cast
> into the sea; and shall not doubt in his heart, but shall believe that
> what he saith cometh to pass; he shall have it. Therefore I say unto
> you, all things whatsoever ye pray and ask for believe that ye have
> received them, and ye shall have them. MARK xi. 23–4 = MATT. xxi.
> 21–2.

Q has this saying in another form; Matt. xvii. 20 = Luke xvii. 6.

> Jesus said to him: That 'if thou canst'! All things are possible to him
> that believeth. MARK ix. 23 (Mark only).
>
> And he said to them, This kind can come out by nothing, save by
> prayer. MARK ix. 29 (Mark only).
>
> Ask, and it shall be given you; seek, and ye shall find; knock and it
> shall be opened unto you. . . . If ye then, being evil, know how to give
> good gifts unto your children, how much more shall your Father
> which is in heaven give good things to them that ask him? MATT. vii.
> 7–11 = LUKE xi. 9–13. (In v. 13 Luke has 'Holy Spirit' instead of 'good
> things'.)
>
> Again I say unto you, that if two of you shall agree on earth as
> touching anything that they shall ask, it shall be done for them of my
> Father which is in heaven. MATT. xviii. 19 (Matthew only).

---

[35] Op. cit., 274.
[36] Matthew only, v. 20.
[37] Mark x. 15.
[38] Matt. v. 45 and Luke vi. 35; Matt. vii. 24–7 = Luke vi. 47–9.

Thus all the different strata of the Synoptic Gospels except the special Lukan passages promise the divine resources in response to believing prayer. Luke gives us something more (x. 17–20); he includes the saying of the Seventy, that 'even the devils are subject unto us in thy name' and Jesus answers, 'I watched Satan fall as lightning from heaven.[39] Behold, I have given you authority to tread upon serpents and scorpions, and over all the power of the enemy: and nothing shall in any wise hurt you'.

In effect this saying contains the same truth as the other passages above, that the divine resources are available for those who are in His 'little flock'. Johannes Weiss regarded this paragraph as unusually valuable for the understanding of the mind of our Lord. 'The rule of Satan is at an end. This conviction of faith may be called the driving force in His religious life . . . Jesus believed in the victory of God, not only in the future but also in the present.'[40] The fall of Satan is the necessary condition for the coming of the kingdom, and they are to rejoice over it. But there is a reason for deeper joy. The names of the 'little flock' are written in heaven. Jesus regarded the knowledge which His followers had been given that they were the children of God, destined to share in His final victory, as more glorious than the spectacular victories over the evil spirits.

In the Pauline and Johannine writings, as in Luke's second volume, the divine resources which are available to believers are summed up in the phrase 'the Holy Spirit', or 'the Spirit', or the 'Spirit of God'. Why are there so few references to the Spirit in the recorded sayings of Jesus? The traditional answer has been to point to the Fourth Gospel. But that does not solve the problem, even if every word in the fourteenth and fifteenth chapters of St. John could be proved to be an authentic utterance of our Lord. In those chapters the gift of the Spirit is regarded as still lying in the future. But according to Jewish expectation the outpouring of the Spirit was one of the chief blessings of the last days. We should

---

[39] See J. H. Moulton, *Prolegomena*, 134, for the justification of the translation of the first sentence.

[40] *Die Schriften* (2nd ed. 1907), 461.

have expected frequent references to the divine activity in a
teaching set within the eschatological framework. The problem
becomes more acute when we consider the quality of life expected
by Jesus in His followers. How can they live in this heroic temper
unless they are endowed with fresh resources of power by the
Spirit of God?

The sayings ascribed to the earthly life of our Lord are only six
in number, apart from the two ascribed to the Risen Christ (Luke
xxiv. 49, Matt. xxviii. 19).

(1) Whosoever shall blaspheme against the Holy Spirit hath never
forgiveness, but is guilty of an eternal sin. MARK iii. 29, with parallel
in MATT. xii. 31.

From a comparison of Matthew xii. 32 with Luke xii. 10, it is
evident that there was another version of this saying in Q, which
was recorded by both the later evangelists.

It has lately been argued that this saying cannot be authentic,
but is a product of the imagination of the apostolic age.[41] The
arguments given are two: first, that the references to the Spirit in
the recorded sayings of Jesus are so few, while belief in the
possession of the Holy Spirit was a cardinal interest of the early
Christian movement; second, that the criticism was probably
levelled at the followers of Jesus after His death that they were
inspired by an evil spirit, and that this is proved by Matt. x. 25:
'If they have called the master of the house Beelzebub, how much
more shall they call them of his household!' These arguments are
unconvincing. The first can equally prove the contrary. The fact
that so few sayings of Jesus referring to the Spirit have been
preserved at a time when the thought of the early Church was full
of the conception of the Spirit, is surely a sign of the scrupulous
fidelity with which the sayings of Jesus were preserved.[42] The
second argument is equally unsubstantial. It is quite probable that
in the years A.D. 30 to 60 Christian exorcists were accused of

---

[41] Branscomb, *St. Mark* (1937), 74.
[42] cf. Easton, *The Gospel before the Gospels* (1928), 90–2.

acting in the power of Beelzebub, and that this reproach was the motive which led to the preservation of the saying before us. But direct evidence for such accusations is lacking. If there is a possible situation in the early Church which might have given rise to this logion about blasphemy against the Holy Spirit, there is a more probable situation in the life of Jesus Himself. The passage reflects the mysterious horror which His extraordinary personal power was likely to arouse.[43]

(2) According to all three Gospels Jesus promises the help of the Spirit in the hour of persecution.

> But whatsoever shall be given you in that hour, that speak ye: for it is not ye that speak, but the Holy Spirit. MARK xiii. 11 (LUKE xii. 12).
>   Again there was a version of this saying in Q. (LUKE xxi. 15= MATT. x. 20.)

Behind any discussion of genuineness here, there lies a question of general probability. First, Jesus had vision and sympathy to put Himself in the place of His disciples. He called His disciples to lose their lives and so to save them.[44] Could He not anticipate for them the perils which were gathering round Himself? Second, what genius was there in the early Church to fashion sayings such as these with their humility, their serenity, their confidence of victory? 'There is nothing overstrained, nothing feverish in the spirit of these first witnesses,' says Wellhausen;[45] 'it is not obstinate or fanatical.' Is it quite incredible that they owed this temper to the remembrance of actual words of their Master? Is not this more probable than that in their danger they fashioned sayings of exquisite beauty and serenity which they proceeded to attribute to Him? It is only after such questions have been satisfactorily faced and answered that we ought to dare to dismiss such a saying as not authentic.

---

[43] So Lohrneyer, *Das Evangelium des Marcus* (1937), 78.

[44] Even Bultmann admits a genuine saying in Mark viii. 35.

[45] *Das Evangelium Matthaei* (1904), 48; in commenting on Matt. x. 16–42.

(3) According to Mark, Jesus introduces the quotation from Psalm cx. I with the phrase: 'David himself said in the Holy Spirit' (Mark xii. 36).

(4) According to Luke (xi. 13) Jesus promises the gift of the Holy Spirit from the Father to those who ask. But the Matthaean parallel has 'good things'. It may well be that the Matthaean version is original Q.

(5) According to Luke iv. 18 Jesus reads Isaiah lxi. I. f. in the Sermon at Nazareth and declares that 'this day' this passage is fulfilled.

(6) According to Matthew's version (xii. 28), Jesus said: 'If I by the spirit of God . . .' where Luke has 'If I by the finger of God . . .'. It is probable that Luke preserves the original form of the saying.

If we are left with only two or three sayings of Jesus which speak of the Holy Spirit, how are we to account for His silence? At least three answers may be advanced. The first is that Jesus said little or nothing because the theme was uncongenial. But surely it is unlikely that He felt that 'an idea like that of the Spirit removed God to a distance or put an abstract power in place of Him'.[46] This would argue Jesus as less skilled in spiritual discernment than Paul, or than hundreds of obscurer saints. The second explanation is purely historical, and has been recently advanced by Dr. Vincent Taylor.[47] Few sayings have reached us, precisely because the conception of the Spirit was dominant and undisputed in the early community. There was no need after Pentecost to quote repeatedly His sayings about the Spirit because all were conscious of perpetual debt to the Spirit. There was no controversy on this issue, nothing to stir the memory to retain the logia which soon perished. It is tempting to go on to the suggestion that in the Fourth Gospel we have a recasting of some such logia, whose original form is irrecoverable. Long ago Matthew Arnold suggested that the surest way to trace original logia in the teaching of the Fourth Gospel was to follow the indication given by the

---

[46] E. F. Scott, *The Spirit in the N.T.* (1923), 79.

[47] In *The Doctrine of the Holy Spirit* (1937), 53–4.

introductory formula Ἀμὴν ἀμὴν λέγω. There are two such logia in the conversation with Nicodemus, referring to the new life which is the Spirit's gift.

These two explanations of the comparative silence of the Synoptic tradition seem inadequate. I venture to offer a third. There are few sayings about the Spirit, because Jesus saw that a richer and profounder understanding of the Spirit was needed than any which His disciples with their lack of insight could glean from the Old Testament; and this re-interpretation of the Spirit's work could only be lived out in His own ministry. So it was with the idea of the Messiahship. He refused the titles which came from popular misconception of His mission; 'no conception of it, current among His contemporaries, answered to His own. It is highly doubtful if He ever used the term Christ of Himself'.[48] This explanation of the problem of the 'Messianic secret' suggests a parallel solution of the problem of the silence as to the Spirit. How easy it was even for His chosen followers to seize upon the lower elements in the Old Testament conception of the Spirit of God is proved by the Acts of the Apostles. At first the stress is on the ecstatic, the abnormal, the transitory. Only after the inseparable bond between His earthly activity and the new life lived in the Spirit's power had been clearly seen, could the deeper truths of the Spirit's working be apprehended and described. Indeed, the whole conception of the Spirit in the Old Testament must needs be baptized into the death of Christ. Calvary was the only gateway to Pentecost.

In support of this position, we may notice that if the word 'Spirit' is not often mentioned by Jesus, the mighty working of God in a new way is not only stated explicitly, but presupposed by all His acts and words. Thus it does not matter whether He said 'by the Spirit of God' or 'by the finger of God' (Matt. xii. 28 = Luke xi. 20). Both phrases have the same meaning.[49] 'God is now mightily active. These deeds of power are signs and tokens of the final overthrow of evil.' So too the sayings about prayer

---

[48] V. Taylor, *Jesus and His Sacrifice*, 20.

[49] cf. Otto, *Kingdom of God and Son of Man*, 168.

prove that in the vision of Jesus God was active. His succour was available; His illimitable gifts were to be bestowed in the time of His final triumph. The givenness of the Kingdom includes the present activity of God.[50] Johannes Weiss once said that the sayings of Jesus on the overthrow of evil could be best interpreted by Luther's verse:

> And let the prince of ill
> Look grim as e'er he will,
> He harms us not a whit:
> For why? His doom is writ;
> A word shall quickly slay him.

We may add that which is lacking in Luther's interpretation by citing a verse of Charles Wesley:

> If what I wish is good
> And suits the will divine,
> By earth and hell in vain withstood
> I know it shall be mine.
>
> Still let them counsel take
> To frustrate His decree,
> They cannot keep a blessing back
> By heaven designed for me.

To the 'little flock' Jesus gave the assurance that they might claim the victory because God's activity was mightily manifest in the world to those who had eyes to see. 'Howbeit rejoice not that the devils are subject unto you, but rejoice that your names are written in heaven.'

In the second chapter I shall endeavour to prove that the connexion of the gift of the new power with a new way of life was immediately recognized by the primitive community.[51] The fellowship in the Spirit was regarded as issuing in social acts. The

---

[50] cf. some excellent pages in H. D. Wendland, op. cit., 129–34, cf. *The Idea of Perfection*, 17–25.
[51] *Infra*, 148–59.

new experience of God was never merely individual. Here we may notice that the new ethical teaching of Jesus must have dawned on the minds of the disciples as a new revelation. This is proved by the care with which the sayings were transmitted, and the distinctive name for the new community. It was a 'Way'. This does not mean a way of a merely individual salvation. All great enterprises and all great revelations create human fellowship. The more surprising and humanly unattainable the gift or calling in which men are united, the more are the hindrances to fellowship swept aside. In their treasuring of the sayings of Jesus and their translation of them into act, the disciples actually gave the world the pattern of a new social structure, even if they did it unawares.

3. The Conception of Messiahship and the Consequent Allegiance

There is a third line of argument which establishes the contention that Jesus is working with a definite idea of an ecclesia. It was inherent in the current idea of the Messiah that he should gather a community in the last days. The conception of Messiahship in the Gospels must be interpreted in the light of the eschatological conception of the Kingdom.

In the first place, it is clear from the data provided by the Gospels that the Kingdom is proclaimed to men as a message of redemption. It is a gift to men, a call to men; it holds out a new righteousness (Matt. vi. 33), and proclaims that the power of evil is being finally broken. In technical language, we may say that the eschatology of the Gospels is a soteriology.[52]

Secondly, since the Kingdom of God is God Himself in His kingly rule, it is not the Messiah who inaugurates the Kingdom, but God who achieves His supreme victory through the Messiah. Jesus Himself in His filial obedience acknowledges the priority of the Father who gave Him the kingdom (Luke xxii. 29). He subordinates His own will at every stage of His ministry to the

---

[52] K. L. Schmidt, in Kittel's *Wörterbuch*, i. 583–4.

will of the Father. Nevertheless He takes the older ideas of the Messianic age and refashions them in His own regal way, confident that through His earthly activity the Father's final purpose is being fulfilled. Again we may say that the Gospel eschatology involves a Christology.

In the third place, since the saving message is directed to Israel, and according to the expectation of Deutero-Isaiah through Israel to all the nations, we should expect that the Gospel eschatology would involve an ecclesiology. So far we have reached the conclusion that Jesus in His Teaching is directing His work to the gathering of a community which is to be the nucleus of the new Israel, that this community is expected to live on a loftier level of achievement than was possible hitherto, and that this life is to be lived out by the power of God, since such a life is His will. Our next step is to trace the connexion between the idea of Messiahship and the idea of the new community.

It was Harnack who laid down, as a postulate of scientific historical study, that Jesus did not intend the Church. Yet in the Harnack *Festgabe* (1921) his famous colleague saw that in the eschatological interpretation of the Kingdom, which Harnack had rejected, lay the germ of the idea of the Ecclesia. Ferdinand Kattenbusch[53] found this in Daniel vii. From this chapter (vii. 13) Jesus took the phrase 'Son of Man' as a description of Himself. But in the same chapter (vii. 27) in the explanation of the vision, the Son of Man is declared to be a symbol of a community, 'the people of the saints of the Most High'. Kattenbusch argued that Jesus must have read the chapter as a whole, that He regarded Himself as the representative of a community, and that for Him His disciples were this community. It was the incomparable greatness of Jesus that into this visionary figure of the Son of Man He breathed a living soul. He brought the vision from heaven to

---

[53] *Der Quellort der Kirchenidee*, 143–72. In the article immediately preceding, Harnack's fellow-Ritschlian, Julius Kaftan, declared (141) that he had been forced to the conclusion that the expectation of the speedy end of the age was the necessary point of departure, if the problem of New Testament Theology was to be solved.

earth, and made it incarnate in a Man, living a human life among men. Jesus and His disciples were a community, joined together in affection, with a faith in God's power working through Him.[54]

Another, and a more drastic expression of the theory which traces the idea of the Ecclesia to Daniel vii, is to be found in the work of Professor T. W. Manson, who maintains that the Son of Man in the Gospels is an embodiment of the Remnant idea. 'The Son of Man, like the Servant of Jehovah, is an ideal figure and stands for the manifestation of the Kingdom of God on earth in a people wholly devoted to their heavenly King.' The mission of Jesus is 'to create the Son of Man, the kingdom of the saints of the Most High'.[55] When Jesus speaks of the Son of Man, he is primarily speaking not of Himself but of a community; it is only as the Cross draws near that He stands alone, and that the title is applicable only to Himself. The view is argued powerfully but is based on a series of improbabilities. To any student to-day the confusion caused by applying the title, now in the sense of a community, now in the sense of an individual, is evident. It is unlikely that Jesus in His teaching of His disciples would clothe His thought in such an ambiguity. Further, the 'community' interpretation is hardly natural in any passage of the Gospels.[56] But in Professor Manson's book there is a valuable stress on the idea of the Remnant as vitally connected with the conception of Messiahship. Without endorsing the common view (against which Manson argues), that Jesus is taking over the conception of the supernatural Son of Man found in the *Book of Enoch*, I would adhere to the view that it is in the highest degree likely that Jesus is using in a unique and original way the phrase which occurs with quite different meanings in Daniel and in Enoch, and is entirely transforming it by His teaching and His life. The real distinction

---

[54] Kattenbusch points out (op. cit., 162) how close is this description to the definition of the Church in the *Apologia* for the Augsburg Confession (*Die Bekenntnisschriften der ev.-luth. Kirche*, 1930, i. 234. Art. vii); societas fidei et spiritus sancti in cordibus.

[55] *The Teaching of Jesus* (1931) 227.

[56] Perhaps in Mark ii. 28.

of His use of the phrase is that He applies it to one who is offering forgiveness to the sinner, companying with a band of chosen followers as a man among men, and treading the path of love which leads to the inevitable Cross. He associates with Himself His followers. It is this connexion of the Messianic Deliverer and the community which is indisputably attested by eschatological passages both in the Old Testament and in the Apocalyptic literature. Even the Man in 4 Esdras, whose fiery breath destroys the wicked, calls unto him another 'multitude of men that was peaceable' (xiii. 12).

Schweitzer has collected some of the evidence.[57] His choice of passages[58] is determined by his view that the members of the community of the Messianic age were predestined for fellowship with one another and with the Messiah, and that their names are inscribed in the Book of Life. It is the _Book of Enoch_ which provides Schweitzer with his most striking illustrations.

> For the Son of Man was formerly hidden, and the Highest kept him in the presence of His power, and has revealed him to the Elect. The community of the Saints and Elect shall be sown [sic], and all the Elect shall stand before him in that day. lxii. 7–8.
>
> The Lord of Spirits shall dwell over them and they shall eat with that Son of Man, shall lie down and rise up to all eternity. The Righteous and Elect shall raise themselves from the earth, and shall cease to cast down their eyes, and shall be clothed with the garment of glory. lxii. 14–15.

We may disentangle the truth which lies in Schweitzer's argument from some of the misleading terms which he uses, such as 'predestination'[59] and 'mysticism'. Jesus takes over the conceptions

---

[57] _The Mysticism of Paul_ (E. tr. 1931) 101–2.

[58] Isaiah iv. 3; Mal. iii. 16–17; Ps. lxix. 28; Daniel xii. 1.

[59] Schweitzer ascribes this concept of 'predestination' to the thought of Jesus. But the predestination does not really predestinate. The election of the saints only becomes a reality if they believe in the preaching of Jesus (op. cit., 180) and their election, he says, 'for Jesus is not an unalterable thing' (106).

of the current eschatology, but He transforms them. He chooses His followers, but they follow gladly, yielding their free consent. The first purpose of His choice is that 'they may be with him' (Mark iii. 14).

'It is simply not the fact that Jesus' preaching dealt with nothing but the nearness of the Kingdom of God and the ethic to be practised during the period of waiting: He also declared that in the fellowship with Him on which they had entered His followers had already the guarantee of future fellowship with the Son of Man.'[60]

He expects that they will suffer with Him. There are special Beatitudes which proclaim the privilege of such suffering (Matt. v. 11–12). There is a kinship between Himself and those who do the will of God, which transcends even family relationship.

> Who is my mother and my brethren? And looking round on them which sat round about him, he saith, Behold, my mother and my brethren! For whosoever shall do the will of God, the same is my brother, and sister, and mother. MARK iii. 33^b–5.
>
> If any man cometh unto me, and hateth not his own father, and mother, and wife, and children, and brethren, and sisters, yea, and his own life also, he cannot be my disciple. Whosoever doth not bear his own cross, and come after me, cannot be my disciple. LUKE xiv. 26–7; MATT. x. 37–8.

The startling form ('hateth not') in which Luke transmits the saying makes it probable that the Lukan version is more original than the parallel logion ('loveth more than') in Matthew. The paradoxical demand for 'hatred' and the inherent probability that Jesus warned His disciples, on the *via dolorosa* which led to the Cross, that any lesser loyalties must take second place, make it highly probable that we have the saying almost as Jesus spoke it. The Hebrew word *sane*, hate, is used in Deut. xxi. 15, Genesis xxix. 31, 33, for 'loving less' one of two wives. That Luke preserves the word 'hate' in a Gospel written for Greek readers who would not be so likely to understand the Semitic hyperbole is another proof of his reverence for the Master's words.

---

[60] Op. cit., 105.

When the historical critic has sifted such sayings as these to the uttermost, there remains something strange, startling, irreducible. A new allegiance was entering into the world, disturbing old traditions, transcending the former sweet loyalties of kindred and home, and destined to outlive all other totalitarian claims, whether those of Caesar in the early centuries, or those of caste and nationality and communism in the twentieth.

Into sayings such as these only a few can enter of those who live in lands where the knowledge of the glory of God in the face of Jesus Christ has been transmitted for generations from soul to soul and life to life. But even now there are children of homes where God has been forgotten who with a new understanding are listening to this solemn music. In India the convert to Christianity from the higher castes has always understood.[61]

But there is another side to this austere demand. The new allegiance is creating a new community.

> Verily I say unto you, there is no man that hath left house, or brethren, or sisters, or mother, or father, or children, or lands for my sake, and for the gospel's sake, but he shall receive a hundredfold now in this time, houses, and brethren, and sisters, and mothers, and children, and lands, with persecutions; and in the world to come eternal life. MARK. x. 29–30.

Those who doubt the authenticity of some of the details in this saying may notice the eschatological form in which the saying is cast.[62] But the new community, even in the present age, is clearly envisaged by our Lord. It is the 'little flock' to which it is the good pleasure of His Father to give the *Basileia*.

In these last two sayings the motive of love for the Messiah is dominant. But the love of the Messiah for His own is presupposed. In the Messianic expectation there is one figure more winning and gracious than the Anointed King, or the unearthly Son of Man; it is the figure of the Shepherd. The Shepherd is a sorrowful figure

---

[61] See the *Life of Theophilus Subramanyam*, by C. H. Monahan.
[62] Bultmann, *Gesch. Syn. Trad.*, 115–16 sees an original saying behind this Markan form.

without his sheep, and some of the pictures of the restored Israel show us God's people as His flock. Even in the *Book of Enoch* (xc.) the Messiah, himself one of the flock, protects and leads it; and in the *Psalms of Solomon* (xvii. 45) he is 'tending the flock of the Lord with faith and righteousness, and he shall suffer none among them to faint in their pasture'.

When Jesus speaks of the lost sheep over whom His soul yearns (Mark vi. 34), or thinks of the individual care of the shepherd, and his long Journey after the lost sheep until he may find it, He is employing the imagery that is most descriptive of personal relationship and tender love. When He quotes Zechariah xiii. 7 (Mark xiv. 27),

> I will smite the shepherd,
> And the sheep shall be scattered abroad,

the words ring like the cry of a wounded heart.[63] It was in love that the Shepherd gathered His flock, and it is the love of their allegiance to Him that will hold the flock together.

Here we shall find the link between the original teaching of Jesus, on the one hand, and, on the other, the thought of the primitive community in Jerusalem, and the profounder Christianity of St. Paul. It is Schweitzer's insight that has enabled us to see this connexion. The preaching of the *Basileia* involves the gathering of the true Israel of God, the little flock. Jesus Himself as the destined Messiah gathered this community in close companionship with Himself. In fellowship with Him now, they have their guarantee of fellowship with the Son of Man hereafter. St. Paul takes up this conception of a corporate relationship of the community with Christ Himself and interprets it by what is misleadingly called his 'Christ-mysticism'. This relationship is no individualistic relationship of the solitary soul with Christ, no 'flight of the alone to the Alone'. It belongs to those in the community. It is an integral part of the idea of the Ecclesia.

---

[63]   Mark xiv. 27. See the excellent discussion of the authenticity in V. Taylor, *Jesus and His Sacrifice*, 145–7.

4. The Message as Constitutive of the Community

The fourth argument may be stated as follows. As the method of gathering the new community, Jesus proclaimed a certain message, the implications of which became clearer to His followers as time went on.

There are three or four terms in the Synoptic Gospels which all point to this conclusion.

The Word of God. The New Testament conception of the Word of God is derived from that of the Word of God in the Old Testament, as the revealed will of God. The very existence of the nation was grounded in the Word or will of God.[64] God spoke in the law and that law was determinative of all the life of the people of God. God spoke through the prophets, and the 'words' were not merely isolated utterances; the whole was present in every single revelation, because every such revelation expressed the divine will which was one, coherent, and continuous.[65] The distinctive characteristic[66] of the Old Testament use of the concept Word of God is that it is directed to human history; it is the will of God for events in time.

> 'To the realism of the natural mind, the spoken word is not a mere articulate sound conveying a meaning; it is a thing, and it does things. . . . The word is a concrete reality, a veritable cause. What was true of the words of men was true in an eminent degree of the words of God. The fiats of God in the first chapter of Genesis are creative forces: 'God said, let there be light, and light came into being.'[67]

This conception is valid both in the Old Testament and in later Judaism.

So in the Gospels Jesus brings the Word of God, which is God's will. 'He that hath ears to hear, let him hear.' In this saying, hearing means obedience and includes action. Where Mark

---

[64] Eichrodt, *Theologie des Alten Testaments* (1933) i. 153.

[65] Köhler, *Theologie des Alten Testaments* (1936) 90–1.

[66] Schniewind, *Euangelion* (i. 1927) 3, 41.

[67] G. F. Moore, *Judaism*, i. 414–15. See Ps. xxxiii. 6, 9; Isaiah lv. 11;4 Esdras vi. 38; tuum verbum opus perfecit.

(iii. 35) writes 'whosoever shall do the will of God', Luke transcribes (viii. 21): 'these which hear the word of God, and do it.' This is true interpretation.[68] But the Word in the New Testament acquires a new solemnity in that it is the final Word, the proclamation of that fulfilment which prophets and righteous men desired to see. The Word is related to the coming judgement:

> Whosoever shall be ashamed of me and of my words in this adulterous and sinful generation, the Son of Man also shall be ashamed of him, when he cometh in the glory of his Father with the holy angels. MARK viii. 38.

Luke (from Q) interprets rightly here: 'Whosoever shall confess me before men.' The person of Jesus is in His word. His word is an event, an act of the will of God.

The Gospel. In the New Testament the determinative expressions are *euangelizesthai*, to proclaim the good tidings, and *euangelion*, the gospel. It is now established by the work of Dalman and Schniewind that the root of the conception is to be found in the later part of the book of Isaiah and especially in ch. lxi. 'One speaks there who says twice of himself that he will "proclaim", and thrice that he is "to bring good news". This was, in fact, the kind and essence of all the preaching of our Lord, according to the very foundation of His purpose. And in that prophetic word, then half a millennium old, lies the most important root of His gospel as well as of ours.'[69]

---

[68] Bultmann, *Glaube und Verstehen* (1933) 273; see the whole of the essay on *Der Begriff des Wortes Gottes im Neuen Testaments*; also the admirable discussion in *Christian Worship* (ed. N. Micklem, 1936) by W. H. Cadman, *The Word of God in the New Testament*.

[69] Dalman, *Jesus-Jeshua* (E. tr. 1929), 55; cf. *The Words of Jesus*, 104. The exposition in the above and the following paragraphs is based on Dalman, also on Schniewind Euangelion, i (1927); ii (1931) and the articles by G. Friedrich in Kittel's *Theologisches Wörterbuch* on *euangelion* and *kerusso*, and is in essential agreement with W. K. Lowther Clarke, Divine Humanity (1936), 87–100: 'What is the Gospel?' These works have taken the discussion beyond the conclusion of Harnack, *Constitution and Law of the Church* (E. tr. 1910), 275–331.

According to our Gospels, Jesus quoted this chapter twice:

(1)   The Spirit of the Lord is upon me,
Because he anointed me to preach good tidings to the poor:
He hath sent me to proclaim release to the captives,
And recovering of sight to the blind,
To set at liberty them that are bruised,
To proclaim the acceptable year of the Lord.
. . . To-day hath this scripture been fulfilled in your ears.
Luke iv. 18–19, 21.

(2)   Go your way, and tell John what things ye have seen and heard;
the blind receive their sight, the lame walk, the lepers are cleansed,
and the deaf hear, the dead are raised up, the poor have the gospel
preached to them. Luke vii. 22 = Matt. Xi. 4–5.

The substantial authenticity of the second logion from Q is
rarely disputed.[70] If Jesus uses the quotation once, might He not
have used it more than once? We may notice the eschatological
setting of both citations. The answer to John's question is indirect,
the declaration in the synagogue at Nazareth is direct. Both
answer and declaration affirm that the word spoken in Israel of
the coming reign of God in the last days is now fulfilled. The
Kingdom is coming in the work and words of Jesus; the climax is
the preaching of good news to the poor. The answer to John would
be meaningless if the *euangelion* were not having an immediate
effect. The poor (who are also the meek, and the lowly, in the
Gospels) were not only hearing the good news but receiving it.
The gospel was the word of God with power, creating faith and
thereby creating a community under the Kingly Rule of God.
'Proclamation and realization are closely connected.'[71]

In Deutero-Isaiah the preaching of the good news of God's
Reign is inseparable from the gathering together of the redeemed
Israel, and the guidance of His flock by Yahweh.

---

[70]   Bultmann admits it, and uses it; Gesch. Syn. Trad., 133 *Jesus and the
Word* (Etr. 1935) 28, 173.
[71]   Dalman, *Jesus-Jeshua*, 53.

> O thou that tellest good tidings to Zion,
>   get thee up into the high mountain.
> Behold, the Lord God will come as a mighty one,
>   and his arm shall rule for him.
> He shall feed his flock like a shepherd.
> Isaiah xl. 9[a], 10[a], 11[a].

> How beautiful upon the mountains are the feet of him that bringeth
>   good tidings . . . that saith unto Zion, Thy God reigneth!
> For the Lord hath comforted his people, he hath redeemed
>   Jerusalem. Isaiah lii. 7, 9[b].

In Isaiah lx. 6 even the heathen come to Zion and proclaim the praises of Yahweh, so great is the power of the word of God.

It is unnecessary to set out in detail all the other passages where the word *euangelion* is attributed to Jesus by the Synoptic Gospels.[72] But a survey of all the evidence which has been assiduously collected and sifted in recent studies, leads, as Dr. Lowther Clarke has pointed out, to a surprisingly conservative result. 'The originality of Jesus was rooted in a revival of the true meaning of Second Isaiah. . . . The Gospel *is* the "Kingdom of God", the message, which is also the reality, that God has ascended the throne and the New Age has begun; further, that the message and the Messenger are one. Eschatology has succeeded to prophecy, the future has become the present.'[73] But one passage deserves special notice:

> Wheresoever the gospel shall be preached throughout the whole world, that also which this woman hath done shall be spoken of for a memorial of her. MARK xiv. 9.

The evangelist does not tell her name, and probably does not know it. It is widely stated that the logion is not authentic, and was formed by the community at the period of the preaching to Gentiles. This statement raises difficulties, and, so far as I can see,

---

[72] Mark i. 14; Viii 35; xiii. 10; Luke iv. 43; xvi 16.
[73] *Divine Humanity*, 96–7.

solves none. There is general acknowledgement of the essential historicity of the incident of the Anointing.[74] Why should a saying be attached without the woman's name? Surely the temptation to give some name would be irresistible for those who were adding to the tradition.[75] Again, Jesus speaks of men (probably Gentiles) coming from the east and the west to sit down with the patriarchs in the kingdom of God (Matt. viii. 11 = Luke xiii. 28–9).[76] The question of St. Paul is as valid for Jesus as for himself: 'How shall they hear without a preacher?'[77] In the third place, we have seen that the 'Gospel' as we have it in the sayings of Jesus was rooted in the thought of Second Isaiah. Are we to conclude that Jesus could not have envisaged any proclamation to the Gentiles and that His vision was narrower than that of the Old Testament prophets?[78]

Whatever be our impression about this logion, the main conclusion stands. Jesus regarded Himself as the bearer of good tidings, of a Gospel which was already powerful, and this Gospel was to be constitutive of the Messianic community. I will only add that the additional conclusion that the new community would, according to Jesus, include Gentiles, whose faith put Jews to shame, is strongly supported by the evidence of the Synoptic Gospels.[79]

The Mystery. But the unbelief of Jews was already a problem in the earthly ministry of Jesus. Linked with the conception of 'Gospel' in our sources is another conception, that of *mysterion*. Some investigation of the word itself and of the idea behind it is necessary if we are to discern the dividing line between the 'little flock' and those who had not received the good news. The word *mysterion* cannot be separated from the well-attested saying (Matt. xi. 25 = Luke x. 21) 'I thank thee, O Father, Lord of heaven

---

[74]   Bultmann, *Gesch. Syn. Trad.*, 37, 69. Branscomb, *St. Mark*, 246.

[75]   Friedrich in *Theologisches Wörtruch*, ii. 725.

[76]   Bultmann, *Jesus and the Word*, 4; 4–5.

[77]   Friedrich, op. cit., 726.

[78]   Isaiah lii. 10; xlix. 6, 12; lx. 6. Malachi i. 11.

[79]   Add to Matt. viii. ll Luke xiii. 29, the story of the Centurion, Matt. viii. 10 = Luke vii. 9. It was faith which Jesus demanded as the essential in His disciples, and the Centurion has it.

and earth, that thou didst hide these things from the wise and understanding, and didst reveal them unto babes'.

The word *mysterion* occurs in the Gospels only in Mark iv. 11[a], and the parallels which have the plural, 'mysteries':

Unto you is given the mystery of the kingdom of God.

The authenticity of the saying has been abandoned by so many leading writers that it may seem presumptuous to dare to question the common verdict. The conclusion that the saying is secondary is usually reached by considering the context, and Mark's theory of the parables. But we may be allowed to disentangle that difficult problem from the discussion of the saying given above as a separate logion. It is indeed difficult to believe that the passage as it stands, Mark iv. 11[b]–12, contains the genuine interpretation of the mind of our Lord about His method of speaking in parables. I believe beneath the form of it the cry of the defeated love of Jesus may be clearly heard, and that His experience was interpreted by Himself in the light of the famous passage in Isaiah, itself full of brokenhearted irony. But for our present purpose verse 11[a] must be considered alone. Even if the authenticity of the allegorizing explanation in iv. 14–20 be given up, this sentence contains an essential idea in the teaching of Jesus.

The chief discussions in English of the word *mysterion* are in J. B. Lightfoot's *Colossians*, 167–8, E. Hatch, *Essays in Biblical Greek*, 57–62, and J. Armitage Robinson's *Ephesians*, 234–40. Lightfoot said that the word was borrowed from the pagan mysteries, and did not even refer to the Septuagint. That opinion is still current.[80] But, as Armitage Robinson demonstrated, there is a deep gulf fixed between a dramatic representation of sacred things which 'the initiated are pledged to keep inviolably secret' and the New Testament sense of 'mystery' as a secret which was once hidden and which God has now willed to make known.

In the Septuagint we find the word used in Daniel ii. of a secret which God reveals to Daniel and which he expounds to the king.

---

[80] Branscomb, *St. Mark* (1937), 78–9.

The Aramaic original is *raz*. The other examples are all in the Apocryphal books (of any secret), but the later Greek translators use it occasionally. Twice it is used of the secret counsel of God.[81] In the Book of Revelation (x. 7) the word is used in a citation of Amos iii. 7, where the LXX translator has avoided it: 'Then is finished the mystery of God, which he declared to his servants the prophets.' This citation carries us back to the eighth century: 'Surely the Lord God will do nothing, but he revealeth his secret (Hebr. *sôdh*) to his servants the prophets.' The Hebrew word[82] means (1) council, Jeremiah vi. 11, Job xix. 19; (2) counsel, a circle of intimate friends, especially the counsel taken by friends in familiar conversation, Psalm lv. 15; (3) the secret counsel of God, which may be revealed, as here in Amos; also, implying familiar intercourse, intimacy; Proverbs iii. 32: 'his secret is with the upright'; Psalm xxv. 14: 'the secret of the Lord is with them that fear him; and he will shew them his covenant'.

Here then we have a fundamental concept of Hebrew religion, including the idea of intimacy with God, and connected with Yahweh's self-revelation. The secret counsel of God is primarily His purpose for human life. In Apocalyptic literature, especially in Enoch, the idea of a mystery to be revealed is frequent.[83] There is a common Aramaic word which Jesus may have used. Finally, the idea of the *mysterion* of the kingdom, the secret of God's final purpose for mankind, is contained in a logion which is undoubtedly authentic:[84]

> I thank thee, O Father, Lord of heaven and earth, that thou didst hide these things from the wise and understanding, and didst reveal them unto babes. MATT. xi. 25= LUKE x. 21.

---

[81]   Theodotion, Job xv. 8 and Psalm xxiv (xxv), 14.

[82]   Brown, Driver, Briggs, *Lexicon*, 691.

[83]   For other references to the 'mystery', some of them pre-Christian, see B. W. Bacon, *The Gospel of Mark* (1925) 142.

[84]   After a searching examination of this saying, Bultmann, op cit., 171–2 comes to the conclusion that there is no reason to refuse it to Jesus.

Indeed, the question is not whether the saying is authentic but whether any religion which offers personal communion with a personal God can exist without this concept of an open secret, whereby God gives Himself to those who are ready to receive Him. 'The secret of the Lord is with them that fear Him.' And when the secret is that the final age has dawned, that it may be apprehended in the person, the words, the deeds, of a living Messenger of God, it will not seem incredible that Jesus said: 'Unto you is given the mystery of the kingdom of God,' and that this gift implied an inevitable contrast with those who had failed to receive it.[85]

According to St. Mark, the 'mystery' was only discerned in its rich meaning at a later stage in the life of our Lord. The revelation that the Son of Man must suffer came after the confession of Peter. In view of the masterly analysis by Dr. Vincent Taylor, *Jesus and His Sacrifice*, it is unnecessary to proceed to the detailed examination of all the sayings which suggest that 'the mystery of the kingdom of God' included for Jesus His death and His resurrection. But certain of the Passion sayings contain an implicit reference to the community which was being constituted in the last days of the life of Jesus.

The two quotations from the Old Testament, 'the Stone which the builders rejected' (Mark xii. 10–11) and the Shepherd (Mark xiv. 27) point to two familiar images of the People of God.[86] The Stone by itself has little meaning. If it is 'the head of the corner' there is contemplated a new house of Jacob. The sheep who are to be scattered abroad, belong to the 'little flock' the nucleus of the new Israel.

In the sayings at the Last Supper the new community is implied, first, in the imagery of the Messianic banquet (Mark xiv. 25);

---

[85] 'The saying may well be based on authentic words of Christ': B. T. D. Smith, St. Matthew (1927) I 37. See Otto, *Kingdom of God and Son of Man* (E. tr. 1938), 138–46 for an interesting interpretation which attempts to do justice to the deep religious significance of the saying.

[86] The house of Israel is so familiar a synonym for Israel that another metaphor can be explained by it: 'The vineyard . . . is the house of Israel' (Isaiah v. 7).

second, in the mention of a covenant (Mark xiv. 24); third by the connexion of this covenant with His atoning death, whereby He gives His disciples a share in that reconciling power.

The content of this 'mystery' is the content of the *euangelion*. The New Age has begun. The future Kingdom is already dawning. Its operation may be seen in the person and activity of Jesus Himself. Those who discern the kingdom in its dawning are pronounced blessed indeed:

> Blessed are your eyes, for they see; and your ears, for they hear. For verily I say unto you, that many prophets and righteous men desired to see the things which ye see, and saw them not; and to hear the things which ye hear, and heard them not. MATT. xiii. 16–17; LUKE x. 23–4.

This saying is accepted by Bultmann[87] as indubitably authentic, and is set in the forefront of his picture of the teaching of Jesus. He denies that the saying originally implied direct reference to the person of Jesus Himself. But in view of his excellent account (already cited on p. 82) of the close connexion between the Word of God and the bearer of that Word, it seems illogical to hold that in the mind of Jesus the proclamation of the New Age now beginning can be sundered from the Person who proclaims it. The Christology of the Church must be rooted in sayings such as this. The Word of God is the Will of God.[88] The message and the acts of the Messenger are the signs of the presence of the new order which is being inaugurated in Him.

The metaphor of 'seeing' the Messianic age has parallels in the New Testament (Luke ii. 30; Hebrews xi. 13; John viii. 56). There is a striking passage in the *Psalms of Solomon* (about 60–40 B.C.) which proves that the saying of Jesus is cast in language intelligible to His hearers:

---

[87] *Jesus and the Word*, 27; *Geschichte der Synoptischen Tradition* (1931) 114, 133.

[88] Bultmann, *Glaube und Verstehen* (1933) 273; *Gesch. Syn. Trad.*, 115, 133.

> Blessed are they that shall be born in those days, To behold the good things of Israel, Which God shall bring to pass in the gathering together of the tribes. xvii. 50.

The saying of Jesus means that the day of the good things of Israel has now dawned. For prophets and kings that day lay still in the future; but now by God's act it is present. He who has ears to hear may hear the good news. He who has eyes to see may behold the dawn.

With this saying goes another, closely related to it, an additional beatitude at the end of His reply to John the Baptist:

> And blessed is he, whosoever shall find none occasion of stumbling in me. MATT. xi. 6; LUKE vii. 23.

This saying is inseparable from the preceding verses. Jesus is preaching the *euangelion* by deed and word, and the 'poor' are receiving it. This final logion implies that some are not receiving the good news; they do not understand the *mysterion*. These are not entering into the Rule of God. Further, we may infer that according to the evangelists John himself was among them; and that he was not satisfied with the reply of Jesus. If there had been any warrant in the tradition, the evangelists would surely have recorded a second homage rendered to Jesus by John. In the discourse on John which follows in the Q tradition, Jesus says that he that is least in the Kingdom of God is greater than John. The impression is confirmed that John did not comprehend the meaning of the *mysterion*.

This beatitude is an appeal from Jesus to John, a cry from the heart of One who knows the sadness as well as the joy of love. There was an 'occasion of stumbling', a *skandalon*, for John the Baptist.

The Greek words (σκάνδαλον, σκανδαλίζεθαι) translated 'offence', 'occasion of stumbling', 'cause to offend or stumble', play no small part in the thought of the New Testament. The noun σκάνδαλον is the later form of a rare Greek word σκανδάληθρον, which originally meant a piece of wood in a trap on which the bait is placed, and which, when touched by the animal, springs up and shuts the trap.[89] In Aristophanes (*Birds*, 527, *Acharnians*, 687) the phrase to set σκανδάληθρα is equivalent to setting a trap. The same meaning is found in the Septuagint, in certain Psalms (lxviii. 23, cxxxix. 6) where the word σκάνδαλον is used[90] as a translation for the Hebrew *môqēsh*, snare. But in three passages in the LXX we find a totally different metaphor – that of stumbling over a stone. This is due to the fact that σκάνδαλον is used as a translation of the Hebrew *mikshôl*, stumbling. The word acquired a special religious significance. It is used for a moral offence, that which renders a man guilty before God, and deserving of punishment;[91] it is an occasion of inner deterioration.[92] In the New Testament the metaphor of the 'trap' or 'snare' persists in a few passages. Thus St. Paul (Rom. xi. 9) quotes Psalm lxix. 22–3; the author of the Apocalypse (ii. 14) regards the teaching of Balaam, to eat things offered to idols and to commit fornication, as a deadly snare. But the dominant metaphor is that of the stone in the path, the occasion of stumbling.[93]

What is the stone of stumbling for John the Baptist according to the mind of our Lord? It must be that Jesus was not the kind of Messiah whom John was anticipating. According to our earliest sources John had proclaimed a mighty Apocalyptic Messiah who would come in the Day of Yahweh and baptize with the fire of judgement. His fan would be in His hand, and He would thoroughly purge His threshing-floor.

---

[89] G. Stählin, *Skandalon* (1930) 15.

[90] Psalms lxix. 2, cxl. 5 in R.V.

[91] Judith v. 20; see Stählin, 74–5.

[92] Prov. xxii. 25 (Sym.); Ezekiel vii. 19 (Sym.); Stählin, 87, 88, 145.

[93] Stählin, 144. The chief passages are Romans xiv. 13; xvi. 17; Rom. ix 33 and I Peter ii. 6 (quoting Isaiah xxviii. 16); I Cor. i. 23 and Gal. v. 11 (the *skandalon* of the Cross); in the Gospels, Luke xvii. 1; Matt. xiii. 41; xvi. 23; xviii. 7. The verb is frequently in Matthew and Mark. The attempt to interpret all the N.T. uses of the verb in the sense of 'setting a trap for' breaks down in the passage under discussion. Carr, *Horae Biblicae*, 58–68; J. H. Moulton, *Expos. times*, xxvi. 331–2; Allen, *St. Mark*, 199–202 (who acknowledges the difficulty of Matt. xi. 6); Moulton-Milligan, *Vocabulary of the Greek Testament*, 576.

He will gather his wheat into the garner,
But the chaff he will burn up with unquenchable fire.
MATT. iii. 12; LUKE iii. 17.

This description is not applicable to any merely nationalist deliverer, nor to a Messianic scion of David's line such as is expected in the *Psalms of Solomon*. Rather is the picture delineated by John that of the Coming One in Malachi, scarcely to be distinguished from God Himself. John could not yet discern the vice-regent of God in a wandering preacher, subject to suffering and perhaps already, like himself, to persecution. If this interpretation is true, the stone of stumbling was the fact of suffering.[94] It is the offence of the Cross, even before the obedience of Jesus to His Father's will had brought Him to Calvary.

Support for this view may be found in the difficult passage in Mark ix. 9–13. Jesus is training His disciples to expect those sufferings. They bring the interpretation of the scribes that the world must be set in order before the Messiah comes. If Elijah is to set all things in order, how is this to be reconciled with the sufferings and humiliation of the Son of Man? Jesus rejects this interpretation. Elijah has come already in the person of John the Baptist. He has been rejected and killed. The predecessor is not exempt from the fate of the Messiah.[95]

The view that John the Baptist doubted the Messiahship of Jesus has been regarded as incredible by the great exegetes of the Church. Calvin regarded it as 'altogether absurd'.[96] But traditional exegesis has underestimated the originality of the idea of a suffering Messiah.[97] The Gospels provide us with evidence that Jesus was concerned to guard the disciples against the danger of stumbling on this rock of offence.[98] His task was the transforma-

[94]   So Stählin, 231–4.
[95]   See Rawlinson, *St. Mark*, 121. The interpretation of Wellhausen is to be preferred to the assumption of a dislocation of the text.
[96]   'Valde absurdum.' cf. Augustine, Serm. 66, 3, 4; So Hilary, Ambrose, Chrysostom and Jerome.
[97]   G. F. Moore, *Judaism*, i. 551.
[98]   cf. Stählin 227.

tion of the current ideal. 'There is no dead lift so heavy as that which is required to change an ideal. We do not wonder that at the moment it was too much for Him and for them.'[99] The gospel which Jesus proclaimed, 'the mystery of the kingdom', included as an essential element the idea of redemption through His suffering, and this idea was explicitly taught by Him towards the end of His ministry. John the Baptist stumbled here. For all his greatness he remained outside. Jesus foresaw that in spite of all His warnings the disciples would also stumble on this offence of the Cross. Yet this message was to be the integrating and constitutive Word of God for the new Israel.

The historical fact that Jesus went up to Jerusalem has been variously interpreted. The theory which has left a deep mark on our records is that He went up because it was predestined. 'The Son of Man must suffer.' For Mark this probably meant that Jesus went up because 'it was written'. But the same evangelist gives us evidence for a profounder view, which also was current in the early Church. The 'must' is not an outward necessity but an inward constraint. The decision to go to Jerusalem, to an almost certain death, was no mere fulfilment of the greatest of the Old Testament scriptures, though Jesus had pondered those scriptures and read His Father's meaning there. His motive was obedience to the Will of God as He discerned that Will in the task to which He was committed, with the divine light shining on it from the oracles of the past.

All our sources agree that His life was a life of obedience; from the moment when the Spirit drives Him out into the wilderness to the dark evening in the garden when He cries, 'Abba, Father, all things are possible to thee: remove this cup from me. Howbeit not what I will, but what thou wilt'. St. Paul and the author of the Epistle to the Hebrews both seize on this clue. 'Being found in fashion as a man, he humbled himself, becoming obedient unto death, yea, the death of the Cross' (Phil. ii. 8). 'Though he was a Son yet he learned obedience through the things which he suffered' (Heb. v. 8). Four times in the Fourth Gospel the phrase rings out:

---

[99]   J. Denney, *The Death of Christ*, 35.

'The will of him that sent me.' 'May thy will be done' is the *motif* of the Lord's Prayer.

It was McLeod Campbell[100] who, more than eighty years ago, insisted that the great key-word on the subject of the Atonement was the text, 'Lo, I come to do thy will, O God'. Discussions of recent years with regard to the eschatological nature of the Kingdom of God enable us to set this motive of obedience against the background of God's final purpose for mankind.

According to the teaching of Jesus it is the Will of God to inaugurate the new age which is to be crowned by God's final victory at the end of human history. The obedience of Jesus to God's Will leads Him to make his final appeal at Jerusalem. But why did He go up, if He knew that His death was certain?[101]

The answer to this question must take account of the general characteristic of the predictive element in Hebrew prophecy. It is moral, and therefore contingent.[102] The prediction of the catastrophe awaiting the Jewish people was intended to influence conduct, and avert the danger threatened. Jesus had prophesied His death. But it was the Will of God that to the end He should continue in the activity in which the Kingdom was already being realized. That activity was a final appeal which conceivably might win a response. If He is confronted by the choice, either to go up to Jerusalem at the time of the Feast, or not to go up, which alternative is He to take? He could have continued the work in 'the borders of Tyre and Sidon', in the villages of Caesarea Philippi, or in the towns of Galilee. But if His aim was a new Israel, or the constitution of a saving remnant, it would naturally be in Jerusalem that the supreme appeal should be made. He was a Jew, and a loyal Jew was expected to be in Jerusalem at the feast of the Passover. 'Sacrifice for the whole nation was accomplished only in her courts, and the nation was world wide.'[103] 'In the pilgrims

---

[100]   *The Nature of the Atonement* (1856) ch. v.
[101]   The answers to this question, bewildering in their variety, are discussed by Montefiore, *The Synoptic Gospels* (1927), i. 190–3.
[102]   A. B. Davidson, art. 'Prophecy' in Hastings, *D.B.*, iv. 125–6.
[103]   G. A. Smith, *Jerusalem*, ii. 397.

from all lands the whole Jewish nation was ideally gathered at the feast.'[104] Thither the tribes went up. From the ends of the earth they would fly instinctively homewards like doves to their windows. They could not forget their home. And in the age to come, according to Jewish belief, Jerusalem would be the religious centre of the world.[105] As a loyal Jew, as a prophet loving His own people, Jesus could not stay away. If He had a message, it must be delivered there, especially at the time when the minds of His hearers might be stirred with sacred memories, and their hearts throbbing with the ancient hope of the final salvation. Only there and at that time could a message be uttered to the Jewish people, which through the pilgrim hosts might be carried to every part of the habitable world. We do wrong to the vastness of the 'spiritual empire'[106] of Judaism, and unwarrantably limit the horizon of our Lord, if we leave out of account the unique opportunity afforded by the gathering of pilgrims at the Passover to One who at once proclaimed and embodied the final purpose of God for mankind.

According to our evidence, He went up to the Passover to carry on and consummate His work, not just to get Himself crucified. On His way He passed through Jericho, and His presence meant a revolution in the life of one outcast. So far from regarding this incident as an interruption, Jesus declares that this was the work which He had come to do. Zacchaeus was one of the lost sheep of the house of Israel. 'The Son of Man came to seek and to save that which was lost.' The Messianic salvation has visited the household, and Zacchaeus is now a true son of Abraham.

This passion for the reconstruction of the true Israel of God is the result of the obedience to the Father's Will, and is the dominating motive of the final ministry at Jerusalem. 'He was not filling in time or merely awaiting the end. All day long He was carrying on His work – cleansing the Temple, answering questions, teaching the people, scattering the seed of the truth. The force of that tremendous assault astonished His adversaries with

---

[104] G. F. Moore, *Judaism*, ii. 12.

[105] ibid., i. 230.

[106] The phrase is that of George Adam Smith, *Jerusalem*, ii. 397.

the fear that He might yet carry all before Him. But with all His energy He was still recollected and quietly competent to judge the quality of everything said and done before Him, and to miss no opportunity of winning any that might be won. If the many refused Him, He did not abandon the few. If they mobilized against Him, He searched their hostile ranks for any son of peace who would receive His gift.'[107]

If His purpose was the delivery of His message and the reconstitution of the people of God, this return to Jerusalem was the only way.

The motive of the cleansing of the Temple has already been interpreted above. It is a Messianic act pointing to the purified worship of Israel which must follow acceptance of the message that the Reign of God is present. But this very act was regarded by the Jewish authorities as an impious challenge to the existing religious order. It was indeed an appeal to the public conscience, a declaration that the religious life of Israel could be reformed. But both appeal and declaration were alike rejected. The message was inevitably confined to a narrow circle of friends at the last.

The decisive saying for the connexion of the message of a crucified Messiah with the reconstituted People of God is to be found in the words of institution at the Last Supper, and particularly in the use of the word *diathēkē*, translated 'testament' (A.V.) or 'covenant' (R.V.). The saying has come to us in various forms, but the two earliest are those in the Second Gospel and in I Corinthians.

> This is my blood of the covenant, which is shed for many.
> MARK xiv. 24.
> This cup is the new covenant in my blood.
> I Cor. xi. 25.

The Markan saying carries in it an allusion to Exodus xxiv. 8 ('the blood of the covenant'), and to Isaiah liii. 12 ('he poured out

---

[107] W. R. Maltby, *The Meaning of the Cross* (1920), 9–10; cf. *Christ and His Cross*, 54–9.

his soul unto death . . . he bare the sin of many'). The Pauline saying also contains an allusion to Exodus xxiv, but points back even more clearly to the new covenant promised in Jeremiah xxxi. 31. It is beyond our power to determine which is the more original form.[108] But the fact of extraordinary significance for the idea of the Ecclesia in the mind of our Lord is the presence in both forms of the saying of the word 'covenant', the traditional word for the divine revelation which constituted Israel, as the People of God.

The Greek word *diathēkē* is almost invariably the translation in the Septuagint of the Hebrew word *berīth*, which is always translated covenant in our English versions. The fundamental meaning is that of an agreement or compact between two parties. But in many other passages, the context excludes the idea of compact, and the idea of setting up a relationship takes its place; this is done by the free act or choice of one party. When the *diathēkē* is between God and man it means a 'disposition' or 'arrangement' made by God in His plenary power. Man may accept this *diathēkē* or reject it, but he cannot alter it.[109] It is an unilateral enactment, rather than a covenant.

For the discussion of the New Testament usage a fresh complication arises. In the papyri and inscriptions the word means 'testament', or 'will'.[110] There seems no exception to this rule in the common Greek of the time. It is possible therefore that in certain New Testament passages the word should be translated 'will'.[111]

---

[108] The discussions in V. Taylor, *Jesus and His Sacrifice*, 131–9 203–6, are valuable and illuminating. But on the whole I regard the Pauline form as more primitive than the Markan. With J. Behm (in *Theol. Wörterbuch*, ii. 136) I think that the Markan version has revised away the difficulties early felt in the Pauline form; especially the description of the cup as the covenant; cf. Lietzmann, *An die Korinther*, 60.

[109] The fullest brief account is by J. Behm, in Kittel's *Theologisches Wörterbuch*, ii. 128–30 but there is a complete survey of LXX usage in the same writer's monograph, *Der Begriff Diatheke im Neuen Testament* (1912), 17–34.

[110] Examples in Moulton-Milligan, 148.

[111] Gal. iii. 15 (though Duncan prefers 'covenant', Galatians, 105); Hebrews ix. 16–18.

But the dominant meaning of *diathēkē* in the New Testament is that of 'unilateral enactment', an arrangement for the people of God, depending on God's initiative, and issuing from His gracious will.[112] We have no English word which can adequately translate *diathēkē* in this, its loftiest sense. 'Arrangement', 'disposition' – these are neutral and lifeless in comparison with the thought of God's redeeming purpose which is essential to *diathēkē*. The word 'testament' is definitely inaccurate and misleading for the great majority of the New Testament passages. The word 'covenant' carries with it too much of the idea of 'compact'. In seven out of the eight instances of the word in the Pauline Epistles and in all the instances in the Gospels and Acts the meaning is that of a 'dispensation' of God, a mighty demonstration of the sovereign will of God in history, by which He establishes a relationship between Himself and His people according to His purpose of redeeming grace. In such a relationship there is necessarily an element of mutuality. Men are free to accept or to refuse His offer. But if we keep the word 'covenant', as we must, the stress must lie on God's initiative rather than on man's assent.

The passage in Jeremiah which Jesus takes up and fulfils at the Last Supper is the highest pinnacle of the idea of the covenant in the Old Testament. For the prophet, a covenant 'was not a contract or bargain but an approach by God to His people, an offer of His Grace, a statement of His Will, and accompanied by manifestations of His power to redeem them'.[113] The New Covenant is an eschatological idea. It is promised for the future. Certain positive features distinguished it from the old. First there was inwardness: 'I will put my law in their inward part'; second,

---

[112]   Detailed proof in J. Behm, *Der Begriff Diatheke*, 37–97; summary by the same writer in *Theol. Wörterbuch*, ii. 132–7; see also a valuable discussion in Burton, Galatians (1921), 496–505. This view has won the assent of Dalman, Bauer, Schlatter and many other writers. Deissmann and W. J. Moulton, art. 'Covenant' in Hastings, *D.A.C.*, argued for the rendering 'testament', on the ground of the contemporary Greek usage. But this view does not do justice to the influence of the Old Testament vocabulary on the writers of the N.T.

[113]   G. A. Smith, *Jeremiah* (1923), 377.

individualism: 'all shall know me'; third, forgiveness of sin: 'their sins will I remember no more'. Dr. Skinner points out that the first of these three truths is predominant in the prophet's mind. It is the inwardness of true religion, 'the spiritual illumination of the individual mind and conscience, and the doing of the Will of God from a spontaneous impulse of the renewed heart. To Christian theology the promise has meant nothing less than this, and the prophecy of the New Covenant has therefore been regarded as one of the profoundest anticipations of the perfect religion that the Old Testament contains'.[114]

We can now see how appropriate for the purpose of Jesus was this citation of the idea of Jeremiah. His own thought, like that of the prophet, was set in an eschatological framework, but with this difference – the supreme day had dawned. What Jeremiah had promised for the future was now being fulfilled. The actual word used by Jesus may well have been the Hebrew *berīth*. 'In Jewish literature (apart from the Targums) there is no Aramaic substitute for *berīth*; the Hebrew word only is used.'[115] For Jesus, interpreting and fulfilling the promise of Jeremiah, the idea of *berīth was correlative to the idea of Basileia*, the reign of God, the new order which He was proclaiming as present. The Kingly Rule of God brought with it a new relationship of men with God, a personal relationship with their Father, an inward consciousness of sonship, a divinely wrought illumination. It was an individual relationship, inasmuch as each of His disciples might enter on it of his own free will, but it was no private possession. It was shared. The 'Kingdom' was given to the disciples as a company, and the gift was based on the reconciliation wrought by the sacrifice of Jesus Himself.

It is tempting at this point to venture on a further step. Could Jesus have had in mind the passages in Second Isaiah which actually identify the covenant with the Servant of God?

---

[114] J. Skinner, *Prophecy and Religion* (1926), 329–30.

[115] Dalman, *Jesus–Jeshua* (E. tr. 1929), 163; the Greek word *diathēkē* is actually used for 'will and testament' in post-biblical Aramaic as a 'loan-word'. Dalan suggests the Aramaic *qeyam* as an alternative which already in Daniel vi. 8 means an 'ordinance'.

I will give thee for a covenant of the people, for a light of the Gentiles; to open the blind eyes, to bring out the prisoners from the dungeon, and them that sit in darkness out of the prison house. ISAIAH xlii. 6, 7.

I will give thee for a covenant of the people, to raise up the land, to make them inherit the desolate heritages; saying to them that are bound, Go forth; to them that are in darkness, Shew yourselves. ISAIAH xlix. 8, 9.

In his last great contribution to theological study, Rudolf Otto, in demonstrating that Jesus must have interpreted His death in the light of the conception of the Suffering Servant, has pointed us to these passages in Second Isaiah, and has ignored the probable reference to the prophecy of Jeremiah.[116] But we cannot prove, from Mark xiv. 24 and I Cor. xi. 25, that Jesus actually had the reference to the Servant in mind. At the same time, the proof that Jesus transformed the contemporary conception of Messiahship in the light of Isaiah liii. is cumulative, and, I think, convincing. If this be accepted we can accept Otto's argument in another form. The passages in Second Isaiah prove that it was possible to unite the idea of the New Covenant with the idea of a Mediator of that covenant. In His own thought Jesus blended these two ideas, knowing that by His passion and death they were being mingled and made one.

The bestowal of a new covenant inevitably implies a community. This is inherent in the use of the word *berīth* in Jeremiah, who uses it of the relationship of God with His people.[117] The prophecy of Jeremiah was a living force at the time of Jesus. This is proved by the existence of the 'Damascus sect', who called themselves 'the men who entered into the new covenant in the land of Damascus'.[118] Their covenant was a covenant of penitence;[119] the adherents relied on an atonement to be made by

---

[116] *Kingdom of God and Son of Man* (E. tr. 1938), 289–95.

[117] Skinner, 325–7.

[118] *Fragments of a Zadokite Work*, ix. 28, in Charles's edition *Apocrypha and Pseudepigrapha* (1913), ii. 785–834.

[119] ibid., ix. 15.

God.[120] They looked for a Teacher of Righteousness to come 'in the end of the days'.[121] The writer of the work which gives us all our information about this sect is conscious that he is living in the last days;[122] he is looking for the advent of a Messiah 'from Aaron and Israel'.[123] Those who will give heed to him when he comes will be 'the poor of the flock'.[124]

The chief interest of the work for our present purpose is that we meet with a close connexion in thought between the idea of the New Covenant and the idea of a renewed Israel. This sect claimed to be the true Israel of God. The old Israel has proved faithless. The new Israel has received fresh revelations. Apparently they claimed to be heirs of all the divine promises. The Temple was their sanctuary. 'Jerusalem and none other was their Holy City, the City of their Sanctuary, and all the cities of Israel were theirs to be instructed in the law of God.'[125] There is a remnant whom God will teach through the Messiah. 'And through His Messiah He shall make them know His Holy Spirit'.[126] These striking resemblances to ideas which we have already traced in the teaching of Jesus afford fresh evidence that the proclamation of the Reign of God as already dawning would naturally carry with it both the idea of a new covenant and the idea of a renewed Israel to be created through the faithful remnant.

If we may look for any one moment wherein the new Israel was constituted, it would be in the act of Jesus at the Last Supper.[127] But even this decisive act should not be regarded in isolation from all that went before and from the Crucifixion, Resurrection, and outflowing of the Spirit that followed after. We may trace various preparatory stages. In His call of the disciples, in His sending them

---

[120]   ibid., vi. 6.
[121]   ibid., viii. 10.
[122]   ibid., vi. I.
[123]   See Charles, 795–6.
[124]   ix. 10; cf. Zechariah xi. II.
[125]   Charles, 793
[126]   ibid., ii. 9–10.
[127]   cf. Kattenbusch, in *Festgabe für Harnack* (1921), 169; see the balanced criticism of Wendland, *Eschatologie* (1931), 187 ff.

forth to preach, in His acceptance of the confession of Peter and His subsequent unveiling of the 'mystery' of the suffering Messiah, He had secured a remnant of Israel, entrusted them with a mission and revealed the purpose of God. But hitherto He had not ceased, in the face of repeated rejections, to appeal to Israel as a whole. The last appeal had been made and refused. He turns to His friends.

> Ye are they which have continued with me in my temptations; and I appoint (διατίθεμαι) unto you a kingdom, even as my Father appointed unto me, that ye may eat and drink at my table in my kingdom; and ye shall sit on thrones judging the twelve tribes of Israel. LUKE xxii. 28–30. (R.V.)

It is probable that we should reject this translation of verse 29. To dine at a king's table is not a sign of sharing his authority.[128] It could equally well be rendered:

> And even as my Father appointed kingly rule to me, I appoint unto you that ye shall eat and drink at my table in my kingly rule.

The connexion between the death of our Lord and His kingly rule is essential to this passage. Only through His suffering will the kingdom be consummated. Jesus desires His disciples to share in the joy of the consummation, but His way to it must be their way. St. Paul is the true interpreter of Jesus here. 'Show among yourselves the spirit which you experience in Christ Jesus' (Phil. ii. 5). 'The vision of rewards in the Kingdom which otherwise would be indistinguishable from a chiliastic dream is stripped of everything gross and earthly.'[129] The characteristic mark of the community which is formed of the friends of Jesus is service, as befits those whose gospel will henceforth contain the story of a Messiah on a Cross.

---

[128] So Creed, *St. Luke*, 269; the interpretation adopted above is also that of Westcott and Hort, Easton, V. Taylor, Moffatt, W. Manson.
[129] W. Manson, *St. Luke*, 245.

5. The Mission of the New Community

The fifth line of argument is taken from the fact that Jesus sent out a chosen body of His disciples on a mission. Jesus 'called' men to discipleship, and this implies a new and unique relationship. Out of the company of disciples He chooses some for a missionary tour, and sends them forth as *apostoloi*. His conception of that mission is a characteristic mark of the community which He was gathering.

The evidence is given by all our sources.

> And he called unto him the twelve, and began to send them forth by two and two; and he gave them authority over the unclean spirits. MARK vi. 7, and parallels.

This passage is closely allied to the choice of the Twelve in an earlier chapter.

> And he appointed twelve that they might be with him, and that he might send them forth to preach, and to have authority to cast out devils. MARK iii. 14 15; cf. the parallels.

Luke preserves the tradition of a mission of Seventy, or Seventy-two, disciples, and records their return. The sayings of Jesus which follow their report of their success reflect the eschatological character of the message with which they were entrusted, and the conviction of Jesus that the final victory of God over the powers of evil was even now being achieved.

> The Lord appointed seventy others, and sent them forth two and two into every city and place whither he himself was about to come. LUKE x. I.
> 17. And the seventy returned with joy, saying, Lord, even the devils are subject unto us in thy name. 18. And he said unto them, I beheld Satan fall as lightning from heaven. 19. Behold, I have given you authority to tread upon serpents and scorpions, and over all the power of the enemy: and nothing shall in any wise hurt you. 20. Howbeit in this rejoice not, that the spirits are subject unto you; but rejoice that your names are written in heaven. LUKE x. 17–20.

There are various difficulties inherent in Luke's account. Matthew x. 5 assigns to the Twelve the charge which Jesus in Luke x. 2–12 addresses to the Seventy. Luke himself (xxii. 35 f.) looks back to x. 4 and assumes that the injunction had been given to the Twelve.[130] It is further urged that the number Seventy has a symbolic value as corresponding with the number of the nations of the earth.[131] But to dismiss the tradition as a construction of Luke, or as a community-legend, raises other difficulties. Why should such a tradition arise in the early Church where the Twelve were accorded an acknowledged pre-eminence? The very preservation of such a tradition in such an environment is an argument for its authenticity.[132] Moreover, the tradition that not only the Twelve, but a larger number, were 'sent out' by Jesus to preach, would help to account for the application of the term 'apostle' to a larger number than the Twelve in the early Church.[133]

We must now endeavour to penetrate to the essential meaning of this 'sending forth'. Recent discussions have added to our knowledge but have not superseded the work of Lightfoot and Hort.[134]

Justin Martyr and Eusebius, are witnesses that systematic measures were taken in Jerusalem by the Jewish authorities to counteract the Christian mission. They sent delegates to the Jews of the Dispersion, to give them correct information about this dangerous movement. It is possible that Paul himself was an apostle of this kind before he became a Christian and an apostle of another kind.

---

[130] Creed, *St. Luke*, 144.

[131] In Genesis x. (70 in Hebrew text, 72 in LXX).

[132] Schlatter, *Lukas* (1931), 274 ff.

[133] Romans xvi. 7; Cor. viii. 23; I Cor. ix. I; xv.5,7; Acts xiv.4, 14.

[134] Lightfoot, *Galatians* (1865), 92–101; Hort, *Christian Ecclesia*, 20–41. Among recent discussions I must name above all those of Karl Heinrich Rengstorf, to which I am especially indebted, art. *Apostello*, and *Apostolos* in Kittel's *Theol. Wörterbuch* (1932), i. 397–448; and his later monograph, *Apostolat und Predigtamt* (1934). See also Harnack, *Mission and Expansion of Christianity* (1908), 319–33; Burton, *Galatians*, 363–84.

Later Judaism, after the destruction of Jerusalem, was familiar
with a legal institution of *shelihim*, called in Latin *apostoli*. These
were financial delegates of the Jewish Patriarch.[135]

But there were far-reaching differences between these officials
and the apostles of the New Testament. In the first place the
Jewish *shelihim* were authorized officials, legal 'delegates', and
not missionaries. The proselytizing work of the Jews at the time
of Jesus was carried on by missionaries to whom the Hebrew
word *shelihim* was not applied, and who had not the official
sanction of headquarters.[136] On the other hand the Christian
apostles were essentially preachers of a message, sent out in the
name of Jesus Himself. Secondly, the Jewish *shelihim* arose out
of the ordinary needs of daily life. Though they were finally given
a religious or ecclesiastical sanction in Judaism by some kind of
ordination,[137] their origin was not specifically religious. But the
Christian apostles take their origin in a new religious movement;
they were disciples called by a religious leader before they became
apostles, and were only apostles in virtue of their personal
relationship with Him.

There is, however, one link between the idea of the later
shelihim and that of the apostles commissioned by Jesus which
determines the meaning of Christian apostleship, and ultimately
the mission of the Christian ecclesia. It is to be found in the
oft-quoted sentence in the *Mishnah*: 'He who is sent by a man is
as he who sent him.'[138] This entrusting of full powers to another
to act in the name of the person who sends him is common both
to the idea of the late Jewish 'apostolate' and to those sent forth
by Jesus. The person 'sent forth' incorporates, as it were, in

---

135 Lake and Foakes Jackson, *Beginnings*, v. 48.
136 Rengstorf, *Theol. Wörterbuch*, i. 418.
137 ibid., 417; Justin Martyr, *Dial.*, 108.
138 *Berakoth*, v.5 [Danby, *Mishnah* (1933),6: 'a man's agent is like to
himself'; Lukyn Williams, *Tractate Berakoth* (1921), 41: 'a man's representative is like himself']. Further evidence in Strack-Billerbeck, *Kom-
mentar* (1926), iii. 3, 4. It is noteworthy that the New Testament of the
Syrian Church translates ἀπόστολος by *shelîha*. See Jerome on Gal. i. I,
quoted in Lake, *Beginnings*, v. 48.

himself the higher authority who sends him.[139] According to a saying preserved by Matthew alone, this principle is set forth by Jesus Himself: 'He that receiveth you receiveth me, and he that receiveth me receiveth him that sent me.'[140]

So too in a saying preserved in different forms by all three evangelists,[141] the disciples are told that when they are delivered up in times of persecution they will be given the word of testimony by the Spirit of God. The reason for the persecution is that they are hated 'for the sake of the name'; they are representing Jesus. The Fourth Gospel penetrates to the heart of this conception of apostleship:

'As the Father hath sent me, even so send I you.'[142] Indeed in the only passage where the word *apostolos* is found in this Gospel (xiii. 16), it is possible that the author has the Jewish 'delegate' in mind.[143] 'A servant is not greater than his lord; neither one that is sent (*apostolos*) greater than he that sent him.'

1. The first distinguishing mark of the conception of apostleship is that those who were sent forth had already been called by Jesus to be His disciples. The relationship between a Rabbi and his disciples was familiar enough in Judaism. Jesus is represented in the Gospels as a Rabbi Himself.[144] But just as the questions at issue between Jesus and the teachers of His day left the Rabbis more conscious of His difference from them than His resemblance to them, so the relationship between Jesus and His disciples transcended, even if it included, the ordinary relationship of the Rabbi to the pupils who surrounded him.[145] The reason for this dissimilarity lies in the difference of the types of truth with which

---

[139] Rengstorf, 415.

[140] Matt. x. 40.

[141] Mark xiii. 11–13; Matt. x. 17–20; Luke xxi. 12–17.

[142] John xx. 21; cf. xii. 44,45; xiii.20.

[143] Rengstorf, 421–2; Bauer, *Johannes evangelium*, 165.

[144] See the essay by C. H. Dodd in *Mysterium Christi* (1930), 53–6.

[145] For the following, compare G. Kittel, *Spätjudentum und das Urchristentum* (1926), 126–31; E. Lohmeyer, *Vom Begriff der religiösen Gemeinschaft* (1925), 4–9; H. D. Wendland, *Die Eschatologie des Reiches Gottes bei Jesus* (1931), 153–6, to which I am greatly indebted.

the Rabbis and Jesus were concerned. The ordinary relationship of teacher and pupil in theological questions is based on degrees of knowledge, sometimes, let us hope, on degrees of insight. The teacher has more knowledge, and imparts it; but he is one with his pupils in looking on the truth as objective; he leads them into truth by wrestling for it, by being profoundly eager to attain to it, and to impart the results of his struggles. But the Teacher-disciple relationship in the Gospels is of another order. The first duty of the disciples is to follow Him who calls. The Teacher makes an absolute demand by proclaiming God's supreme offer. He Himself embodies His message. The Rule of God comes to actuality and visible presence in Him. Knowledge for the disciples is dependent on a decision in presence of an urgent divine message. In this relationship the Teacher stands, not side by side with His disciples, in the search for truth, but over against them as One who has the truth. He asks what God asks. He teaches the will of God, and His will is one with God's will. The relationship of the Rabbi to his disciples is based on the ground of knowledge; the relationship of Jesus to His disciples is based on unconditional faith. Knowledge is promised in this relationship, but no advance in knowledge can ever bring the disciples beyond their Master. He calls; they follow, and they will remain followers to the end. So Jesus says: 'Be not ye called Rabbi: for one is your teacher and all ye are brethren.'

Hence it is that, in the Gospels, discipleship does not rest on any special spiritual equipment of those who are called, nor indeed on their own decision, but on the initiative of Jesus. This becomes clearer as we study the words used for 'call' and 'follow'.

The use of the word 'call' as summoning to participation in the salvation of God is especially common in Second Isaiah.[146] As we have seen above in the case of the word 'to preach the gospel', the roots of the religious meaning of this word lie in the oracles of 'the most evangelical of the Prophets'. In Second Isaiah the call is to Israel, but there is a hint of a call more individual and appealing.

---

[146]   Isaiah xl. 9; xlii. 6; xlvi. 11; xlviii. 12, 15; and above all 1. 2 and li. 2. See art. καλέω, by Karl Ludwig Schmidt, in Kittel, iii. 489–92.

'I have called thee by thy name, thou art mine.'[147] So those who were destined to be 'sent' heard the summons to repentance, one by one, and embraced the opportunity with eagerness. But before they could be sent they must learn. They were disciples before they were apostles. The religious and ethical teaching of Jesus, such as is preserved in the Sermon on the Mount or in the Lukan parables, is an indispensable preliminary to their mission.

It is characteristic both of the teaching and the method of Jesus that He regards the new order as involving first of all a call to individual men of the kind formerly made by the prophets to the nation. 'The Kingly Rule of God becomes concrete through the call of Jesus which is followed by obedience.'[148] The demand made on men is that they should follow. The word translated 'to follow', when it occurs in the form 'they followed him', has a far deeper religious meaning in the New Testament than in its common usage to-day. It is more than ethical allegiance, or respectful admiration, or an attempt at imitation of a matchless character by one who is afar off. In the LXX the word is hardly ever used except with a conventional meaning,[149] and there are apparently no real parallels in popular Greek. The word is one of those which were baptized into Christ and thereby acquired a meaning completely original and distinctive. It is found only in the four Gospels in its religious sense apart from one passage in the Apocalypse.[150] The new meaning is due to the fact that for the early Christians there was only one discipleship possible and therefore only one way of following. Jesus was the Messiah, and His followers shared in the salvation which He brought,[151] shared in His earthly vicissitudes,[152] and shared in the hope of the high calling which was theirs in Him. This is no mere *imitatio*

---

[147]   xliii. I; cf. xlv. 3.

[148]   H. D. Wendland, *Die Eschatologie des Reiches Gottes bei Jesus* (1931), 152.

[149]   Art. ἀκολουθέω by Kittel in his *Theol. Wörterbuch*, i. 211.

[150]   Rev. xiv. 4; Kittel, 214.

[151]   Mark ii. 14 is the call of the Messiah; cf. Luke ix. 61–2; Mark x. 17, 21.

[152]   Matt. viii. 19–20; Mark viii. 34 and parallels.

Christi. This is a complete and absolute dedication of all life to
One who is bringing the fulfilment of the final purpose of God
for human life. It involves entrance into a new fellowship and a
new community. Contrast the idea of 'following God' which we
find in Marcus Aurelius[153] and Epictetus[154] or in the noble
utterance of Cleanthes:[155]

> Lead thou me on, O Zeus and Destiny,
> To that goal long ago to me assigned.
> I'll follow and not falter; if my will
> Prove weak and craven, I will follow still.

On this side, a brave acquiescence, a stalwart individualism, a
proud self-sufficiency; on the other, an active self-dedication to a
purpose of love, an entrance into a new commonalty of the people
of God, an independence of the world through dependence on
Jesus.

Those who followed Jesus were 'disciples'. The 'apostles' were
selected out of this larger company,[156] and it is not necessary to
assume that even in the lifetime of Jesus the apostles were only
twelve in number.[157] The wider meaning given to the term apostle
in the early Church is best explained by some justification for it
in the earthly life of Jesus Himself.[158]

2. The second decisive act in the making of apostles was the
decision of Jesus to send a number of His disciples on a missionary
tour. Here we may leave out of account the question whether the
number sent out was twelve or seventy, or whether the two

---

[153] *Meditations*, vii. 31.

[154] *Discourses*, I, xx. 4.

[155] At the end of Epictetus, *Encheiridion*.

[156] So Luke vi. 13, 17; xix. 37; and probably Mark iii. 13–14; Matt. v. I.

[157] See the interesting discussion of Johannes Weiss, *The History of
Primitive Christianity* (E. tr. 1937), 673 ff. I am not convinced that Mark
vi. 30 and Matt. x. 2 give sufficient warrant for the statement that, for
the first two evangelists, 'the Twelve' and 'the Apostles' are in all respects
identical.

[158] cf. Rengstorf, 425.

numbers are evidence for two such missionary tours.[159] The act of Jesus was distinguished by the bestowal of ἐξουσία, authority; this is attested by all three of the Synoptists. His messengers are invested with full power to carry out their mission. The authority is defined as power to cast out evil spirits;[160] and the mission is further defined as preaching the gospel of the kingdom and healing disease. The authority which He gave to His missionaries was possessed by Jesus Himself in virtue of the advent of the Rule of God which was manifested in His own activity. The fact that the demons were subject to those whom He had sent out was greeted by Him as a further sign of the overthrow of the realm of evil. Thus the authority with which He endowed them is insepasably bound up with the message which they preached.[161] Both in their preaching of the message and their power to vanquish evil and disease the messengers were as the One who had commissioned them. 'He who is sent by a man is as he who sent him.'

There are two further pieces of evidence that Jesus endowed His disciples with this power.

> John said unto him, Master, we saw one casting out devils in thy name: and we forbade him, because he followed not us. But Jesus said, Forbid him not: for there is no man which shall do a mighty work in my name, and be able quickly to speak evil of me. For he that is not against us is for us. MARK ix. 38–40

John was one of the candidates for greatness in the coming Reign of God. His words may reflect a feeling that the personal prestige of the disciples is imperilled by this action. But it is more likely that behind his complaint is the fact that the man had not received due authorization. He was an outsider, and had no right to exorcize 'in the name' of Jesus unless Jesus Himself had given him the power.

---

[159] The history of the modern discussion of the authenticity of the mission of the Twelve is summarized in Schultz, *Apostel und Jünger* (1921), 71–4.

[160] Mark iii. 15; vi.7; Matt. x. I; Luke ix. I.

[161] Foerster, art. ἐξουσία in Kittel, *Theol. Wörterbuch*, ii. 566.

A further saying follows in Mark's account, and there are similar sayings in Matthew and Luke.

> For whosoever shall give you a cup of water to drink because ye are Christ's, verily I say unto you, he shall in no wise lose his reward. MARK ix. 41.
>
> He that receiveth you receiveth me, and he that receiveth me receiveth him that sent me. He that receiveth a prophet in the name of a prophet shall receive a prophet's reward; and he that receiveth a righteous man in the name of a righteous man shall receive a righteous man's reward. M\ATT. x. 40–41.
>
> He that heareth you heareth me; and he that rejecteth you rejecteth me; and he that rejecteth me rejecteth him that sent me. LUKE x 16; cf. JOHN xii. 44 f., xiii. 20.

The thread on which these logia are strung is the idea of the authorization of an 'apostle'. 'He who is sent by a man is as he who sent him.' No wonders or victories over devils are mentioned here, and the word 'apostle' has no place in any of the sayings. In the Markan and Matthaean sayings the slightest service to those who are speaking or working in the name of Jesus is regarded as service to Jesus Himself. He took the idea of the final salvation and the idea of the duty of humble service and united them so that they are eternally one.

Further, in all these sayings Jesus is identifying Himself with His followers in a way that points forward to the Pauline doctrine of union with Christ and to the Johannine teaching of the unity of the Vine and the branches. The Lukan saying with its solemn warning is an unmistakable sign that Jesus is convinced of the absolute finality of His own mission.[162] Implicit in this saying, as in the rest, is the principle that the function of the apostle is to carry the word of God as Jesus proclaimed it. To reject the messenger is to reject Jesus and to reject God Himself. The proclamation of this word is not one among many functions, like the various duties which might fall to the lot of an official, but the sole function of those whom Jesus sent forth. The exorcism

---

[162] cf. W. Manson, *St. Luke*, 125.

of demons, the healing of the sick – these are but outward manifestations of the Word which proclaims that God's Reign is now present in the activity of Jesus, that the powers of the New Age are even now available for the destruction of evil, and that Jesus, by His very commission to His messengers, is summoning a community to live beneath God's kingly Rule. These three declarations determine the character of an apostle in the early Church, and contain the essential characteristics of the Christian ministry for all time. First, there is the proclamation of the Word; second, the power given in the New Age for the fulfilment of the tasks laid upon His messengers; and third, the gathering together of the new community, the people of God. Word, Spirit, Church – these three determine the nature of the ministry.[163] Such creative ministerial work is actually constitutive of the Church.

It is now clear that we cannot speak of the apostle as holding an 'office' in the later sense of the word; neither is apostolate confined to the Twelve. The traditional view which has governed the thought of the Church for centuries is expressed in Justin Martyr:[164]

> From Jerusalem twelve men went out into the world, and these uneducated, and without great ability in speech, but by the power of God they proclaimed to every race of men that they were sent by Christ to teach all men the word of God.

A similar view is found in Ignatius and in Clement of Rome, but both add St. Paul to the number of apostles.

The view that Jesus appointed twelve men, and twelve only, to the office of apostles cannot be substantiated by the New Testament evidence. The statements in Luke vi. 13 ('he chose . . . twelve, whom also he named apostles') and Acts i. 2 ('the apostles whom he had chosen') do not prove that the author of Luke-Acts believed that the number of apostles is confined to

---

[163] So Kögel, *Das geistliche Amt im neuen Testament* (1929).
[164] *Apology* I, 39.

twelve.[165] In Acts xiv. 4, 14, he calls Paul and Barnabas apostles. His use of this word, as of many others, is variable. As against modern theories the conclusion of Bishop Lightfoot still stands.[166] 'In the account of the foundation of the apostolate, and in the language used in the Gospels of the Twelve, there is no hint that the number was intended to be so limited. It is true that twelve is a typical number, but so is seven. And if the first creation of the diaconate was not intended to be final as regards numbers, neither is there any reason to assume this of the first creation of the apostolate.'

In the light of the foregoing discussion we may venture to qualify Lightfoot's use of the word 'office' in speaking of the apostles. If 'office' is regarded as possessing a *character indelebilis*, the act of Jesus in sending them forth affords no warrant for the use of the term. Certainly the Twelve possessed one prerogative which was not shared, and which could not be taken from them. They had been 'with him'. They had shared His wanderings, and they had continued with Him in His temptations. This prerogative was incommunicable. If 'office' is regarded as including authority for the government of the new community, again the term is inadmissible at this stage. As Hort said:[167] 'There is no trace in Scripture of a formal commission for government from Christ Himself.' This has been criticized as one of 'those subtle super-refinements which occasionally detract from the value of Dr. Hort's work'.[168] But no

---

[165] This is against the view of Lake, *Beginnings*, v. 51, who gets rid of Acts xiv. 4 and 14 by assuming that the editor of Acts found this in his source and left it unaltered; cf. W. L. Knox, *St. Paul and the Church of Jerusalem*, 363. 'The view that the number of Apostles is confined to Twelve and that there can be neither more nor less, appears in Acts i. 2 seqq. and apparently also in xii. 17.' Canon Knox regards James the Lord's brother as having been elected to fill the vacancy caused by the death of James the son of Zebedee.

[166] *Galatians* 95

[167] *The Christian Ecclesia*, 84.

[168] A. J. Mason in *The Early History of the Church and Ministry* (1918), 41. Dr. Mason quotes 2 Cor. x. 8. But Hort is referring to the earthly life of Christ.

evidence is adduced to prove that in His earthly life Jesus gave to the Twelve any formal commission for government. The solitary passage which might be quoted is the difficult saying[169] which Luke attributes to our Lord at the Last Supper and which Matthew reports as spoken in answer to Peter's question about the reward of the Twelve:

> Ye shall sit on thrones judging the twelve tribes of Israel. LUKE xxii. 30.
>
> Verily I say unto you, that ye which have followed me, in the regeneration when the Son of Man shall sit on the throne of his glory, ye also shall sit upon twelve thrones judging the twelve tribes of Israel. MATT. xix. 28.

In the original Lukan text the number of thrones is not given. If the Lukan version is the more primitive form of the saying this may be no more than the apocalyptic expectation which reappears in the Pauline verse: 'Know ye not that the saints shall judge the world?'[170] In that case the promise would not be exclusively confined to the Twelve. In any case, even on the improbable hypothesis that the Matthaean form is the authentic version of the saying, the promise would not refer to the government of the community in the interval between the close of our Lord's earthly life and the end of human history.

It is likely that the preservation of this saying was due to the desire to justify the position of authority which was naturally accorded to the Twelve in the early Church. But as it stands it

---

[169] Hort mentions this (29), as an 'indication that a distinctive function was reserved for the Twelve throughout, over and above their function as the chiefest disciples'.

[170] I Cor. vi. 2; Rev. xx. 4; cf. Wisdom iii. 8: the righteous 'shall judge nations, and have dominion over peoples'; Enoch cviii. 12: 'I will bring forth clad in shining light those who have loved my holy name, and I will seat each on the throne of his honour.' The chief passage is Daniel vii. 22: 'Judgement was given to the saints of the most High . . . the saints possessed the rule.'

does not convey a formal commission of authority for government.[171]

Summary

I may now sum up the result of this inquiry. Did Jesus in His earthly life declare by deed and word that He had a community in view, and that this community would be a new kind of community?

The answer depends first on the nature of the Kingdom of God which was the central theme of all the preaching of Jesus and determined all His activity. We have seen that the Kingdom is not to be identified with Utopia, or with any ideal order to be set up on earth by human effort. Nor is the Kingdom of God on earth to be identified with the Church. That equation is only found many centuries later. The Kingdom of God is the kingly Rule of God. It is eternal, but it has yet to be fully manifested. It is present in the activity of Jesus Himself, and yet it is still to come. In the distinctive sense in which it is used by Jesus it is an eschatological concept. The Reign of God is the deliverance promised by the prophets for the last Days. That deliverance has now begun. The signs are given to John the Baptist, and are manifest in the success of the Seventy.

That Kingdom is primarily, then, the Rule of God; secondarily (33–35), since the Rule of God does not operate in the void, it is a domain into which men can enter, in which they accept God's

---

[171]   Professor C. H. Turner, *Catholic and Apostolic* (1931), 285–6, criticized Bishop Headlam for neglecting this saying in his Bampton Lectures, *The Doctrine of the Church and Christian Reunion* (1920, 2nd ed. 1923, xi). Dr. Headlam replies that his argument, which is essentially a re-statement of that of Hort, is both positive and negative. 'On the one side I pointed out that in no case is authority given specifically to the Apostles or to the Twelve as such – it is given to the disciples; on the other hand that warnings are given specifically to the Twelve against the assumption of anything in the nature of authority.'

kingly rule. Thirdly we have seen (35–40) that though the Rule of God is not a community, it implies the gathering of a community.

Next the problem was faced whether, in view of the expectation of the nearness of the end of human history, there was time enough allowed for the existence of any community of a new kind. The answer was that there was a sufficient interval, and that Jesus expressly disclaimed knowledge when the Last Day would dawn. He definitely looked forward to a future in time and in this earth in which His followers would have to live and work.

The fivefold argument, which has just been concluded, has been designed to gather up the various elements in the teaching and activity of Jesus into a coherent and intelligible unity. First, His appeal was to Israel, but Israel must be purged and reconstituted. His hope therefore lies in the Remnant, and this Remnant is the 'little flock' to which much of His teaching is addressed.

Second, that teaching is ethical and therefore social, as well as individual. By its very nature it presupposes that the Remnant will be characterized by a new way of life, and that fresh power is available for the fulfilment of the demands which Jesus makes. The Remnant will live on a new and higher level because of the divine resources available in the New Age. This presupposition is, in fact, the gift of the Spirit, though the word is rarely used.

Third, the conception of Messiahship essentially involves the gathering of a community.

Fourth, the message of Jesus was meant to be constitutive of the community.

Fifth, the mission on which Jesus 'sent forth' some of His disciples contains His conception of the mission of the new community.

Jesus then envisaged a new Israel, to be formed through the little flock, and living beneath God's kingly Rule in a new era. His followers were committed to a new way of life and were promised the divine power to enable them for it. They owned allegiance to a Messiah who was treading the path of suffering. The message which they accepted and which the rest of Israel rejected was that of God's final salvation; to accept this message was to go into the

Kingdom, while to reject it was to stay outside. Their mission was to deliver this message, in full reliance on the divine power manifested in the New Age; and in the delivery of it they were fully commissioned representatives of the Son of Man, so that to reject them was to reject God Himself. A community which can thus be described is surely the *ecclesia*, the people of God, Israel as God intended Israel to be.

Chapter Four

The Promise to Peter

It has been possible to arrive at the above conclusions without taking into account the only two passages in the four Gospels where the word *Ecclesia* is found.

The first of these is the famous promise following on Peter's confession (Matt. xvi. 17–19):

> 17. And Jesus answered and said unto him, Blessed art thou, Simon Bar-Jonah; for flesh and blood hath not revealed it unto thee, but my Father which is in heaven.
>
> 18. And I also say unto thee, that thou art Peter, and upon this rock I will build my church; and the gates of Hades shall not prevail against it.
>
> 19. I will give unto thee the keys of the kingdom of heaven; and whatsoever thou shalt bind on earth shall be bound in heaven: and whatsoever thou shalt loose on earth shall be loosed in heaven.

It is idle to deny that the authenticity of this passage is under grave suspicion. Recently, however, there have been great attempts to remove the doubts which prevent many modern students from accepting this as a genuine utterance of our Lord in His earthly life.[1]

---

[1] The late Professor C. H. Turner seemed to believe in the authenticity of this saying: *Catholic and Apostolic*, 283 ('in substance trustworthy'); but he assumes (193–4) that in the early tradition it formed part of a postresurrection narrative, like that of John xxi. This may be so, but the

Two questions are involved: first, the relation of Jesus to the Church; second, the position of Peter in early Christianity.

The main arguments[2] against the authenticity of this passage will be familiar to readers of recent English commentaries, though an answer to those arguments is not so readily accessible.

The attempt of Harnack to prove that the passage is an interpolation into the original text of the First Gospel, made in Rome about the time of Hadrian (A.D. 117–138), has completely broken down. We have no Greek manuscript and no ancient version in which Matt. xvi. 17–19 or at least xvi. 18 is wanting.[3] Further, the Semitic colouring of these verses is unmistakable. The opening beatitude, the designation of Simon by his father's name, the Rabbinic expression of 'binding and loosing', the eschatological struggle with the powers of the underworld – all these are indications of a primitive origin for the whole paragraph. Suspicion falls on it chiefly because it does not occur in Mark or in Luke.[4] But the sayings are not proved unauthentic because the other evangelists do not record them. As Linton observes,[5] other sayings peculiar to one or other of the evangelists are not so severely handled. There are, however, three arguments on which the rejection of this pericope rests, and which call for some reply.

The first is that the word *ecclesia* is attributed to Jesus only here and in Matt. xviii. 17, and that both passages are under suspicion. This Linton calls the 'argument from statistics'. The answer to this must be the whole argument which has been

---

conjecture removes the saying from the framework of the earthly life. The most vigorous defence of the authenticity comes from those who are firmly convinced that the teaching of Jesus must be placed in an eschatological setting; Schweitzer, *Mysticism of Paul*, 103–4; Kattenbusch, art. in *Festgabe für Harnack (1921); Gloege, Reich Gottes und Kirche*; and, above all, K. L. Schmidt, *Die Kirche des Urchristentums* (1932), a reprint from *Festgabe für Deissmann* (1926), 259–319; and art. ἀκκλησία in Kittel's *Theol. Wöurterbuch*, iii. 522–30. There is a summary of Schmidt's views in W. K. Lowther Clarke, *Divine Humanity* (1936), 158–60.

[2]　Linton, *Das Problem der Urkirche* (1932), 169.
[3]　K. L. Schmidt, *Die Kirche*, 283.
[4]　Linton, 158.
[5]　Op. cit., 175.

developed above. If the fact of Church is to be found in the teaching of Jesus there may very well be a name for it. There are synonyms used in the Gospels and by Jesus. There is the little flock (*poimnion*, Luke xii. 32). There are the 'disciples' But the reply can be carried further still. The word *ecclesia* is used in the Septuagint to translate *qahal*, the 'people' of God. Jesus may well have used this Hebrew word, or the Aramaic *q'hālā*. Schmidt has advanced an attractive suggestion that the word used was *kenishta*, the commonest Rabbinic word for 'synagogue'. The Sinaitic Syriac version translates *ecclesia* by *kenushta*.[6] It is possible that this word was used not only for the local community meeting in a particular synagogue, but also the whole 'Israel of God'. Certainly each local community regarded itself as one with the whole of the Jewish people and as a microcosm of Judaism.

The second argument is that the idea of the ecclesia cannot be fitted into the framework of eschatology within which the teaching of Jesus falls. Again, the answer must be found in the fivefold argument already developed. If the idea of the Remnant, the ethical teaching of Jesus, His idea of Messiahship, His conception of His message, all involve the idea of the community which He is gathering, then this objection to authenticity falls to the ground. But at this point it is essential to point out that no true interpretation of this passage can be reached if the assumption, so common in this country, is maintained that the Church is in verses 18 and 19 identified with the Kingdom of God. No proof of this widespread fallacy has been brought forward.[7] The only convincing

---

[6] Matt. xvi 18 is not preserved in this version, but xviii. 17.

[7] The only passage which might be adduced to this effect is in the *Odes of Solomon*, xxii. 12, one of the Odes which became incorporated in the *Pistis Sophia*.

> Thou didst bring thy world to corruption;
> That everything might be dissolved and renewed,
> And that the foundation for everything might be thy rock,
> And on it thou didst build thy Kingdom;
> And thou becamest the dwelling-place of the saints.

If this were addressed to Christ it might be a direct reminiscence of Matt. xvi. 18. But almost certainly the Ode is addressed to God. God Himself is the rock.

proof would be a demonstration that in the first or second centuries or both the Church was ever identified with the Kingdom of God on earth. The *Basileia* creates a community, and uses a community as an instrument. Those who enter the *Basileia* are in the *Ecclesia*; the *Ecclesia* lives beneath the kingly rule of God, acknowledges it, proclaims it, and looks for its final manifestation; but the *Ecclesia* is not itself the *Basileia*. Since the Church is gathered under God's rule, death will have no power over it.[8]

The third argument is drawn from the facts of the subsequent history of the early Church. Peter did not occupy the authoritative position which would have been inevitably secured for him by such a saying of Jesus. This argument depends on the adoption of one particular interpretation of 'the power of the keys', which will be discussed below. In any case Peter did occupy a position of acknowledged moral authority in the early Church, though the primacy in administration and government seems to have belonged to James the brother of the Lord.

The difficulty of accepting the verses in the framework in which Matthew has placed them lies in the blessing pronounced in verse 17, where Jesus hails Peter's confession with joy. In Mark the word 'strictly charged' conveys rather the idea of rebuke. 'The evidence of the Gospels goes to prove that to Jesus Messiahship was a burden; no conception current among His contemporaries, answered to His own.'[9] But there can be no reasonable doubt that Jesus believed Himself to be the Messiah, the instrument and embodiment of the Reign of God. Otto says, I think rightly, that the common belief that Jesus brings the kingdom is completely foreign to Jesus Himself. 'On the contrary the kingdom brings Him with it . . . He Himself is in His actions the personal manifestation of the inbreaking divine power.'[10] Let us assume that Peter, either at Caesarea Philippi or on some other occasion, was granted an insight into the meaning attached by Jesus Himself to the idea of Messiahship. For the first time he had entered into

---

[8]   'The gates of Hades' is probably a synonym for Hades.

[9]   V. Taylor, *Jesus and His Sacrifice*, 20.

[10] Otto, *Kingdom of God and Son of Man*, 103, 104.

'the mystery of the reign of God' and he was the first of the disciples so to enter.

The words of Jesus which follow include a beatitude and three separate declarations. I should like to put forward two governing principles for the interpretation of this paragraph which may be justified if the paragraph can thereby fall naturally into its place as part of the teaching of Jesus.

First, the beatitude governs the thought of all three declarations. Second, the three declarations say different things. They are not three different ways of saying that Peter is to be the principal person in the new community, but they are three different results of the revelation which has been made to Peter.

First, the idea which governs the whole passage is that of a personal revelation to Peter. The special position given to him is not first bestowed in the declaration of the building of the Church but has already been vouchsafed to him by God. It follows that the interpretation of the passage is not affected by questions as to his faith or his boldness in making his confession. To adduce against the authenticity of this passage a 'psychological' argument which asserts that the description 'rock' does not fit the character of Peter is irrelevant, and misconceives the situation. Even if Peter were unstable, even though his faith was actually proved fluctuating, it was to such a man that the divine revelation came.

If we do not know the exact nature of the revelation made to Peter, we know that it issued in a confession of the Messiahship that went beyond the thought of his contemporaries, and involved a personal illumination. He saw God's purpose in a new light. This, as Jesus said, was the gift of God. In later times when a man has been given such an integration of his life in God through Jesus Christ, we know that such an one becomes a person to be reckoned with, one to whom others who are seeking naturally turn. This is the way in which the Christian Church is built. 'On this rock I will build my Church.' It is on Peter, a man who now is as good as his name that the next stone will be placed and many another stone after, in the building of the spiritual house of the Church, a house not made with hands.

The difference in gender between *Petros*, Peter, and *petra*, rock, has led Protestant commentators to draw a distinction between Peter and the quality of his confession, and to interpret the rock as the confession of the Messiahship. This view cannot be sustained by the linguistic evidence. There is only one word in Aramaic and, except where it is used as a man's name, it is always feminine. The rock is more likely to be Peter himself as one to whom a momentous revelation has been made by the Father, than the abstract confession of Messiahship. Jesus was deliberately playing on the name He had given to His disciple; it is dangerous to be too subtle in such a play on words.

Harnack protested[11] that those who interpreted this verse as meaning that Peter was the first stone in the new house, and that his primacy therefore was a primacy in time, were treating 'rock' as equivalent to 'stone'. Again it may be answered that to press this distinction is over-subtle. Peter is not merely one stone among many; he is a rock on which many other stones will be placed. A true parallel is found in the Rabbinic parable[12] which likens God to a king wishing to build himself a house, finding no sure foundation, and digging deep down, till at last he found a rock. 'So when God saw Abraham who was to arise, he said: Now I have found a rock on which to build and establish the world.' In this passage Peter is to be as it were the forefather of the new Israel, as Abraham was the forefather of the old.

In I Cor. iii. 11 x. 4, Christ Himself is spoken of as the foundation, and is identified with the rock which according to Jewish legend followed the Israelites in the wilderness. In Ephesians the apostles and prophets – the inspired preachers of the early Church – are the foundation of the spiritual edifice which God is building, Jesus Christ Himself being the chief corner-stone. In I Peter believers are living stones, and Christ is the living stone which is the head of the corner. We may, if we like, regard these as indications of a different view of the Church from that found in Matthew xvi. 18 and thereupon reject the Matthew passage as

---

[11] *Sitzungsberichte d. preuss. Akad.* (1918), 646–7.

[12] Quoted in G.F. Moore, *Judaism*, i. 538; see B.T.D. Smith, *St. Matthew*, 152–3.

the product of early Christian controversy. But it is also at least a tenable view that Jesus Himself spoke a word to Peter which was misunderstood, and that both Paul and Peter too (if he wrote the first Epistle which bears his name) were careful to remind their readers that there was only one possible foundation for the Christian Church.

Again, the assertion (Eph. ii. 20) that the Church is built on the foundation of apostles and prophets is an historical statement, and is not irreconcilable with Matt. xvi. 18. If the Church is built on Peter in virtue of a revelation of God given to him, others to whom the same revelation is given may become, like Peter, the foundation of the Church. Such were in fact the missionaries and inspired preachers who took the chief part in building up the community.

The second declaration: 'I will give thee the keys of the kingdom of heaven', cannot refer to the right to admit to and exclude from the Church, unless Church and Kingdom are regarded as synonymous terms, just as it cannot make Peter the porter at the gates of heaven, unless the Kingdom is to be identified with the future life. There are two possible interpretations which may be justified by the biblical use of the metaphor.

First, a picture is given in Isaiah (xxii. 22) of a Grand Vizier, or major-domo, into whose hands is committed 'unlimited authority over the royal household, carrying with it a similar authority in all affairs of State.'[13] Of this unlimited authority the key is the symbol. This passage was applied in the early Church to our Lord Himself.[14] 'These things saith he that is holy, he that is true, he that hath the key of David, he that openeth and none shall shut and that shutteth and none openeth.' If the power of the keys implies such absolute administrative authority, the promise cannot be authentic. The whole history of the early Church contradicts this interpretation. According to the Acts, Peter comes naturally to a position of spiritual leadership in the Church. But the leadership is shared. It is no unlimited authority. It is not Peter

---

[13] J. Skinner, *Isaiah*, i. 170.
[14] Rev. iii. 7.

alone who exercises the right of admission to and excommunication from the Christian community. He is even withstood by St. Paul, and called to account for his actions by the Church at Jerusalem.[15] He is the pioneer advocate of the social equality of Gentiles and Jews within the new brotherhood, this too in virtue of a vision which he regards as a divine revelation. But there is no trace in his attitude to others of the authority of a Grand Vizier.

There is a second possible interpretation in another saying of Jesus.

> Woe unto you lawyers! for ye took away the key of knowledge: ye entered not in yourselves, and them that were entering in ye hindered. LUKE xi. 52.
>
> Woe unto you, scribes and Pharisees, hypocrites! because ye shut the kingdom of heaven against men: for ye enter not in yourselves, neither suffer ye them that are entering in to enter. MATT. xxiii. 13.

The key of the kingdom is here the 'knowledge' which makes entrance to the kingdom possible. The word 'knowledge' or *gnosis* is used in the Septuagint with a rich religious and ethical content. It is 'a spiritual possession resting on revelation'.[16] In Luke i. 77 (the only other occurrence of the noun in the Lukan writings) it is insight into the meaning of the final Messianic salvation, and is linked with the idea of forgiveness of sins.[17] This 'key' therefore is far more than intellectual knowledge. A Rabbinic saying illustrates the quality which alone can open the door of religion: 'He who has knowledge of the law without reverence towards God, is like unto a treasurer who has been given the inner key, but not the outer key. How can he enter?'[18]

It is therefore from another saying of our Lord, and not from the passage in Isaiah, that this promise to Peter is to be interpreted. The key is the spiritual insight which will enable Peter to lead others

---

[15] Gal. ii. II; Acts xi. 3.
[16] Bultmann, art. γινώσκω in *Theol. Wörterbuch*, i. 699.
[17] Bultmann, 706.
[18] About the third century A.D.; Strack-Billerbeck, i. 737.

in through the door of revelation through which he has passed himself. It is the true understanding of the open secret, the mystery which has been hidden from the wise and understanding, and is now revealed unto babes. The power is not in its essence governmental authority. Jesus Himself said (Mark x. 42–3) in reference to this kind of authority: 'Their great ones exercise authority over them. But it is not so among you.' The principle of ministry in the new household of God is the service of humble love.

> Love is the key of life and death,
> Of hidden heavenly mystery:
> Of all Christ is, of all He saith,
> Love is the key.

And this key is not the exclusive possession of Peter, though on the day of Pentecost by common consent he was the first to use it. It belongs to every confessor of the Son of God.[19]

If this interpretation be accepted, instead of the usual view which regards the power of the keys as authority to exercise ecclesiastical discipline, the saying falls into place with the conception of apostleship already described above. When He 'sent forth' His disciples on a missionary tour they went as His representatives carrying the Word of God. So here Jesus entrusts Peter first of all, and other disciples later, with the power for the communication of the open secret which has now been revealed. This is entrance into the Kingdom. The power of the keys is thought of primarily as the power to admit, as when a modern Christian says of another to whom he owes his very soul: 'he has the key, and he opened Christianity to me as by an inner door.' Doubtless the power to admit may also involve the power to exclude, which is implicit in the story of the Council of Jerusalem. But this power to exclude is in the background, and secondary. Those who accept Peter's message and Peter's Lord enter the kingdom. That is the authority entrusted to Peter.

Thus we have already in these two verses three characteristics of the Ecclesia, three aspects of the one fact. To be built on the

---

[19]   cf G. G. Findlay, *The Church of God as set forth in the N.T.* (1893).

first stone, on Peter, means to belong to the community, and this
in turn implies entrance into the kingly rule of God.

The third promise made is parallel to that in Matt. xviii. 18:

> Verily I say unto you, what things soever ye shall bind on earth shall
> be bound in heaven: and what things soever ye shall loose on earth
> shall be loosed in heaven. MATT. xviii. 18.

This is spoken to the disciples, according to Matt. xviii. I. The
meaning of 'Heaven' is quite different from that of 'the kingdom
of heaven'. It means the dwelling place of God, and so in Matthew
is often used for God Himself, in His transcendence.[20] The words
'binding' and 'loosing' reflect a Rabbinic phrase, which means
'forbidding' and 'allowing' practical questions of conduct. The
saying therefore means that the inspired decisions of the apostles
will be accepted by God. They will apply the revelation of God's
will which they have received to the various problems which
confront the community and will be given discernment to decide
what is right and what is wrong.

Owing to the context in which Matthew places this verse
(xviii. 18) it is often argued[21] that the binding and loosing have
to do with exclusion from or admission to the community.
Naturally as in the council at Jerusalem, the power of deciding
what is right and what is wrong includes the power of decision
about those who shall be admitted to the Church. On the other
hand, many of the sayings in the First Gospel owe their position
to the Evangelist. It is more likely that the saying has a general
meaning.[22]

If the view were accepted that the saying deals with the
admission to the community, a possible view is that no legislative
authority is intended, and that there is no allusion to decisions in

---

[20] Dalman, *Words of Jesus* (E. tr. 1902), 92–3.

[21] As Strack-Billerbeck, i. 738–42.

[22] cf. T. W. Manson in *The Mission and Message of Jesus* (1937), 502–3,
who points out that the use of the neuter plural both in xvi. 19 and xviii.
18 makes a general sense more likely than the admission and excommunication of persons.

cases of moral perplexity. The binding and loosing would be the inevitable result of the apostolic preaching which was the word of judgement.[23] The saying would then be parallel to Luke x. 16:

> He that heareth you heareth me;
> And he that rejecteth you, rejecteth me.

The hearing would correspond to 'loosing', and the rejecting to 'binding'. The loosing, or acceptance in the community, follows naturally on the hearing; the binding, or exclusion from the community, follows inevitably on the rejection. Both loosing and binding are ratified in heaven.

No final decision can be made between these different interpretations. But if the promise to Peter be regarded as authentic, it cannot be separated from the promise to the larger company of disciples, nor can the promise be regarded as unconditional. There is no contradiction between the 'Thou' of xvi. 19 and the 'ye' of xviii. 18. The community which is built on Peter has his privileges and his duties, and both the privileges and the duties are determined by the mission of Peter and his fellow apostles, which is the age-long mission of the Church of God, to carry the divine revelation to mankind.

Conclusion

If the argument of Part I be accepted, the Church is a new creation of Jesus. It is old in the sense that it is a continuation of the life of Israel, the People of God. It is new in the sense that it is founded on the revelation made through Jesus of God's final purpose for mankind. It begins with the call of the first disciples. 'He called them out in order that through them and on them He might lay the foundation stone of a new edifice. . . . He gathered His own, the people that were "His", and in them He planted the conscious-

---

[23]   So H. D. Wendland, op. cit., 179–81; Schlatter, *Die Geschichte des Christus* (1923), 387

ness that they were a separate community. The question whether Jesus Himself founded the Church may be answered in the affirmative, not only in the dogmatic sense but in the historical sense. He founded the New Covenant, not as an *ecclesia invisibilis*, as those who regard the Church purely as an invisible spiritual body would have us believe, but as a real community, a people, however unassuming it may have seemed at first, whose constitution is "the blood of the New Covenant".[24]

Note

It is probable that doubt will always remain as to the authenticity of Matt. xvi. 17–19. The weight of the case against lies not simply in the fact that they are only attested by Matthew, but in the fact that they appear in Matthew as an apposite expansion of the Markan Confession of Peter. If Mark knew these sayings why did he omit them?

I have tried to meet this argument by liberating these sayings from their context in Matthew, and by showing that the ideas in them are congruous with the teaching of our Lord. This defence of their genuineness allows for the possibility that they may have been spoken on some other occasion or occasions, that they may have persisted in oral tradition, and that they may have been combined and set in their present frame by the author of the First Gospel.

---

[24] E. Brünner, *The Mediator* (E. tr. 1934), 558–9.

Part Two

The Primitive Church

The Death of Jesus on the Cross, His Resurrection and Ascension, the coming of the Holy Spirit – these events created an entirely new situation for the disciples of our Lord. It is therefore the more striking to find essentially the same description of the nature of the new community reappearing in the preaching of the early Church, as we have already found in the teaching of Jesus. Indeed, the same description underlies the variations of the doctrine of the Ecclesia in the Pauline epistles, the Johannine writings and First Peter. If this can be established, the conclusion will be forced upon us that the idea of the Ecclesia as a community, on earth, indwelt by the Spirit of God, carrying the word of revelation, unique alike in its origin, its fellowship, its allegiance, its message, and its mission, is essential to Christian theology if theology is to be measured by the writings of the New Testament.

What conception of the Ecclesia do we find in the earliest days after the Resurrection? For evidence we must rely on the second volume of Luke's work, The Acts, and especially on the Petrine speeches. Professor C. H. Dodd has based his investigation[1] into the content of the primitive preaching on the view made probable

---

[1]   *The Apostolic Preaching and its Developments* (1936).

by the linguistic discussions of Torrey and De Zwaan, that the
early chapters of Acts (especially i. to v. 16 and ix. 31 to xi. 18)
contain a large element of Semitism. We may infer that the writer
made use of Aramaic sources, whether written or oral, and that
the speeches attributed to Peter in these chapters are based on
material which proceeded from the Aramaic-speaking Church at
Jerusalem.[2] 'We may with some confidence take these speeches to
represent not indeed what Peter said upon this or that occasion,
but the *kerygma* of the Church at Jerusalem at an early period.'[3]
As Peter, according to these same sources with supporting evidence from the Gospels and St. Paul, was ready in speech, the
leader of the Twelve, the natural representative of the Jerusalem
Church when its message had to be declared, it is only a further
inference to find in these speeches the substance of what Peter
used to say.

---

[2] Op. cit., 35–6.
[3] Op. cit., 37.

Chapter Five

The Church as the Israel of God

On the day of Pentecost, to the question: What shall we do? Peter replies:

> Repent ye, and be baptized . . . and ye shall receive the gift of the Holy Spirit. For to you is the promise, and to your children, and to all that are afar off, even as many as the Lord our God shall call to himself. ACTS ii. 38, 39.

The promise is that of Joel, to the Israel of the last days. Peter has spoken to his hearers as 'men of Israel' not 'Jews' or 'Judaeans'; thus he deliberately uses the religious designation of the people of God. The promise is not to Jews as members of a nation. In the passage from Joel, immediately after the words quoted in Acts ii. 17–21 comes the limitation:

> For in mount Zion and in Jerusalem there shall be those that escape, as the Lord hath said, and among the remnant those whom the Lord doth call. JOEL ii. 32.

Here then the promise is to the remnant, to the little flock. From the beginning the early Christians regard themselves as the true Israel, inheriting all the promises of God made through the prophets. Peter is envisaging a wider company to be joined to the 'little flock'. Those who are 'afar off' will be Jews of the Diaspora, and not Gentiles.[1] The 'call' is that of God Himself. It is charged with the same authority as the call which had come to the disciples by the Galilean lake. Obedience to the call is regarded as being saved from 'this crooked generation'. The phrase comes from the Song of Moses (Deut. xxxii. 5), where the children of Israel are arraigned for their rebellion against God.

> They are not his children. . . .
> They are a perverse and crooked generation.

To reject Peter is to reject the call of Jesus which is the call of God, and to remain in the crooked generation of those who are not God's children. But 'he that heareth you heareth me'. To hear Peter is to hear the call of Jesus; it is a decisive act setting a man in the remnant which through this very obedience is apart from the rest of the nation. The new community is not separated from Israel, but it is separate from those who forfeit their privileges in Israel. It is the true Israel of God. As Hort said, 'the crooked generation of the unbelieving present, which perverts and misinterprets the ancient covenant, is the evil sphere to be abandoned'[2]

> Ye are the sons of the prophets, and of the covenant which God made with your fathers, saying unto Abraham, And in thy seed shall all the families of the earth be blessed. Unto you first God, having raised up his Servant, sent him to bless you, in turning away every one of you from your iniquities. ACTS iii. 25, 26.

The blessing spoken of at the establishment of the covenant with Abraham (Genesis xxii. 18) is explained by Peter, as by Paul afterwards, as referring to Jesus Christ.[3] The thought of Peter travels back from Moses (ii. 40, and iii. 22, 23) to Abraham. Moses had already declared of Jesus, 'To him shall ye hearken in

---

[1] I follow Wendt, *Apostelgeschichte* (1913), 95–6, rather than the majority of modern commentators.

[2] *The Christian Ecclesia*, 43, 44.

[3] Galatians iii. 8, 9. This is a singular illustration of the unity of the apostolic *kerygma*. cf. Knowling in *Expos. G. T.*, ii. 119.

all things'. In this speech the view already implicit in the phrase 'this crooked generation' is explicitly announced. 'Every soul which shall not hearken to that prophet shall be utterly destroyed from among the people.' Those who rejected Jesus had thereby ceased to be Israelites. This conclusion is grounded by Peter on the meaning of the original promise to Abraham. When God announced blessing to all the nations through Abraham's seed, He meant the final blessing through His Servant Jesus. The proud claim to the exclusive possession of the original covenant is unmistakable. The Jews in those early years regarded Christianity as a Jewish sect,[4] and modern writers have sometimes so described the infant Church.[5] But that was not the view of the original disciples. A sect is a party or school within Israel. But the disciples *were* Israel. They were the Church or People of God. They did not separate from Israel. They could not. It was the rebellious sons of Israel who forfeited their covenant by rejecting Christ.

The same conviction is encountered in the use of the term 'saints' or *hagioi* as a description of the early Christian community. There are three ideas inherent in the use of this word in Judaism which contribute to the meaning of the word in the New Testament.

First, there is the thought of Israel as 'holy' and as separated in the purpose of God from the world, because Israel is God's own people. Second, the word is used in an eschatological sense. 'The holy' are those who have been delivered from the rule of darkness, and who share in the glory of the Messianic age. A third and derivative use of the term is connected with the idea of keeping the commandments of God. These are holy, as derived from Him, and so those who keep the laws can be holy too.[6]

---

[4] Acts xxiv. 5, 14; xxviii. 22. Schlier, art. αἵρεσις in *Theol. Wörterbuch*, i. 182, points out clearly the reason for the Christian repudiation of the term.

[5] Headlam, *Doctrine of the Church*, 50; Dobschütz, *Christian Life*, 145; Wernle, *Beginnings*, i. 134.

[6] Asting, *Die Heiligkeit im Urchristentum* (1930), 133–9; Procksch, art. ἅγιος in Kittel, *Theol. Wörterbuch*, i. 108.

This third, or ethical idea is not apparent in the Acts, where the plural form is used four times as a title for Christians.[7] All these instances occur in the story of Paul's conversion, but though the word is the usual name for Christians in the Pauline Epistles, we need not conclude that the occurrence of the word in Acts is due to Pauline influence. The conception of the people of God, especially when assembled for worship, as holy, is firmly established in the Old Testament,[8] and is based on the holiness of God. He it is who makes His people holy.[9] The idea acquires a richer meaning in Second Isaiah, because of the declaration that the Holy One of Israel is also the Redeemer.[10] At a later stage, therefore, it was natural to describe the redeemed people of the new age, or those who were expecting the final judgement, as the holy ones, or saints.[11] Christians are 'the saints', first, because they are the true Israel; and second, because they are living in the new order, under the Reign of God, and awaiting the return of Christ as Judge.

It is the combination of these two conceptions which distinguishes the early Christian doctrine of the Church as the New Israel. If we lay all the stress on the continuity of the new community with the ancient People of God, it would seem incorrect to use the phrase New Israel at all.[12] But the claim to be the true sons of the covenant, the legitimate heirs of the promises, is dominated by the conviction that the Messianic Age had already

---

[7]   Acts ix. 13, 32, 41; xxvi. 10. Compare ἡγιασμένοι in Acts xx. 32.

[8]   Exodus xix. 5, 6 (the *locus classicus*, as O. C. Whitehouse calls it, *E.R.E.*, vi. 758, because the covenant idea underlies the description of the people as holy); see also Deut. vii. 6; xxvi. 19; Lev. xix. 2; Psalm lxxxix. 5; Wisdom xviii. 9.

[9]   Exodus xxxi. 13.

[10]   Isaiah xli. 14; xliii. 3; xlvii. 4.

[11]   Daniel vii. 18, 22; Enoch xxxviii. 4, 5, &c.; full list of references in Asting, 71.

[12]   Harnack, *Mission and Expansion*, i. 240–1; H. F. Hamilton, *The People of God* (1912), ii. 24–39; criticized by P. G. S. Hopwood, *The Religious Experience of the Primitive Church* (1936), 231–2.

dawned and that the last days were at hand. It is this conviction which makes the idea of a new Israel inevitable. It was new because it was founded on a fresh act of revelation, inaugurating the final era.

The passages which prove this for the primitive community, are:

(1) The connexion of the idea of the *Basileia* with the promise of the Father, and the baptism of the Spirit. ACTS i. 3–5.

(2) Acts ii. 16–21 is a quotation of an eschatological passage from Joel ii. 28 ff., introduced by the formula declaring that the present is the time of fulfilment: 'this is that which was spoken by the prophet'. The phrase 'in the last days' is introduced in ii. 17, although it forms no part of the LXX original. There are other passages proving that the gift of the Spirit was a sign of the last days (e.g. ISAIAH xliv. 3).

(3) In Acts iii. 19–25, Peter distinguishes between the present manifestation of the new age, which had been prophesied by all the prophets from Samuel, and the future 'seasons of refreshing', the times of the restoration of all things, when the Christ would be sent from heaven.

We may thus conclude that the Christian message from the beginning was dominated by the conviction that the New Israel was already being constituted because the new era had already dawned. This is the mark which distinguishes the claim of the Christian Ecclesia from that of the Damascus sect. This was the disturbing element in Christian doctrine when the gospel was presented to the Greeks. At Athens Paul is represented as delivering a skilful speech which for the most part covers the common ground between a Christian missionary and a contemporary Greek philosopher. When he proclaims his eschatological message the audience interrupts and some begin to mock. Yet, as Professor A. D. Nock points out, this disturbing element was fundamental. 'The central fact in the teaching of Jesus was not a novel doctrine of God or man but the heralding of the kingdom. . . . The business of those who heard the message was to labour to prepare Israel for the Day of the Lord. Israel was unwilling to be prepared, and the New Israel took its place. But even so, and even when the expectation of the final act of the cosmic drama became fainter, the Church was in the last analysis not an organization for the sanctification of souls in the present so much as a nursery for the people of the future.'[13]

---

[13]   *Conversion* (1933), 242–3.

Chapter Six

The Church is the Company which Shares in the Gift of the Spirit

The language of the Acts is that they received power (i. 8), were all filled with the Holy Spirit (ii. 4) received the gift of the Holy Spirit (ii. 38–39). What did this mean for the community?

There are two accounts of the gift of the Spirit; the account in Acts ii, and that in John xx. 22–3. Both agree in the supreme fact that the Spirit is given by Jesus Himself after the Resurrection. According to John, who has no account of the Ascension,[1] this takes place on the first Easter Day; according to Luke, on the fiftieth day. In view of the fact that the other accounts of the Resurrection appearances tell us nothing of the gift of the Spirit on the day of the Resurrection, the Lukan narrative is to be preferred.

According to Jewish belief the Spirit of God was given to the prophets. Professor Lake raises the question whether the phrase to receive the Holy Spirit does not mean 'to become prophets'.[2] In support of this view we may note that in the quotation from Joel the result of the gift of the spirit is that 'your sons and your daughters shall prophesy', and even slaves and handmaids shall share in this gift.

Pentecost would then be the fulfilment of the devout wish of the founder of Hebrew prophecy: 'Would God that all the Lord's

---

[1]   Though he presupposes it: vi. 62; xx. 17.
[2]   *Beginnings*, iv. 26. The suggestion is built on the evidence in Strack-Billerbeck, ii. 127–9.

people were prophets, that the Lord would put his spirit upon them' (Num. xi. 29). But against this view must be set the fact that a new order of prophets speedily developed in the Christian Church, distinct from apostles, and distinct from those who possessed the gift of speaking with tongues. It is not likely that the author of Acts, who knew well what a Christian prophet was, would have intended us to infer that all those who received the Holy Spirit became prophets in this sense. But there is a vital historical truth in this connexion of the new community with the gift of prophecy. Can we set down in some definite way what the Church received at Pentecost, apart from the unique phenomena which Luke probably knew full well had not been repeated?

It is not enough to conclude that 'the apostolic circle in Jerusalem underwent a deeply moving psychological experience. It was of the nature which to that and many later generations was known as inspiration.'[3] That the Spirit inspired the apostolic circle seems a strangely inadequate verdict for scholarship to pass on one of the greatest moments in the history of religion.

The gift of the Spirit brought a conviction of the activity of God Himself in the present. They already knew that God had revealed Himself in the life and death and resurrection of their Lord. They were firmly convinced that Jesus was to come again. Given these two convictions they would have had history and eschatology, memories of one revelation now past, and hopes of another still in the future. Now came a fresh revelation that their Lord, though exalted, still cared for them. 'He hath poured forth this which ye see and hear.' At no moment in the interval between Pentecost and the consummation of all things were they to be bereft of the active grace of God. This revelation may be described, in Dr. Anderson Scott's words, as the uprush of Life. It brought to them 'life of a new quality, life which quickened deeper levels of personality, and related men to one another and to God in a bond which neither death nor life could break'.[4]

---

[3] Lake, *Beginnings*, v. 120.
[4] *The Fellowship of the Spirit* (1921), 46.

According to the Lukan account (ii. 4) all the members of the community received the gift of the Spirit. On the ground that in i. 8 the promise is spoken to the Eleven apostles, the conclusion has been reached that the gift of the Spirit was conferred in the first instance by Jesus on the Apostles, and by the Apostles on the other Christians.[5] But Luke certainly gives no hint of this discrimination. According to the Joel quotation, all flesh – sons and daughters, young men and old men, slaves and handmaids – all receive the divine gift. The distinctions of sex and age and caste are bridged. There is no aristocracy of the Spirit. Again, the Spirit is bestowed that power may be given to bear witness to the Resurrection (i. 8), and there were many more witnesses than the Eleven (1. 23; I Cor. xv. 6). Peter says (ii. 32), 'This Jesus did God raise up, whereof we all are witnesses'. It seems therefore certain that Luke regards the Eleven as representing the whole community when the promise is made to them. All the believers received the gift on the day of Pentecost.

The significance of this fact for the idea of the Ecclesia is far-reaching. The Church was not divided into two classes; those who have received the Divine Spirit and those who have not. Not all may be prophets, but all may share in that intimate knowledge of God and His purpose which the Hebrew prophets in their measure shared, and which was their special endowment for their work. 'The Christian consciousness might be not unfairly described as the democratization of the prophetic consciousness through the gift of the Holy Spirit. This is true whether we think of the cruder side of prophecy in its psycho-physical phenomena, or of its moral and spiritual side realized by the greater prophets. This consciousness includes a new experience of God (through Jesus Christ), a new emphasis on the supernatural, a new sense of power.'[6]

These three characteristics are discernible in the early history of the Church at Jerusalem. The exaltation of Jesus to the right

---

[5] Lake, *Beginnings*, v. 110, following on the note in iv. 17.
[6] H. Wheeler Robinson, *The Christian Experience of the Holy Spirit* (1928), 14.

hand of God meant that now and henceforth they believed in God through Him, and they lived in the consciousness that through Him God was achieving His final victory. A new day had dawned in which the impossible became possible; there was a new emphasis on the supernatural. The new sense of power is apparent both in the witness borne to the Risen Christ and in the new way of life which (as is proved by the preservation of the sayings of Jesus) the early Christians believed that they must live.[7] These three convictions have no meaning except as found in determining the lives of individual men and women. They must be regarded as marks of the religious 'experience' which was the result of the revelation given at Pentecost.

We do not know how this revelation was appropriated and understood by individual believers. There is evidence that crude and unworthy conceptions of the action of the Spirit still persisted. But it is impossible to understand the religious experience of the Early Church, or indeed of the Church at any time when faith was alive and victorious, if we merely proceed on a maxim borrowed from biology. Religious life does not necessarily evolve from the lower forms to the higher, from the unethical to the ethical, from the outward and material to the inward and spiritual. It is unjust to the evidence to declare that Paul 'ethicized' the idea of the Spirit, as though that idea had been non-ethical before. We do not minimize the spiritual and intellectual greatness of Paul if we insist that he was not the first to discern what the Holy Spirit is and does.[8] In modern scholarship the view has won wide acceptance that in the early Church before Paul the Spirit is regarded as the mysterious wonder-working power of God, which is not con-

---

[7]   The evidence for these three characteristic marks is:

    (1)   Acts ii. 32–3; iii. 16; iii. 19–20; iv. 10–12. The new consciousness is directly connected with Christ, and faith in Him.

    (2)   ii. 19, 43; iii. 12; iv. 10, 30; v. 12.

    (3)   i. 8; ii. 44–7; iv. 13, 19, 31–7. See the discussion of 'The Way' on pp. 156–9.

[8]   cf. Büchsel, *Der Geist Gottes im Neuen Testament* (1926), 250–3; Feine, *Der Apostel Paulus* (1927), 307.

nected in their minds with the normal religious acts of daily life, nor with the interpretation of the divine purpose in history.[9]

This view leaves out the one dominant fact. The new revelation of God's working in the world is read in the light of the revelation already given through Jesus. He it is who gives the Spirit. The gift comes to those who have been called by Him, taught by Him, commissioned by Him. It is therefore incredible that they should merely have reproduced the current popular views. In the first place, if the Spirit is the gift of Jesus, it is the gift of One whose own activity was the evidence and embodiment of the final purpose of God for human history. Secondly, it is the gift of One who had taught them what faith neant, and prayer, and self-sacrifice, and courage, and above all, love. In the Acts (ii. 43–7) stress is laid on their public and their private worship, on their new mode of life as well as on the wonders and signs. Thirdly, the experience was not regarded by them as that of a mysterious Power of which no intelligible account could be given. They did not merely point to the wonders wrought. The notable fact in the second chapter of Acts is that an explanation was given. From the ancient expectation in the prophecy of Joel the mind is carried direct to Jesus, His Resurrection, His Exaltation to be both Lord and Christ. The confidence of those early speeches and their argumentative cast, are evidence that no violence had been done to the minds of the first Christian witnesses. On the contrary, their minds had been satisfied, quickened, exalted, and were thus made ready from the first to begin the interpretation of the new Fact. In the fourth place, we notice that the Spirit is never regarded as a private possession. From the beginning the new experience is shared. The Spirit is given to the community. This fact differentiates the New Testament belief from that of Israel and later Judaism, where the Spirit is only bestowed on certain special individuals, and where there is a hope of a general outpouring in

---

[9] This view goes back to Gunkel, *Die Wirkungen des heiligen Geistes* (1888, 3rd ed. 1909), 8, 12, 20; detailed criticism in H. von Baer, *Der heilige Geist in den Lukasschriften* (1926), 183–92, and, briefly, in my book, *The Idea of Perfection*, 46, 47.

the last days.[10] This characteristic mark of the New Testament belief is to be traced back to the activity of Jesus in His earthly life. It was He who had called disciples to be with Himself, and had established with them, as with a newly constituted Israel, the new covenant; it is to Him that they now attribute their new power, which is shared by all. To the question: 'What happened at Pentecost?' we may answer, a fresh revelation of God's activity in the present, which resulted not only in a new experience of God through Christ in the lives of all believers, but a new quality of fellowship. It is of the whole community that Luke writes:

> They continued steadfastly in the apostles' teaching and fellowship, in the breaking of bread and the prayers. ACTS ii. 42.

There are several possible ways of explaining the word *koinonia* or 'fellowship'. It may be (1) 'contributory help' (as in Hebrews xiii. 16; Rom. xv. 26; 2 Cor. viii. 4) almost equivalent to almsgiving; or (2) the common life, described in verse 44, and thus equivalent to κοινότης, which was later used of a communist order of society. (3) It is just possible that the word may be a translation of a current designation of the Church, the community understood in a particular sense. (4) The word may be spiritual fellowship, in a general sense: the sharing in the gift of the Spirit, the brotherly relationship. (5) As a variant of this explanation it is suggested that the words may be translated: 'in the teaching and fellowship of the Apostles' (so A.V. and R.V.): or that (6) 'fellowship' may be in apposition to, and thus equivalent to, 'the breaking of the bread' (cf. the Vulgate).

Against the second and third suggestions is the lack of support. 'If κοινωνία was ever a current designation of the Christian Church, perhaps anterior to the use of the word "ecclesia", it has left no other trace' (T. A. Lacey, *The One Body and the One Spirit* (1925), 247). The word is rarely used for social life in Classical Greek (Aristot., *Pol.*, 1252 *a* 2), and still more rarely in Hellenistic Greek (perhaps in Marcus Aurelius, v. 16; Epict., *Fragm.* 1), but never for a particular type of society (Seesemann, *Der Begriff Koinonia im N.T.* (1933) 42). These facts tell against the attractive suggestion of Dr. Anderson Scott, that the word in Acts ii. 42 is used as an equivalent of the Aramaic word *chabura*, a group of companions or partners, sharers

---

[10]   Gunkel, op. cit., 29.

in a common life (*Christianity according to St. Paul*, 159–61). The word is used in the Tractate Pesachim (vii. 3, 13) to describe the group of friends who might unite to celebrate the Passover Feast in common. The Hebrew form, *cheber*, is used of a company in Hosea vi. 9, on the coins of John Hyrcanus and his successors to designate Israel; in the Damascus Fragments it is used for the community of the new covenant. But these uses of a Hebrew word give us no warrant for supposing that the Aramaic *chabura* was used as a designation for Jesus and His friends. And the word κοινωνία seems to be never used as equivalent to a community, or *societas*. The dominant sense of the word is the inner relationship which constitutes fellowship. It is used with reference to marriage in an Oxyrrhyncus Papyrus. The closest parallel in the N.T. for the absolute use here is Gal. ii. 9, 'the right hands of fellowship'.

The most probable of the many meanings set out above are the fourth and the fifth. If the fifth be adopted we have two pairs which balance one another. They continued steadfastly in the teaching and the fellowship of the apostles – the stress here is on adhesion to the Twelve, – and in the Breaking of the Bread and the Prayers – this would be the rite whose central feature was the breaking of bread accompanied by common prayers, such as those which we find in the *Didache*.[11]

But the fourth alternative is perhaps the most probable of all. 'They continued steadfastly in the teaching of the Apostles and in fellowship.' The word would be used absolutely,[12] without the limiting reference to the Apostles, and would express the idea of the fellowship in which the Church is united, not without a hint of the acts of fellowship in which the fellowship is realized. The fellowship was 'the unity in which the whole Body was constituted and maintained'.[13] It was the inward bond which necessarily called for outward acts in which it could be expressed.

---

[11] So C. H. Dodd in *Christian Worship* (ed. N. Micklem, 1936), 68–70.

[12] Seesemann, *Der Begriff Koinonia*, 89; Wendt, *Apostelgeschichte* (1913), ad. loc.; Bauer, *Wörterbuch*, 687; Carr in *Expositor* (1913), 458–64.

[13] J. Armitage Robinson, in Hastings, *D.B.*, i. 461; cf. Hauck in *Theol. Wörterbuch*, iii. 809–10.

The author of the Acts clearly intends the word to point forward to the sharing of material goods and the mutual supply of material needs, as well as to the fellowship in Temple worship, in united prayers, and in the private ritual acts of the community.[14] Christian fellowship at its highest has always been of this quality, uniting the practice of common worship with care for the material needs of those who were poorer or in want. Such fellowship in the Spirit derives from Him who gave the Spirit, and who in His earthly life taught His followers to share with one another all that they had received from God.

From the Acts alone we learn little of the nature and meaning of the chief ritual act, the Breaking of the Bread. It is private or domestic, and so is distinguished from the public worship in the Temple. It was not an ordinary meal, like the eating of the bread in Luke xiv. I, 15; thus apparently Luke intends to distinguish an ordinary meal from 'the breaking of the bread'. Nothing is said about a cup, or about any connexion between this special meal and the death of Christ. In the oldest surviving Eucharistic prayers, preserved in the *Didache*, the death of our Lord is not even mentioned. It is Paul who lays stress on the proclamation of the Lord's death in this sacrament, but it is unlikely that he was the first so to do. Probably he is recalling the Corinthians to the original significance of the rite, which they had forgotten. The symbolic act of the breaking of the bread was inseparably connected with Christ's gift of Himself to His own. In partaking of the bread the early Christians shared in the benefits of His self-giving, and the thought of His death could never have been far away.

The fellowship in the gift of the Spirit involved outward expression not only in prayers but in the conduct of daily life. This we have already seen exemplified in the sharing of material possessions. But it is probably included also in the phrase 'the apostles' teaching'. It is difficult, and indeed impossible, to draw a rigid distinction between 'preaching' and 'teaching', between *kerygma* and *didache*, throughout the various writings of the New Testament. The two are undoubtedly distinguished in the Pauline

---

[14] ii. 44–6; iv. 32–7.

Epistles; probably also in Hebrews and the first two Johannine Epistles. Luke, too, draws a distinction between the function of teaching and the function of preaching in such a way as to suggest that the content of the *didachē* is distinguished from the content of the *kerygma*. At the end of Acts (xxviii. 31) Paul in his hired dwelling is preaching the kingdom of God, and teaching the things concerning the Lord Jesus. But clearly the content of *kerygma* and *didachē* must overlap. He could not preach the kingdom as Jesus preached it if he did not preach concerning the Lord Jesus. In Acts xv. 35, Paul and Barnabas remain in Antioch 'teaching and preaching the word of the Lord'.[15] In v. 42, the Apostles 'ceased not to teach and to preach Jesus as the Christ'. Teaching no doubt was largely occupied with proofs from the Old Testament. But in the speeches of Peter which contain the *kerygma*, the proof from Scripture continually finds a place. 'According to the Scriptures' is certainly an integral element in the apostolic preaching. There are other passages where we see the distinction between *didachē* and *kerygma* wavering. In Acts xiii. 7, Sergius Paulus 'sought to hear the word of God'; in xiii. 12 he was 'astonished at the teaching of the Lord'. The word of God which was 'proclaimed' at Salamis (xiii. 5) is taught to Sergius Paulus at Paphos. In Luke iv. 15 and 31 Jesus teaches in the synagogues. But between these two verses comes the account of His proclamation of the good news in the synagogue at Nazareth. It is difficult to believe that Luke would have excluded such preaching as this from the content of the synagogue teaching elsewhere.

In Acts ii. 42 the word *didachē* must include the ethical teaching of Jesus as related to the new Message which was being preached.[16] The originality of the word 'teach' in the Gospels and

---

[15] Is Lake's translation justified? *Beginnings*, iv. 183: 'teaching and with many others telling the good news of the word of the Lord.' 'The word of the Lord' may be the accusative to the two participles (so Moffatt). In that case the content both of the *didachē* and the *kerygma* is the divine revelation given through Jesus.

[16] See art. διδάσκω, διδαχή by Rengstorf, in *Theol. Wörterbuch*, ii. 141 ff., 147–50, 166.

Acts lies in the fact that it is bound up with the person of Jesus.[17] The teaching is never merely intellectual. It is directed to the end of securing the complete obedience of the hearers to the whole revelation made through Jesus. In the Apostles' teaching would be included, for Luke, all that Jesus began to do and to teach. We may fortify this conclusion by noting that for Matthew (xxviii. 20) one function of the Apostles is to teach whatever Jesus commanded them. This ethical teaching is also distinguished from the preaching of the Gospel. So in the Pauline Epistles the Pauline teaching on questions of conduct is grounded on the message of the Cross, and the obedience and love manifested there.[18] If teaching such as this, including a wrestling with the scriptures of the old dispensation, and a drawing out of the implications of the gospel preaching, is a characteristic mark of true Christianity from the beginning, Professor Nairne[19] was justified in setting 'scholarship' between worship and evangelism in his description of the proper work of the Ecclesia.

The Way

In one of the earliest titles applied to Christians we may find further evidence, first, that they were conscious of possessing the supreme revelation of God's purpose, which other Jews had failed to appropriate; and second, that they knew this revelation involved a new and loftier level of conduct. Six times in the Acts occurs the term 'the Way', or 'this Way'. Paul journeys to Damascus to arrest

---

[17] Rengstorf, 144; compare Denney's exposition in *The Way Everlasting* (1911) 103–4.

[18] Rengstorf, 150; Harnack's article in *Sitzungsberichte d. preussischen Akad. Berlin* (1928), 124–8, is of great importance for the understanding of Pauline ethical teaching. He shows that Paul did not give his churches the Old Testament as the Christian handbook for their instruction in Christian conduct, but that the decisive fact for his ethical teaching was the teaching and the Cross of Christ.

[19] *The Book of Job* (1935), ix.

'any that were of the Way' (ix. 2). The title is introduced casually, as though it were already well known. In the reply of Paul before Felix to Tertullus, Paul says that he serves 'the God of our fathers after the Way which they call a sect'.[20] Tertullus had called Christianity a sect. It is a fair inference that Christians repudiated the title of a sect, and called themselves 'the Way'.[21] In Acts xviii. 25, 26, it is further defined as 'the way of the Lord', 'the way of God'. In the first of these two titles we may perhaps see the original and distinctive use of the term, and in the second, the statement of the absolute nature of the revelation through Christ which all the early Christians would have accepted, and which marked them off from all other Jews. As Peter said in his speech to the rulers and elders and scribes (iv. 12): 'In none other is there salvation: for neither is there any other name under heaven, that is given among men, wherein we must be saved.'

It is not open to us to take the traditional explanation, that Jesus called Himself the Way (John xiv. 6), and that the Christians therefore called themselves the people of the Way. But Matthew records a saying of Jesus contrasting the narrow way of salvation with the broad and easy way which led to destruction.[22] It is probably from the current teaching about the Two Ways that the term came to be applied to the Christian message as the only Way. There seems to be no parallel in Greek literature for this use of the word as applied to a religion,[23] and the Rabbinical citations speak usually of 'the ways' of the Gentiles. [24] The nearest approach to the Christian use of the phrase is in the *Pirqe Aboth* (vi. 4). In the second century A.D. Rabbi Judah ha Nasi, and in the first century Rabbi Jochanan ben Zakkai, discuss 'the straight

---

[20] xxiv. 14.

[21] The other examples are xix. 9 and 23 (in Ephesus); xxii. 4 (Paul on the steps of the castle, addressing the Jewish mob); xxiv. 22, where Felix has more accurate knowledge of the Way, which turns out to be uncomfortably ethical in its demands (verse 25).

[22] Matt. vii. 13–14. It is probable that Luke (xiii. 24) preserves the more original form of this saying.

[23] See Liddell and Scott, *Lexicon* (new ed. 1932), 1199.

[24] Strack-Billerbeck, ii. 690.

way', 'the good way',[25] to which a man should cleave. R. Jehoshua ben Levi in the third century lays down 'the way of the Torah'. In none of these utterances is there any consciousness of living in the Messianic age, or in view of a coming Judgement. The 'way' is observance of the Law, and the expression is natural enough. There is no real parallel to the Christians' title for themselves.

The roots of the idea may possibly be found in certain sayings of the prophets:

> Thus saith the Lord: Behold, I set before you the way of life and the way of death. JEREMIAH xxi. 8.
> Thine ears shall hear a word behind thee, saying, This is the way, walk ye in it. ISAIAH xxx. 21.
> An high way shall be there, and a way, and it shall be called The way of holiness. ISAIAH xv. 8.

In these oracles, the last two of which are eschatological, there breathes the sense of urgency, the necessity of choice. So, too, for the Christians, adhesion to their community is a matter of life and death. The Christian 'Way' is not one road among many. It is the only way.[26] But the term also implies a consciousness of vocation to a new way of life, a life in accordance with the sayings of the Lord.

The preservation of the daring demands such as we find in the Sermon on the Mount was only possible in a community which was taking those sayings seriously. Indeed, every saying of Jesus is a witness to the ideals and convictions of the early Church. 'The proud sense of belonging to the "little flock" is morally possible only when it is combined with the consciousness of being pledged to do extraordinary deeds.'[27] But we must add that such a pledge

---

[25] Compare the sayings already quoted, Matt. vii. 13, 14; Acts ii. 40, iii. 23.

[26] The brief discussions in *Beginnings*, iv. 100; V.391–2, admit the Jewish origin of the title, and hazard the guess that the term was applied to Christians in Greek-speaking Jewish circles.

[27] Johannes Weiss. See the whole section in *Primitive Christianity* (E. tr.), i. 77–82.

becomes idle, and indeed meaningless, if it be not joined to a conviction that power has now been granted, whereby the righteousness of the followers of Jesus may exceed the righteousness of the scribes and Pharisees. The Beatitudes of the Great Sermon, the condition of childlikeness, the forgiveness of enemies, the love which is like the love of God Himself – all these go to the interpretation of that phrase 'the Way of the Lord'. And not one of them can be entertained by weak human nature unless it be read in the light of that other saying of Jesus: 'With men it is impossible but not with God: for all things are possible with God.' The power of the Spirit is the presupposition of the Sayings which the early Christians preserved.[28]

---

[28] cf. the argument in *The Idea of Perfection in Christian Theology*, 18–21.

Chapter Seven

The Church is Constituted Through its Allegiance

The Resurrection and Exaltation of Jesus to the right hand of God are two essential elements in the revelation which preceded Pentecost. As we have seen in the foregoing description of the gift of the Spirit, the Lordship of the Risen Christ both makes possible the gift and determines its nature. From this point we may proceed to the next inference drawn by the apostles – that the Lordship of Christ is the constitutive fact for the Church. The doctrine of 'the Crown Rights of the Redeemer' is to be found in the earliest traditions as to the nature of the Christian community.

Johannes Weiss has pointed out the significant order of the convictions born in the minds of the disciples as the result of the appearances of the Lord. First they were convinced that he still lived. But immediately they went on to the further inference that He was now the Messiah. This is a singular fact. The only immediate inference from the fact of Resurrection is 'that the powers of death have been conquered: Hades was not able to hold Him fast. But this was no proof of Messiahship for and in itself. . . . How this conviction should thus arise immediately, and as it were, spontaneously, can only be explained if within the oldest group of disciples the question of Messiahship was already central, even before the death of Jesus'[1] Every theory which denies

---

[1] *The History of Primitive Christianity*, i. 31.

that our Lord ever accepted any form of Messiahship for Himself makes shipwreck on this indubitable fact.[2] The Christian Church was constituted by this apostolic conviction that Jesus was Messiah, and exalted to the right hand of God.

> Let all the house of Israel therefore know assuredly,
> That God hath made him both Lord and Christ,
> This Jesus whom ye crucified.
> ACTS ii. 36.

The fresh word here is Lord, *Kyrios*, which is joined with Christ. The word is found in Psalm cx. 1:

> The Lord said unto my Lord,
> Sit thou at my right hand.

This Psalm, quoted in the speech of Peter, is frequently cited by New Testament writers, and was used in His teaching by our Lord Himself.[3] Contributory evidence that the title was primitive is to be found in the second of the two Aramaic prayers which were probably used in the early Christian assemblies, *Abba* and *Marnatha*. The words *Marana tha* mean either 'the Lord is come' or 'Come, Lord'. The first meaning is probably traceable in Phil. iv. 5, 'The Lord is near' and the second in Rev. xxii. 20, 'Come, Lord Jesus'. In liturgical history such brief sentences are often perpetuated and carried forward untranslated from one language to another, and the presence of *Abba* and *Maranatha* in the epistles of St. Paul speaks strongly for their use from the very beginning of Christian worship.[4] Thus we have additional evidence that prayer was addressed to the exalted Christ.

---

[2] cf. the arguments of Bousset, *Jesus* (E. tr. 1906), 168–9, and Sanday, *Life of Christ in Recent Research* (1907), 75–6, against the theory of Wrede. The arguments hold against the resuscitation of Wrede's views in R. H. Lightfoot, *History and Interpretation in the Gospels* (1935).

[3] Mark xii. 35–7; cf. Acts vii. 56 (Stephen); I Cor. xv. 25; Hebrews i. 13; Eph. i. 20; Col. iii. 1.

[4] Fabricius in the *Seeberg-Festschrift* (1929), 21–2.

The allegiance of the Jerusalem Church to Jesus could hardly be expressed by any loftier titles than these two, 'Lord and Christ'. There is little trace of 'development in Christology' as the story of Acts proceeds. But there are traces of mental movement, as though Peter or the Church at Jerusalem were feeling after fresh forms in which to clothe their adoration of their Lord. Thus in the third chapter new titles appear. Jesus is the Servant, of Isaiah liii. He is the Holy and Righteous One. He is the Prince of Life. He is the Prophet of whom Moses spoke. He is the fulfilment of the covenant granted to Abraham, and it is through Him that all the families of the earth will be blessed. In the fourth chapter He is the stone set at nought by the builders, and now made the head of the corner. His is the only name under heaven wherein we must be saved. In the prayer of the church (iv. 24–31) He is the king prophesied in the second Psalm, and yet He is the holy Servant of Isaiah liii. 3. In the fifth chapter (29–32) He is not only Prince, but Saviour. In the seventh chapter Stephen calls Jesus both Lord and Son of Man. It is a singular testimony to the fidelity of the author of Acts to the traditions which he had received that he does not once introduce the title 'Son of God' in his first eight chapters, though he might have conjectured that the title 'Son' would be probable if the second Psalm was used as a testimony to Jesus. Only when Paul begins his preaching in the synagogues is Jesus said to be proclaimed as Son of God.

The close connexion of some of these titles with the assembling of a community has already been discussed.[5] The designation, 'Head stone of the corner' has no meaning unless there is a house to be built. The titles Saviour and King imply the reconstitution of the People of God. In the Septuagint the word Prince (*archēgos*) is applied to the political or military leader of the whole people, and is the translation of nine different Hebrew words. It is found once[6] in a phrase structurally like that of Acts iii. 15 in the sense of 'one who inaugurates', who through His example gives an impulse to others to follow. Here it is One who

---

[5]   See above, 74–80.
[6]   Micah i. 13, ἀρχηγὸς ἁμαρτίας.

inaugurates the era of new life, who 'through His resurrection gives the warrant that His followers will share the lot of their heroic deliverer'.[7]

But the title 'Lord' remains the dominant description. 'Jesus is Lord' became the first Christian Creed.[8] The part played by this creed in the constitution of a new community is clearly seen in the foundation of the Church at Antioch, the Church which originated the Gentile mission. The words of Hort[9] deserve to be quoted:

> Here was a great capital, including a huge colony of Jews, in close relations with all the Greek-speaking world and all the Syriac-speaking world; and in its midst a multitude of Christian disciples had come into existence in the most casual and unpremeditated way. No Apostle had led or founded a mission; no Apostle had taught there. But there the congregation was.

The origin of the congregation was due to Christian refugees, men of Cyprus and Cyrene who overstepped the usual limitations observed by most of the brethren and spoke to Greeks as well as to Jews, 'preaching the good news of Jesus as the Lord'.[10] Barnabas was sent as the delegate of the apostles, and he saw in the very fact of the congregation so gathered the grace which was of God. The disciples therefore were recognized by their common allegiance as part of the true Israel of God.

The first outward and visible sign of allegiance was Baptism. The sudden appearance of this initiatory rite on the day of

---

[7] Delling, art. ἀρχηγός in *Theol. Wüorterbuch*, i. 486.

[8] Acts ii. 36; I Cor. xii. 3; Rom. x. g; Phil. ii. 11.

[9] *The Christian Ecclesia*, 59.

[10] Acts xi. 20, Lake's translation. Lake's note, *Beginnings*, iv. 129 (cf. Cadbury's note, v. 360), offers no explanation of the origin of the title *Kyrios* but seems to assume some variant of Bousset's theory. Of such a view that this title was derived from Hellenistic usage, and was first applied to Jesus in the Gentile Church, Professor C. H. Dodd writes: 'Seldom, I think, has a theory been so widely accepted on more flimsy grounds.' *Apostolic Preaching*, 25.

Pentecost raises doubts in the mind of the historian which are
not readily allayed.[11] The Synoptic Gospels give us no hint that
Baptism was the way of entrance into the circle of the disciples
of Jesus. The earliest disciples had probably been baptized by
John the Baptist,[12] but neither this probability, nor the undoubted fact that Jesus Himself was baptized by John nor the
doubtful tradition of a command of the Risen Lord,[13] gives a
satisfactory historical basis for the immediate and spontaneous
adoption of this rite on the day of Pentecost. On the other hand,
the dismissal of the account in the Acts raises greater difficulties
for the historian. The attempted constructions of the supposed
process by which Baptism afterwards became naturalized in the
Church are purely conjectural. It seems more reasonable to
assume that the Fourth Gospel, in spite of its apparent contra-
dictions at this point, preserves a genuine tradition. In iii. 22 and
iv. I, 'Jesus was baptizing'. In iv. 2, 'Jesus Himself was not
baptizing but his disciples'. If the fact underlying these discrep-
ancies was that Jesus did not baptize, but He allowed His
disciples to baptize, we could then trace an intelligible sequence
of events. First, Jesus Himself was baptized with the baptism of
John, a baptism of water, which not only was the first step in the
gathering of a new community of those who were preparing for
the Day of the Lord, but also pointed forward to a baptism with
the power of the Spirit. Those who afterwards became the
disciples of Jesus were also baptized by John. Jesus allows them
to baptize, though He does not Himself baptize. On the day of
Pentecost, when the Spirit was given, the apostles, remembering
that Baptism had been linked with the idea of the forgiveness of
sins, ask for submission to this rite as a sign of repentance. But
since Jesus is now recognized as the exalted Messiah, and has
fulfilled the ancient expectation of an outpouring of the Holy

---

[11] For these see J. Weiss, op. cit., 50–1; Foakes Jackson and Lake,
Beginnings, i. 337–44

[12] W. K. Lowther Clarke, *Divine Humanity*, 69.

[13] Adopted in a modern form by Oepke, art. βαπτίζω, in *Theol. Wörterbuch*, i. 536–7

Spirit, the baptism must be 'in the name' of Jesus, as a token of allegiance to Him.[14]

The reluctance to admit that the phrase 'in the name of Jesus' could be used in baptism at this stage, is difficult to appreciate. It is used in sayings of Jesus; it is so thoroughly Semitic in form, that no exact parallel has been traced outside Biblical Greek.[15] The Semitic phrase may have two senses; it may mean 'with reference: to' something that will be, or 'with reference to' something that is. The first is a final, the second a causal sense. In the saying: 'receive a prophet in the name of a prophet', the phrase has a causal sense. The man who listens to or entertains a prophet in the name of a prophet, does so because he is a prophet. Thus in Matt. xviii. 5 the phrase 'in my name' means 'for my sake'.[16] In Mark ix. 41 whosoever shall give you a cup of cold water to drink in the name that ye are of Christ, is rightly translated in the R.V., 'because ye are Christ's'. It means 'with reference to', or 'thinking upon' Jesus.[17]

So here, in Acts ii. 38, Baptism in the name of Jesus is baptism because Jesus is what He is, the exalted Messiah, and because He has done what He has done, poured forth the promised gift of the Spirit. From the beginning Christian Baptism means taking Jesus Christ for all that He is. It is therefore a sign both of the supreme allegiance and of admission into the Ecclesia. The minister in Baptism was perhaps an Apostle or one of the Seven, or one who like Ananias is simply described as a disciple. It is curious that

---

[14] For this explanation, cf. J. Leipoldt, *Die urchristliche Taufe im Lichte der Religionsgeschichte* (1928), 29–35; it goes only two steps beyond that of Lietzmann, *The Beginnings of the Christian Church* (E. tr. 1937), 80–1, who dismisses John iv. 1–2 as unhistorical, but believes that it indicates 'the direction in which we must look for a solution of the problem'; he also thinks that the formula 'in the name of' was introduced later.

[15] Moulton-Milligan, *Vocabulary*, 451–2; though Deissmann claims one, *Bible Studies* (E. tr. 1903), 197–8, in an inscription which has the simple dative, without a preposition.

[16] Strack-Billerbeck, i. 590–1.

[17] Dalman, *Words of Jesus*, 305–6.

neither on the day of Pentecost nor in the success of Philip at Samaria (viii. 12–13) nor after the conversion of Paul, does the tradition explicitly record who administered the rite. In Caesarea, Peter commanded the Gentiles to be baptized in the name of Jesus Christ. The deduction to be made is that apparently it was competent for any baptized Christian himself to baptize. But one fact is certain from the evidence: the minister in baptism acted as one commissioned by Christ, and guided the convert to fix his gaze on Christ alone. The value of Baptism does not depend on the activity or office of the minister. It is Christ who acts and gives.[18]

---

[18]   cf. Schlatter, *Die Geschichte der ersten Christenheit* (1926), 33. It is unnecessary for our purpose to discuss the different views of the nature of Baptism which have been discovered by some scholars in the Acts; see *Beginnings*, v. 134–7; Hopwood, *The Religious Experience of the Primitive Church* (1936), 277 ff.

Chapter Eight

The Message of the Primitive Church

The message is Christ. Luke uses various objects for the verb *euangelizesthai* – 'that Jesus is the Christ' (v. 42), 'the word' (viii. 4) 'concerning the kingdom of God' (viii. 12), 'Jesus' (viii. 35), 'peace through Jesus Christ' (x. 36), 'that Jesus is the Lord' (xi. 20), 'the word of the Lord' (xv. 35), 'Jesus and the resurrection' (xvii. 18). The one truth shines through these varieties of language, that the promised Rule of God is now present in Jesus.

Professor C. H. Dodd, in his brilliant demonstration of the essential unity of the Apostolic preaching, has begun with this, its determinative element. First, 'the age of fulfilment has dawned. . . . Secondly, this has taken place through the ministry, death, and resurrection of Jesus. . . . Thirdly, by virtue of the resurrection, Jesus has been exalted at the right hand of God, as Messianic head of the new Israel. . . . Fourthly, the Holy Spirit in the Church is the sign of Christ's present power and glory. . . . Fifthly, the Messianic age will shortly reach its consummation in the return of Christ. . . . Finally the *kerygma* always closes with an appeal for repentance, the offer of forgiveness and of the Holy Spirit, and the promise of "salvation", that is of "the life of the Age to Come" to those who enter the elect community.'[1] The detailed evidence for this analysis is given by Professor Dodd, and need not be repeated here. For our present purpose we may note (1) that the idea of the Ecclesia is essential, pre-supposed

---

[1] *The Apostolic Preaching and its Developments* (1936), 38–43.

and indeed explicit, in three out of the six articles in the primitive *kerygma*, the third, the fourth, and the sixth; (2) that the idea of the *Basileia* which is the theme of the first and second proclamations involves the correlative and subordinate idea, that of the Ecclesia; (3) that the proclamation of the end of human history in the Return of Christ implies Judgement (cf. x. 42). It is the destruction of the evil (cf. iii. 23). It is the Return of Christ to His own people (iii. 21), and the consummation of that perfected fellowship in the final victory of God. Thus at every point of the *kerygma* we see the idea of the Ecclesia declared or implied.

But we can also trace clearly in Acts the characteristic relation between the Message and the Ecclesia, which we have already seen in the teaching of Jesus. The *kerygma* contains the idea of the Ecclesia, but it also creates the Ecclesia. The Word of God, the supreme and final revelation of His will for mankind, is the constitutive fact for the Church. In one of his summaries, by which he links the various units of his narrative, the author of Acts expresses the universal conviction of the New Testament writers.

> And the word of God increased; and the number of the disciples multiplied in Jerusalem , exceedingly; and a great company of the priests were obedient to the faith. ACTS vi. 7; cf. xii. 24, xlx. 20.

The growth of the Word of God is used as a synonym for the growth of the Ecclesia. There is a dynamic force in the Word. The Christian gospel declared authoritatively in the power of the Spirit is living and active.[2] It effects a result wherever it meets obedience.

In the traditions of the *kerygma* preserved in the Acts there are hardly any hints of the meaning of the death of Christ, and no direct allusions to the Last Supper with its decisive establishment of the New Covenant in His blood. The fact of the death of Christ in all its shame and tragedy is asserted. That fact clearly implied a judgement on those who put Him to death.

---

[2] cf. Hebrews iv. 12–13.

Him, being delivered up by the determinate counsel and foreknowledge of God, ye by the hand of lawless men did crucify and slay; whom God raised up, having loosed the pangs of death: because it was not possible that he should be holden of it. ACTS ii. 23, 24[a].

Ye denied the Holy and Righteous One, and asked for a murderer to be granted unto you, and killed the Prince of life; whom God raised from the dead; whereof we are witnesses. ACTS iii. 14, 15[a].

Jesus Christ of Nazareth, whom ye crucified, whom God raised from the dead. ACTS iv. 10; cf. iv. 25–8; vii. 51–3.

These speeches are not addressed to the few who were primarily responsible for the Crucifixion, but generally to the representatives of the old Israel, who have been guilty of rejection, but still have an opportunity of repentance. There is no statement of any saving significance in the sacrifice of Calvary unless it is implied in Philip's exposition of Isaiah liii., in Acts viii. 30–5. There is apparently no connexion between 'the breaking of the bread' and the death of Christ, though, as I have suggested above, the thought of Christ's gift of His body, and so of Himself in death, could hardly have been altogether absent from the primitive conception of the rite. Are we to conclude that the earliest believers had no sense of the saving power of the Cross? Or that the author of Luke-Acts was uncertain about it himself?[3]

It is possible to lay too much stress on the argument from silence. In the first place, we have definite evidence that the death of Christ was part of the *kerygma*, and that a meaning was read into it. On the one hand it was part of the eternal counsel of God; on the other hand, as an historical fact it meant Israel's rejection of God's purpose, and therefore liability to judgement. Secondly, Luke is writing a second volume, and cannot be expected to repeat what he has already stated in the first. Even if he himself has no *theologia crucis*, he knows the pity of the Cross and the power of it, when it is preached at the centre of a gospel. No one who was without feeling for the power of the Death of Christ could have

---

[3] See the statement of the problem by J. Weiss, *Primitive Christianity*, i. 113–16; cf. 59–62. The difficulty is not new; see R. W. Dale, *Atonement* (1875, 5th ed.1876), 110–17, and especially his answer, 112.

written the Passion narrative in the Third Gospel. In the third place, evangelical preachers do not find it always necessary to establish the relation of the death of Christ to the forgiveness of sins, before they bring their hearers to repentance and to faith in Jesus Christ as Lord. Both Peter and the author of the Acts regarded the death of Christ, not as an accidental event, but as an essential fact in the divine purpose. Both see that penitence, confession, and acceptance of a divine offer, are essential to Christian faith. Modern theologians demand too much, both of their sources and of the Apostles, if they require the deeper meaning which Jesus read into His own sufferings to be immediately translated into the message and the theology of the early Church. But already in that Church the death of Christ is preached as within the divine purpose, and as part of the divine revelation; forgiveness and cleansing are offered in the name of the One who died and rose again. The inner connexion between the various elements in the message will be seen later. But the Cross of Christ is there, at the heart of the *kerygma*, and always viewed in the light of the Resurrection. It is to the Resurrection that the Apostles bear witness, as the culminating fact in their gospel.

Witnesses of the Resurrection

The word 'witness', *martys*, has a special meaning in the Acts,[4] a part from two passages (Acts vi. 13; vii. 58) where it is used in the ordinary legal sense of witnesses at a trial. The other eleven passages[5] in which the word is used all refer to those who are eye-witnesses of the Resurrection. These include, of course, the Apostles and their friends (Luke xxiv. 13, 18 33), and Paul himself. The name is given to Stephen, not in the later sense of martyr, but in virtue of the special vision of Christ given to him

---

[4] The study of this word by Professor R. P. Casey, in *Beginnings*, v. 30–7, is the basis of the following paragraph.

[5] Acts i. 8, 22; ii. 32; iii. 15; v. 32; x. 39, 41; xiii. 31; xxii. 15,20; xxvi. 16; compare Luke xxiv. 46–9.

at the time of his death.[6] Another characteristic of the witness is that he has been specially chosen before by God for this privilege.[7] There then we have the conception of a limited body of witnesses who are specially chosen by God to bear their testimony to the cardinal fact in the *kerygma*.

Professor Casey claims that the Pauline Epistles show a broader conception of the content of Christian testimony, which would include not only the Resurrection, but the whole substance of the revelation dispensed by the Spirit.[8] But I do not think that the linguistic evidence warrants us in going quite so far. In the crucial passage, I Cor. xv. 14, 15, the primary reference of apostolic testimony is to the Resurrection: 'If Christ hath not been raised, then is our preaching (*kerygma*) vain, your faith also is vain. Yea, and we are found false witnesses of God; because we witnessed of God that he raised up Christ.' Taken in connexion with the opening verses of the chapter which contain the list of the various appearances of the Lord, this verse would support the view of Luke that the 'witnesses' to the Resurrection were in the nature of things a limited company, and that their testimony was the constitutive fact for the Christian Ecclesia.

---

[6] Compare Acts xxii. 20 with vii. 54–6 where the testimony is offered.
[7] Acts x. 41; xx. 14; xx. 16.
[8] *Beginnings*, v. 33.

Chapter Nine

The Mission of the Ecclesia

'From the very beginning the original church was a missionary church.'[1] The justification for this statement must be found in the preceding description of the nature of the Ecclesia. As the nucleus of the true Israel, and so destined to be God's instrument in His fulfilment of His purpose in the last days, the Ecclesia must fulfil the age-long mission of the Remnant. It must be a saving Remnant. The conversion of Israel is the first task. Since the Ecclesia is equipped for the task by the gift of the Spirit, the mission is that of prophecy, or inspired preaching. 'Even upon my bond-servants, both men and women, at that time will I pour out my Spirit and they shall, prophesy.'[2] The gift of the Spirit is the mark of the Messianic community; as the function of the Messiah was to gather the redeemed community, so those who received His gift direct from His hands must testify to their allegiance to Him, by sharing that allegiance with all whom they could win. And this could only be done by the proclamation of the supreme Word of God, the *euangelion*, the message which was at once simple, coherent and intelligible, – the declaration, in the power of the Spirit, of certain redeeming facts which embodied the *euangelion* of Jesus concerning the Reign of God. The Word is proclaimed in public preaching, and also in solemn acts of worship, in Baptism and Eucharist and in private or public

---

[1] Lietzmann, *The Beginnings of the Christian Church*, 90.

[2] Acts ii. 18.

assemblies for prayer. The Word is also proclaimed in the daily life of the community, in the new ventures of fellowship to which the Church is called, in the care for the sick, the impoverished, and the bereaved. The Church is therefore missionary, from the very beginning, in virtue of the divine revelation with which it is entrusted. At every point the Word determines the mission. The Ecclesia is a believing community, a witnessing community, a worshipping community, and a community pledged to a new Way of life.

The scope of the mission was to be indefinitely widened; but of this expansion and its consequences the first believers could not be fully aware. There are hints even in the early preaching of the Jerusalem Church that the message could not be confined to Palestine. The Spirit was to be poured 'on all flesh'. The promise was not only to those present in Jerusalem but 'to all that are afar off'. The ancient covenant promised that in Abraham's seed all the families of the earth should be blessed.[3] Jerusalem was already the centre of a spiritual empire. As the Old Testament scriptures were reread in the light of God's supreme act in Jesus Christ, the consciousness of a mission to the nations might penetrate into the mind of the Church. But for the period preceding the death of Stephen, only indirect evidence can be adduced for the way in which the mission was interpreted. The preservation of the Mission Charge to the disciples is a probable indication that the early missionaries went out two by two, avoiding the roads which led to the Gentiles and the cities of the Samaritans.[4] Their first task was to go to the lost sheep of the house of Israel, to gather fresh disciples into the 'little flock' for the reconstitution of Israel under the consummated Rule of God. Thus their vivid consciousness that the followers of Jesus were alone the true Israel, and that they alone possessed the final Word of God, was saved from the peril of fanaticism; every Jew was a possible member of the new Ecclesia. But it was from the Greek-speaking Jews in the Church at Jerusalem that the impulse

---

[3] Acts ii. 18; ii. 39; iii. 25.
[4] Matt. x. 5–23; xv. 24.

for expansion was to arise. It is to one of the Seven, rather than to the Twelve, that a clearer vision was granted of the result of the continued Jewish rejection of Jesus as the Christ.

The Speech of Stephen

'The general character of the speech seems to fit in very well with the theory that it represents either a good tradition as to what Stephen really did say, or at least what a very early Christian, not of the Pauline school, would have wished him to say.'[5]

For our present purpose it does not matter which of these alternatives we adopt. The speech may be accepted as representing fairly the doctrine of the liberal party of Greek-speaking Christians in the Church of Jerusalem.

There are three ideas dominating the thought. First, as we should expect, is the central proclamation of the primitive *kerygma*, the Messiahship of Jesus. There are two characteristic marks of Stephen's exposition. The starting point is the covenant made with Abraham (vii. 2–8). The doctrine of Israel as the people of God is the background of the Messianic idea. On the other hand, the historical result of Messiahship is rejection at the hands of the Hebrew people, a fate already foreshadowed by the rejection at the hands of the patriarchs, and by the rejection of Moses, their appointed deliverer in the second great act in their history, the Exodus from Egypt (vii. 25–9; 35–7). Moses was like the promised Christ. Rejected by the People of God, he was their deliverer none the less. Again they rebelled, and paid the penalty in exile (vii. 41–3). Thus Stephen dealt with the question which must have been discussed in every synagogue in the controversies of the followers of Jesus with other Jews: how could Jesus, who was rejected and crucified, be the Messiah?

The second leading idea is the supersession of the Temple. The illustrations from the past are drawn from the lives of the Jewish Fathers who had no part in the Temple worship. The tabernacle

---

[5] Lake, *Beginnings*, iv. 70.

was a true copy made by Moses of the true Idea which he had seen in the Mount. Solomon himself, who built the Temple, admitted the essential spirituality of all true worship, and the temporary nature of this new house of God (vii. 44–50). This is the only answer which Stephen makes to his accusers, who had brought against him the same charge as was made against Jesus. 'We have heard him say, that this Jesus of Nazareth shall destroy this place.'

The third idea of the speech is only made explicit in the climax, the resistance of the Jews to the Holy Spirit. 'As your father did, so do ye.' In the persecution of the prophets, in the failure to keep the divinely given law, the Jews had demonstrated their rejection of the Word of God. And now they had betrayed and murdered the Righteous One Himself.

Beneath these three leading ideas lie three positive principles for the doctrine of the Ecclesia. (1) There is a divine purpose in history for the people of God, a purpose which cannot be thwarted by rejection. The call of Abraham was the first unveiling of the divine will for Abraham's seed, and that will is consummated in Christ. The corollary is that the despised Christians are the true children of Abraham. (2) The time of the supersession of worship at the Temple is drawing near. The corollary is that the people of God, the true Ecclesia, is not bound to any one place. There is a new edifice, made without hands. The language recalls the saying of Jesus already discussed in a previous chapter.[6] (3) The Spirit of God is creating a new people, those who have not rejected the divine Word, and who therefore will take the place of those who have simply followed their fathers in rejecting the messengers of God.

There is in this speech no new doctrine of the Ecclesia. But there is evidence of a powerful mind wrestling with the history of Israel, and interpreting the common *kerygma* in a sense which no doubt was unwelcome to some of the leaders of the Church, perhaps to James himself. Stephen does not reject the Law. On the contrary, his counter-charge against the Jews is that they have not kept it.

---

[6] *Supra*, pp. 55–8.

But so far as we know, he was the first to draw the conclusion from the saying of Jesus that the time for the supersession of the Temple-cultus was drawing near. The next step was the universality of the Gospel, the equality of Jew and Gentile in the newly constituted Ecclesia, without reference to the traditional Jewish practices of circumcision and Temple-worship. Apparently this deduction was not explicitly drawn by Stephen. But the Jewish authorities were justified in their conviction that his liberal doctrine was a danger to the Judaism which they had known.

The persecution which followed enabled the Church to realize its missionary character in fresh fields and on untrodden ways. The rapid expansion of the Church was not due to the work of the Apostles; 'they are specially excepted by St. Luke'[7] The missionary to Samaria is Philip the Evangelist, one of the Seven, who only in later tradition is called an Apostle.[8] Suddenly, and without previous warning, we read of a Christian community in Damascus.[9] In ix. 31 we read that 'the Church throughout all Judaea and Galilee and Samaria had peace, being built up; and walking in the fear of the Lord and by the invocation of the Holy Spirit was multiplied'. The Ecclesia has a wider range; it is no longer the Church of a single city, but it is still one Church.

The 'casual and unpremeditated way' in which the Church was extended among Gentiles[10] has been lit up by an imaginative page written by Dr. T. R. Glover.

> The Gospel was preached instinctively, naturally. The earliest Christians were persecuted in Jerusalem, and were driven out. I picture one of them in flight; on his journey he falls in with a stranger. Before he knows what he is doing, he is telling his fellow-traveller about Jesus. It follows from his explanation of why he is on the road; he warms up as he speaks. He never really thought about the danger of doing so. And the stranger wants to know more; he is captured by the message, and he too becomes a Christian. And then this involuntary

---

[7] Hort 53.
[8] Eusebius, *Ecclesiastical History*, iii. 31.
[9] Acts ix. 1, 2, 19–22.
[10] Acts xi. 19–21; Hort, 59.

preacher of the Gospel is embarrassed to learn that the man is a Gentile; he had not thought of that. I think that is how it began – so naturally and spontaneously. These people are so full of love of Jesus that they are bound to speak. (Acts viii. 4). 'One loving heart sets another on fire.'[11]

[11]   *The Jesus of History* (1916), 89.

Chapter Ten

The Ministry of the Ecclesia

So far I have ventured to analyse the idea of the Ecclesia, as we meet it in the preaching and life of the primitive community. The conclusion must be that it corresponds to the idea of the Ecclesia already outlined in the sayings and actions of Jesus in His earthly life. Later we shall see that the same outline can be traced in subsequent teaching, in the Epistles of St. Paul, in the Fourth Gospel and in I Peter. But hitherto there has been little discussion in this essay of the ministry of the Church. In most English work on the subject the Ministry is given more attention than the Ecclesia itself.[1] There are historical reasons in the Christianity of Great Britain for this singular disproportion. Since the various communions are divided from one another by varying convictions as to the ministry, it is assumed that discussion must be concentrated on questions of the origin and nature of the ministry of the Church. But the New Testament shows us a better way. It is surely more important, both for the attainment of historical truth and for the discovery of the way of reconciliation, that attention should first be concentrated on the essential nature of the Church which the ministry serves, and only after that, on the relation of the ministry to the Church. We may now proceed to the secondary question. In what sense is the ministry essential to the Church or constitutive of it? We need only glance at the further and subor-

---

[1] See, for example, Dr. A. C. Headlam's Bampton Lectures; C. Gore, *The Church and the Ministry* (1889, new ed. 1919).

dinate question: does a study of the primitive community encourage the belief that any one form of ministry must always and everywhere be regarded as constitutive of the being of the Church?

The primary question here is the place of the Apostles in the primitive community. This involves the problem of the nature of the Ecclesia. Did the early Christians conceive of the Church as an organized legal institution, with duly appointed rulers who already exercise a formal judicial function?

The Apostles

It seems unlikely that modern scholarship, after the closest scrutiny of our documents, can do more than establish two statements as to the place of the Twelve in the Primitive Church.[2] First, they were accorded a certain pre-eminence in the counsels and leadership of the community; second, the exact nature of their authority was undefined. Their general pre-eminence they owed:

(1) to their close companionship with Jesus in the days of His flesh;[3]
(2) to their privilege of witnessing the Resurrection;[4]
(3) to the fact that they had been sent forth to preach by Jesus Himself in His earthly life;[5]
(4) to the fact that Jesus had given them 'authority' to cast out devils.

These last three privileges they shared with others.[6] The first was in its nature incommunicable, and only eleven men shared in it. It is therefore in the first privilege that we must find the decisive reason for the singular pre-eminence of the Twelve. It is probable

---

[2] See the statements in W. L. Knox, *St. Paul and the Church of Jerusalem* (1925), 6, and J. Weiss, *Primitive Christianity*, 48.
[3] Mark iii. 14, endorsed by Acts i. 21.
[4] Acts i. 21–2; cf. I Cor. ix. 1.
[5] Mark iii. 14, 15.
[6] I Cor. xv. 5–8; Luke x. 1,19.

that Matthias was brought in to fill the place of Judas because he had enjoyed intimate fellowship with Jesus in His earthly life.[7] A similar reason lies near at hand for the association with them at an early date of James, the brother of the Lord. But the other brothers of the Lord were not given a corresponding position, at any rate in the early days. Here, then, it is probable that we should look not only to his blood-relationship to Jesus, and his intimate knowledge of Him, but also to the special appearance of Christ to James,[8] as the explanation of his early advance to the leadership of the Church of Jerusalem.

The record in Acts of the activities of the Twelve seems to be sufficiently explained by the four privileges detailed above. On the day of Pentecost Peter stands up with the Eleven and on their behalf preaches the message, which is confirmed by the apostolic witness to the Resurrection. Those who are added to them continued steadfastly in the Apostles' teaching (ii. 42), which was given in virtue of their close association with Jesus in the days when He taught them. Wonders and signs were done by the Apostles (ii. 43), just as the devils had been subject to them during the lifetime of Jesus. One illustration is given in detail (ch. iii–iv), together with the preaching given in explanation of the healing. The election of the Seven was due to the conviction of the Twelve that they themselves had been set apart for a special ministry of the word of God, and were therefore to be exempted from ordinary administrative duties (vi. 2). The Seven are ordained for their special task by the Apostles. This rite apparently signifies the solemn transmission to the Seven of the one administrative duty which was discharged in the early period by the Apostles, that of the distribution of the money from the common fund to those in need.[9] In the discharge of that task supernatural insight had been granted to Peter to detect the duplicity of Ananias and Sapphira.

---

[7]   For the election of Matthias to the vacant place, see W. K. Lowther Clarke, *Divine Humanity*, 194–8, against the widespread view (e.g. J. Weiss, *Primitive Christianity*, 47–8) that this is an ecclesiastical legend.

[8]   I Cor. xv. 7.

[9]   Acts vi. 6, compared with iv. 34–5.

Peter's harsh treatment of Sapphira is the culminating difficulty of this unsavoury story,[10] which is a doubtful foundation for the view that he was exercising any judicial functions here. The *motif* of the tradition is to show the terror of the sin against the Holy Spirit, rather than to illustrate the function of an apostle. It is another of the 'wonders and signs'. If the sin of Ananias was 'the attempt to gain admission to the Church under false pretences',[11] the function of Peter here is to admit or reject the candidates for membership. We know nothing of the method employed in sifting such applications, but the Apostles as the pastors of the new community may have had the determining voice.

The advent into the Ecclesia of the Samaritans, so hated by the Jews, naturally called for the approval of the Apostles. They sent Peter and John, whose prayers resulted in the gift of the Holy Spirit to the Samaritans, through the laying on of hands.[12] But this does not point to any special prerogative of the Apostles. When Paul is given the Holy Spirit, it is through the laying on of the hands of 'a certain disciple', otherwise unknown, who is not an Apostle at all. When Peter is called to account for his conduct in eating with the new Gentile converts, 'we hear nothing of any formal assertion of authority, either by St. Peter himself. or by the Apostles generally, or by the Apostles and brethren together. St. Peter simply seeks to carry the whole body with him by patient explanation of the circumstances and considerations belonging to the case'.[13]

This survey of the familiar passages proves how scanty is the evidence for any formal or legal exercise of the authority of the Twelve over the primitive Church. Only Peter and John are mentioned, and John is a silent partner. It is James who is the leader of the Church at the time of Peter's release from prison.[14]

---

[10] J. A. Findlay, *A Portrait of Peter* (1935), 223–5; Foakes Jackson, *Acts* (1931), 41–3.
[11] W. L. Knox, *St. Paul and the Church of Jerusalem*, 19.
[12] Acts viii. 14–17.
[13] Hort, 58, on Acts xi. 2–18.
[14] Acts xii. 17.

When a formal decision is chronicled at the Council of Jerusalem, it is James who makes the decisive speech.[15] It is probably true that Protestant exegetes and historians have been inclined to under-estimate the position of Peter among the Apostles, and in the primitive community.[16] But it is equally true that if we were to call any Apostle 'pope' in a primitive hierarchy, it would be, not Peter, but James.[17] The Twelve disappear from the pages of the Acts after the Council of Jerusalem. According to the Travel-Document used in the last part of the book, Paul meets James and the elders when he visits Jerusalem for the last time. Paul speaks once only of the Twelve.[18] But in Galatians Paul mentions James and Cephas and John as the 'so-called pillars' of the Church,[19] and the others are ignored. It is with these three only that 'the gentlemen's agreement' is made.

The question of the position of the Twelve is still a living issue in the modern debate, largely owing to the brilliant essay of Karl Holl.[20] 'We meet in the Christian community from the beginning onwards, a legalized hierarchy, a divinely ordained order, a divinely sanctioned ecclesiastical law, a Church as an organized institution, into which individuals were received. A strictly circumscribed group of Apostles (i.e. James and the Twelve), possesses a permanent divine prerogative to be obtained by no one else, and is therefore authorized for leadership. The Church stands on their testimony, which is regarded as real testimony, as the

---

[15]   It is not certain whether the words in Acts xv. 19, ἐγὼ κρίνω mean 'I decree', or 'I give my vote', 'I recommend'; Hort, 80, Lake, *Beginnings*, iv, ad loc.

[16]   Harnack, *Constitution and Law of the Church* (1910), 7.

[17]   Karl Holl, *Gesammelte Aufsätze* (1927), ii. 54.

[18]   I Cor. xv. 5; the reference in Gal. i. 17 suggests the Twelve, but others may be included.

[19]   Gal. ii. 9. The phrase is not ironical. See Burton, *Galatians* (1921), 72, and G. S. Duncan, *Galatians*, 39–40, 50–1.

[20]   *Der Kirchenbegriff des Paulus in seinem Verhältnis zu dem der Urgemeinde* (1921), republished in *Gesammelte Aufsätze* (1927), ii. 4447. Lietzmann's view is not greatly dissimilar; *Beginnings of the Christian Church*, 84–5.

rehearsal in the power of the Spirit of that which they had themselves experienced. Every development of spiritual life is conditioned by their testimony. In virtue of this they are called the pillars of the Church.'[21] Holl regards this conception of the Church as radically different from that in the Pauline Epistles.

The essay of Karl Holl marks a complete reaction from the work of Rudolf Sohm, who regarded legal authority as completely incompatible with the very nature of the Christian Church as a spiritual society, based on the divine revelation.[22] Sohm's view cannot be sustained. The first thesis of Holl, then, we may regard as justified. If the Church is a visible society of men, it cannot dispense with some kind of form, with some rules, however loosely framed, some generally received order of life which controls action in cases of perplexity. If 'law' be interpreted in this sense, there is already a divinely sanctioned law in the Christian community from the beginning. Such a 'law' would be derived from the teaching of Jesus, and would be interpreted in the teaching of the Apostles in the light of the gift of the enabling power of the Spirit. But the 'law' of the Christians is not a mere code, but a new 'way' of life in the Spirit. Karl Holl has not given sufficient emphasis to this controlling principle.[23] The apostolate is not analogous to any 'office' in any other society. The work can only be carried out in full reliance on the gift of the Spirit which has been granted to all in the new community. This is shown by the fact that there are recognized 'signs of an apostle, miracles, wonders, deeds of power'.[24]

---

[21] ibid., 54.

[22] The discussion between Sohm and Harnack may be followed in Harnack's book, *The Constitution and Law of the Church* (E. tr. 1910); see also Sohm, *Outlines of Church History* (1909), 32–40. Holl's results, following on the work of Harnack, are accepted in the main by Gerke, *Die Stellung des ersten Clemensbriefes innerhalb der altchr. Gemeindeverfassung* (1931), 9–14, but criticized by Lake, *Beginnings*, v. 55–6.

[23] cf. the criticism of Rengstorf, art. ἀπόστολος, in *Theol. Wörterbuch*, i. 434, note 169.

[24] 2 Cor. xii. 12.

In the second place, the thesis is justified that the Church is regarded as an organized institution into which individuals are admitted. This again implies order, and a certain rule, which may well have been administered by the Twelve. But the organization of a community whose basis is a new divine revelation in an historic Person, and whose life is the charismatic life of the Spirit, is essentially different from the life of a community based on a code. The organization of the Ecclesia must conform to the essential nature of the Ecclesia, and not to that of preceding or contemporary institutions.

Thirdly, the thesis that the Ecclesia possesses a legalized hierarchy is misleading. The word 'hierarchy' is inextricably bound up with later ecclesiastical development. The pre-eminence of the Apostles was due to the amazing privilege of intimate personal companionship with the Messiah, to the special commission once given them in His earthly life to preach and cast out demons, and to the renewed commission from the Risen Lord to be His witnesses. This is a 'hierarchy' the like of which the world has never seen. But for that very reason a fresh word is wanted. The term conveys associations of earthly rule which were expressly repudiated by Jesus Himself. We do not see the Apostles exercising the kind of rule against which He warned them. In the crucial instance of the letter written from the Council of Jerusalem to the brethren in Antioch and Syria and Cilicia, the Apostles and the elders associated with them do not lay stress upon their own position. We cannot improve on the statement of Hort. They send 'a strong expression of opinion, more than advice and less than a command. . . . A certain authority is thus implicitly claimed. There is no evidence that it was more than a moral authority, but that did not make it less real. . . . It was a claim to deference rather than a right to be obeyed'.[25]

---

[25] The *Christian Ecclesia*, 83, 85. In the light of the foregoing discussion, it is unnecessary to answer the contention of Karl Holl, which is an essential part of his argument, that the Apostles in Jerusalem claimed the right of taxation (ein gewisses Besteuerungsrecht, op. cit., 62) over the whole Church. Compare Lietzmann, *Beginnings*, 93; 'a complete parallel

Fourthly, the view Twelve, together with James, formed a strictly circumscribed group cannot be substantiated. The chief argument on which Karl Holl relies is his interpretation of 'all the apostles' in I Cor. xv. 7 as including only the Twelve and James. But in I Cor. ix. 5–6 there can hardly be any doubt that Barnabas and the Brethren of the Lord are ranked among the Apostles. It may therefore well be that the phrase 'all the Apostles' includes all the Lord's Brethren. May not Barnabas also have been among those to whom the Lord appeared? His name should not be summarily excluded from a Pauline list which speaks of Apostles. May not some of the Seventy have become witnesses of the Resurrection? For reasons given above,[26] the tradition of a mission of the Seventy can be regarded as historical. It is difficult to account for the preservation of such a tradition in a community in which the Twelve were raised to a position of pre-eminence, unless the Seventy had actually been commissioned by our Lord. According to a tradition preserved in Clement of Alexandria,[27] Barnabas was one of the Seventy. Andronicus and Junias were 'notable among the Apostles', and they were Christians before Paul.[28] It is not incredible that they were among the Apostles to whom Christ appeared.[29] In such a question no certainty is attainable. But if this appearance may be identified with that of Luke xxiv. 33–49 there were others present as well as the Eleven.

---

to the temple tax which was sent to Jerusalem by Jewish communities in the diaspora'. This view is based by Holl on an elaborate attempt, to prove that the word ἅγιοι was a synonym for πτωχόι, and that both were the current designations for Jerusalem Christians. This means the denial of the rich content of the word ἅγιος (see above, p. 142, and Procksch, art. ἅγιος in *Theol. Wörterbuch*, i. 107, note 59). For a sensible view of the 'Collection for the Saints', see Dodd, *Romans* (1932), 229–33; G. S. Duncan, *St. Paul's Ephesian Ministry* (1929), 229–35.

[26] *Supra*, p. 108.

[27] *Strom.*, ii.20; Eusebius, *Eccl. Hist.*, i. xii. 1.

[28] Rom. xvi. 7.

[29] Karl Holl's argument dismissing them has been fully answered by Olof Linton, *Das Problem der Urkirche*, 87. Lightfoot's argument (*Galatians*, 98) still stands.

To all of them the commission was given to preach in the name of Christ, and the commission was universal. The same author who preserves the tradition that the Twelve were given pre-eminence in the life of the primitive community of Jerusalem, preserves another tradition whereby the Risen Christ empowers others together with the original eleven for the special work of Apostleship. This view corresponds, on the one hand, with the historical situation as we see it in the Synoptic Gospels, and, on the other hand, with the data provided by the Pauline Epistles. In the Gospels there is an inner circle of twelve, and a wider group of disciples. In the Pauline Epistles a certain preeminence of the original companions of Jesus is acknowledged, but the Twelve are distinguished from 'all the Apostles' in a passage (I Cor. xv. 1–8) in which Paul is adhering most closely to the received tradition.

It follows that the theory that the Twelve together with James formed an exclusive hierarchy, and that no one could be admitted to their privilege of government, is not proven. But we may regard certain conclusions as highly probable.

1. The privilege on the basis of which the Eleven, and in a modified degree, Matthias, and James, the Lord's brother, were accorded an undisputed pre-eminence in the Jerusalem Church, was their intimate association with Jesus in His earthly life. But in the case of all privileges was incommunicable.

2. The 'authority' claimed and exercised by the Twelve corresponded closely to the injunction laid on them, according to the Lukan tradition, at the Last Supper.[30] It was moral rather than legal. They made no attempt, so far as our knowledge goes, to 'exercise lordship' over the community. But they certainly exercised 'an ill-defined but lofty authority in matters of administration and government',[31] and this was directly due to the moral authority with which they were clothed by the commission given to them by Christ to be His witnesses. It is only in the Church in Judaea that we have clear evidence of their leadership in administration. How far was the authority of the Twelve acknowledged in the commu-

---

[30] Luke xxii. 24–7; cf. Mark x. 42–5.
[31] Hort, 84.

nities beyond? For the earlier period of the Gentile mission this question cannot be fully answered. But another question may perhaps serve to prove both the wisdom with which the Twelve exercised their responsibility, and the limits of their authority. What would have happened if the Jerusalem leaders had refused to recognize Paul? 'The answer can scarcely be in doubt. He who had received from God Himself both his Gospel and his commission to preach it was not likely now to disobey God at the dictates of man. . . . Fortunately the "authorities" dealt more wisely with Paul than their successors dealt with Luther and Wesley.'[32]

3. The Apostles formed a compact group, which originally included others beside the Twelve. This seems proved by the expression 'All the Apostles' in I Cor. xv. 7. Whether Barnabas, Andronicus, and Junias are to be included in that original group, is an open question. It may be that these three, and the 'Apostles of the Churches' in 2 Cor. viii. 23, owe their title to a commission from a local ecclesia.[33]

4. The chief sign of an Apostle was that he had received his commission to preach direct from the Risen Lord, in one of the Appearances. But the Appearances are regarded as an unparalleled series of events which were concluded by the Ascension.[34] They are not to be classed with 'visions' which are on another plane. So too for Paul the experience on the Damascus road was solitary, unique, decisive. It is not to be named in the same breath with the visions and revelations of the Lord which have their parallels in pre-Christian Jewish literature, and which Paul only reluctantly names when controversy compels him to meet his antagonists on their own ground. It is not on momentary experiences such as these, modes of the pure inner life of contemplation, that he bases his apostolic authority. But the Damascus experience was an Appearance on the same level as those to the original

---

[32] G. S. Duncan, *Galatians*, 54; cf. Hort, *The Christian Ecclesia*, 85, commenting on Galatians ii. 6; Paul 'was not prepared to obey if the Twelve had insisted on the requirement of circumcision and the law.'
[33] cf. W. L. Knox, op. cit., 367.
[34] K. Holl, op. cit., 50.

disciples, and the last of all, as to one born out of due time. This Appearance, like that in Luke xxiv. 44–9, Matt. xxviii. 16–20, conveyed, not 'unspeakable words which it is not lawful for a man to utter', but an intelligible commission to proclaim the Word .[35] The messengers thus empowered became Apostles. For their task, those that were sent became as He who sent them.

The Seven

The general view that Luke gives an account in Acts vi. of the origin of the later office of the diaconate cannot be regarded as certain, or even probable. Three linguistic points call for notice:

1. The word translated 'neglected' is not used elsewhere in the Greek Bible, and primarily means 'slighted'. It may therefore have a wider reference than 'being passed over in the distribution of alms', or 'receiving less than the Hebrew widows at the common meals'. It is possible that behind this dispute lies some question of the observance of the Law, some point of ceremonial purity, in connexion with the common meals.[36]

2. The word *diakonos* is not used. But the corresponding verb appears in the phrase 'to serve tables', and the noun in the phrase, 'daily ministration' (vi. 1) and 'ministry of the word' (vi. 4). There is a contrast between 'serving tables' and 'the serving of the word' (vi. 2, 4). But singularly enough when we do hear of the subsequent activity of any of the Seven, they are preaching the Word, or expounding the Old Testament Scriptures, or working wonders and signs, like any Apostle. The contrast in vi. 2 does not necessarily imply a disparaging judgement on the serving of tables. The word διακονεῖν had already been given a rich religious meaning by the time at which Luke was writing. The verb is not used in the Septuagint, and the transformation is entirely due to Christianity. To the question, 'Who is the greater, he who sits at the table, or he

---

[35] See Rengstorf, art. ἀπόστολος in *Theol. Wörterbuch*, i. 431, especially the section *Der urchristliche Apostolat als Gabe des Auferstandenen*; and the same writer's *Apostolat und Predigtamt*, 28–30.

[36] H. W. Beyer, art. διακονέω, in *Theol. Wörterbuch*, ii. 84.

who serves?', the natural man, and the Greek most of all, returns one unhesitating answer, and the Christian another.[37]

But the contrast is probably due to the conviction of the Apostles that their primary function is to bear witness to the Resurrection, to proclaim the *kerygma*, and that this function would be impaired if they became involved in the dispute about meat and drink. In view of the use of the word 'tables' here, the probability is that 'the daily ministration' refers to common meals[38] rather than to a daily dole of food. But in view of the Jewish system of the daily distribution of the *Tamhui* or Tray, to those who were in actual need of food for the coming day, a decision is doubtful.[39]

3. We do not know what is meant by the phrase in vi. 3 'whom we may appoint *over this business*'. The word χρεία, translated business, means sometimes in Hellenistic Greek 'office',[40] sometimes 'matter in hand', 'business',[41] but usually in the New Testament 'need'. In view of the preposition used, the choice is really between the second and third of these meanings.[42] But we are not enabled to judge what the business or need was. Was it an appointment to a permanent or a temporary office? Were the Seven deputed to be Charity Commissioners, to superintend all the charitable meals and philanthropic work, or only to settle the particular dispute which had arisen?

There are some other considerations which may help us to a decision on this question. The dispute was dangerous because it threatened the fellowship of the community at a most vulnerable point. The Jews of Palestine, and the Hellenistic Jews of the Diaspora who had settled in Jerusalem, formed two elements in the new community which were with difficulty reconciled. There was a tendency on the part of the native-born Jews to look down

---

[37] cf. Beyer, 82–4; Hort, 202–8.

[38] Wendt, ad. loc., 131.

[39] See G. F. Moore, *Judaism*, ii. 176; Lake, *Beginnings*, v. 148–9.

[40] Bauer, *Wörterbuch*, 1410.

[41] Moulton-Milligan, *Vocabulary*, 691.

[42] Blass-Debrunner, *Grammatik*, paragraph 234 and note 5; see Matt. xiv. 45; xxv. 21; Acts viii. 27; Rom. ix. 5.

on the later comers. It is all the more significant that the Seven who were appointed all bore Greek names. It is a persistent conviction of scholars that this fact must have some significance. Harnack conjectures that the Seven were 'Hellenistic rivals of the Twelve, who did not in the last resort overthrow the authority of the Twelve, but contributed greatly to the progress of Christianity, because in the spirit of Jesus they turned against the Temple, and began the mission to the Samaritans, and their followers the mission to the Gentiles'.[43] It is possible to accept this description of their achievement, without regarding them as rivals of the Twelve. Such a view can only be maintained, if we accept a theory which is a direct descendant and heir of the Tübingen theory of Ferdinand Christian Baur and his school, that the author of Acts has carefully edited his traditions to gloss over the bitter hostility between the two sections of the early Church. Actually Acts tells us that 'the whole multitude' chose the Seven. Another view of the function of the Seven is that they represented the interests of the Hellenistic widows only.[44] But as it stands the narrative favours the view that in their generosity and disinterestedness the Hebrew Christians allowed trustworthy and outstanding Hellenistic Christians to be appointed to settle the dispute, and probably to superintend the charities of the Church.

For the conception of the Ecclesia, we draw four main conclusions from this narrative. First, an advance was made in the organization of the community. The appointment of the Seven was a sign that 'the Ecclesia was to be an Ecclesia indeed, not a mere horde of men ruled absolutely by the Apostles, but a true body politic, in which different functions were assigned to different members, and a share of responsibility rested upon the members at large, each and all; while every work for the Ecclesia, high and low, was of the nature of a "ministration", a true rendering of a servant's service.'[45]

---

[43] *Constitution and Law of the Church*, 30–1; against this see Lake, *Beginnings*, v. 150.

[44] Lietzmann, *Beginnings*, 89; W. L. Knox, op. cit. 49.

[45] Hort, 52.

Second, the appointment of the new ministry was controlled by the essential and constitutive principles of the Ecclesia. The principle of the supremacy of the ministry of the Word is recognized (vi. 2). All the Seven are full of the Spirit, who both inspires the preaching of the Word and the other services rendered to the community. Thus from the beginning every ministry in the Ecclesia is 'charismatic'.

Third, the appointment of Hellenistic Jews, one of whom was a proselyte, is a step towards the complete emancipation of the Ecclesia from Jewish narrowness and particularism.[46]

Fourth, the ministry arises as the Ecclesia fulfils its mission. In this instance the mission was the expression of its fellowship in the alleviation of poverty and distress. Out of this task the new office comes.

Presbyters

The interest of the author of the Acts lies more in the mission of the Ecclesia than in the various ministers who aid in the fulfilment of the mission. We hear nothing of the Presbyters or elder brethren till the eleventh chapter, where suddenly they appear as responsible officials at Jerusalem, receiving the charitable contributions of the Famine Fund which had been raised at Antioch. From this time onward they appear side by side with the Apostles,[47] and presbyters are appointed in every church on their first journey by Barnabas and Paul.[48] But before any mention of the office, there is perhaps a hint of a natural division of the Ecclesia into older and younger in the word νεώτεροι, 'the younger men', in Acts v. 6, who are employed in an unpleasant but necessary service.[49] The 'older men' in the community are accorded the Jewish reverence for age which was naturally carried over into the new community. The nomina-

---

[46] cf. Lightfoot, *Galatians*, 297.
[47] Acts xv. 2, 4, 6, 22, 23; xvi. 4; xxi. 18.
[48] Acts xiv. 23.
[49] Schlatter, *Geschichte der ersten Christenheit* (1926) 92.

tion of presbyters from among the older men to care for the community is a sign of ordered life, and a natural paralle to Jewish custom.[50] Lightfoot conjectured that the office of presbyter arose after the persecution following on the death of James (Acts xii. 1, 2).[51] If the Twelve were dispersed on a wider mission, the presbyters would be required to take their place.[52] Again we note that the development of the office is directly due to the mission of the Ecclesia. So, too, in the new Churches presbyters are appointed (xiv. 23), as overseers, *episkopoi*, in order to conserve the results of missionary preaching and to feed the flock of Christ.[53] The name *presbyteros* has yielded to *episkopos* in Phil i.1. In First Peter, Christ Himself is described as Episkopos and Shepherd, and the function of the presbyters is described as the tending of the flock, the exercising of 'oversight'. It is likely that in Eph. iv. 11 the word shepherd, *poimenes*, refers to the presbyters.

The chief passage is in Paul's speech to the Ephesian elders, in Acts. xx. 27–8.

> I shrank not from declaring to you the whole counsel of God. Take heed unto yourselves, and to all the flock, in the which the Holy Ghost hath made you bishops, to feed the Church of God, which he purchased with his own blood.

From this and the other N.T. passages, we see, first, that the presbyters are all bishops, *episkopoi*. The first title denotes their

---

[50] The usual explanation finds the provenance of the presbyterate in the elders of the synagogue, who were not, however, the rulers of the synagogue. A recent theory traces the two offices of presbyters and deacons to the ἀρχισυνάγωγος and the ὑπηρέτης (Goetz, *Zeitschrift J.T. Wissenschaft*, 1931, 91). A remarkable parallel is found in the Damascus-sect, where, as Charles says, the Censor corresponds to the *Episkopos* of the early Christians. See W. K. Lowther Clarke, *Divine Humanity*, 199–203; Beyer, art. ἐπίσκοπος, in *Theol. Wörterbuch*, ii. 614.

[51] *Philippians*, 193.

[52] The absence of any mention of the Apostles in Acts xi. 30 is best explained by the assumption that they were elsewhere.

[53] Acts xx. 27, 28.

office, and the second their function. The function is also described as tending or feeding the flock.[54] Second, there are several bishops in each local church, and there is no distinction of rank between them. Third, their appointment is ascribed to the Spirit of God. They may have been commissioned by an Apostle, perhaps by Paul himself, or elected by the Church. But the decisive act is the divine working of the Spirit. There is no distinction between a local ministry and a charismatic ministry. Fourth, the Church for which they are to care has been constituted by the redemptive work of Christ upon the Cross. The ministry of the Word is supreme for the Ecclesia.[55]

The Missionary Ministries

So far the only ministries mentioned have been those which were first found in the Church at Jerusalem. But the two persecutions, following on the death of Stephen and the death of James, gave an impetus to the missionary expansion of the Ecclesia, and resulted in the growth of new missionary ministries. There is a list in I Corinthians xii.: apostles, prophets, teachers, workers of miracles, healers, helpers, administrators, those who speak with 'divers kinds of tongues'. In Romans xii. there is an even wider catalogue, which shows that 'Paul made no such hard and fast distinction between clerical and lay ministries as later emerged in the Church. His point is that whatever talent a member of the Church may possess is a gift of the grace of God'.[56] In Ephesians iv. there are apostles, prophets, evangelists, pastors, teachers. In Acts xv. 22 the prophets Judas Barsabbas and Silas are called 'leaders', the title given in Hebrews to the rulers of the Church,[57]

---

[54]   Peter ii. 25; v. 2.

[55]   cf. Beyer, in *Theol. Wörterbuch*, ii. 612.

[56]   C. H. Dodd, *Romans*, 195.

[57]   The ἡγούμενοι of Hebrews xiii. 7, 17, 24, belong to a later stage of development; there are two classes in the community, these rulers and the ἅγιοι. See Büchsel, art. ἡγέομαι, in *Theol. Wörterbuch*, ii. 909–10.

but in the Council's letter the phrase simply means leading men. The chief of these new ministries were the Prophets, the Evangelists, and the Teachers. They all illustrate the variety of gifts, the spiritual freedom within an ordered life, and the supremacy of the Word of God, the divine revelation, for the Ecclesia, and they actually were a powerful unifying force as the message was carried farther afield. Some explanation of their significance for the mission of the Ecclesia must be given.

The early Christian Prophet was like his counterpart in the old Israel, a gife from God to the People of God. His function was to declare the divine will, as the prophets at Antioch declared the message of the Holy Spirit for the mission of Barnabas and Saul.[58] Agabus, Judas, Silas, the four daughters of Philip are also specially mentioned.[59] We have no record of the missionary labours of the prophets. We know that their function was inspired preaching, which was intelligible, in contrast to 'the speaking with tongues'. Their preaching promoted the growth in holiness and knowledge of individual members of the Church, and availed also for the conversion of the outsider and the unbeliever.[60] They have the divinely inspired gift of insight into religious truth, of piercing to the innermost recesses of the conscience and awakening in unregenerate hearts the adoration of God. The origin of Christian prophecy is to be sought in Jewish apocalyptic circles,[61] and the gift was associated with the coming of the last days. The common conviction of the early Christians, that the new era had already dawned, is the explanation of the special characteristics of the New Testament prophets. They receive the revelations of the

---

[58] Acts xiii. 1–3; cf. I Tim. i. 18; iv. 14.

[59] Acts xi. 28; xxi. 10; xv. 32; xxi. 9.

[60] I Cor. xiv. 22–3. The two verses are in apparent contradiction. Either Paul had not thought, when he dictated 22, of what he was to dictate later (J. Weiss, ad loc.), or the word 'sign' 22[a] as in Luke ii. 34, 'a sign to be spoken against', is a means for confirming the unbelieving in their unbelief (W. F. Howard, ad loc., in *Abingdon Commentary*; cf. Anderson Scott, *Footnotes to St. Paul* (1935), 122).

[61] cf. Bousset, *Religion des Judentums* (ed. 3, 1926), 394–9.

Spirit which had also been promised for the new era, and which had been given at Pentecost.[62]

The Evangelist was one who brought the first news of the gospel message. The word is only used three times in the New Testament.[63] It is possible that, as Harnack suggests,[64] the word is inserted into the usual list of Apostles, Prophets, and Teachers because the circular letter which we call 'Ephesians' is addressed to Churches which had been founded by missionaries who were not Apostles; and that the word 'evangelists' is inserted after prophets, because the combination of Apostles and Prophets was too well established to be disturbed. The word denotes function rather than a definite office.[65] Philip who is 'one of the Seven' is an evangelist in virtue of his work in Samaria and elsewhere. Timothy is charged with the work of an evangelist in addition to his other duties. The word does not occur in the *Didache*, probably because by that time the word 'apostle' was regarded as including it. The next step is that Philip the Evangelist is called an Apostle in the later tradition.[66] In the New Testament every Apostle is an Evangelist, but every Evangelist was not an Apostle. A direct personal commission from the Risen Lord in one of the series of Appearances was the chief differentiating mark of an Apostle.[67]

The Teachers rank after the Apostles and Prophets in the first Pauline list. In Ephesians, they are closely joined with the Pastors (*poimenes*), a sign that the local officials are naturally entrusted with the function of teaching. In the *Didache* they are a separate though cognate class; honour is to be given to the 'bishops and deacons' because they too minister the ministry of the prophets and teachers.[68] The function of the Teacher was to expound the

---

[62]   Acts ii. 17; καί προφητεύσουσι.

[63]   Eph. iv. 11.; Acts xxi. 8; 2 Tim. iv. 5.

[64]   *Mission and Expansion*, i. 321 note 4, 338.

[65]   Certainly not so definite an office as that of 'local preacher' in the Methodist Church.

[66]   Eusebius, *Eccl. Hist.*, iii. 31.

[67]   See Friedrich, art. εὐαγγελιστής, in *Theol. Wörterbuch*, ii. 735, for the later meanings of the word.

[68]   xv.1.

inspired revelation which had been proclaimed by Apostles and Prophets. Apparently in Acts xiii. 1 the Prophets can also be Teachers. The word, like the word evangelist, denotes primarily a function rather than an office. The function was possibly to interpret the primitive *kerygma* in the light of the Old Testament scriptures, but certainly to apply the *kerygma* to the needs of common life.[69] Already we have seen that the teaching of the Apostles (Acts ii. 42) is to be understood in this sense. The function of teaching is exercised within the Ecclesia rather than towards those that are without.

It was the recovery of the *Didache* that first opened the eyes of scholars to the meaning of these missionary ministries in the early church. The evidence was already there in the New Testament, but now with the aid of the *Didache*, which as Lietzmann observes,[70] is the best commentary on the Pauline lists, we can advance to certain generalizations.

(1) All these ministries are for the Church as a whole. Like the Apostles the Evangelists were itinerants. They must travel continually; their gift is for the world. The Prophets too may travel, but they may settle down if they choose.[71] The Teachers are sometimes resident in a local church, but they may travel.[72] In any case their gift is for the Church as a whole. Of course any ministry in the community was for the whole Ecclesia, whether exercised by those who wandered far or by those who stayed at home. But it would be difficult to overemphasize the part played by itinerant preachers in fostering the sense of unity and creating the homogeneity of the Ecclesia. Apart from their work the local churches would have become isolated, and stagnant, gradually losing the

---

[69] Rengstorf, art. διδάσκαλος in *Theol. Wörterbuch*, ii. 160 cf. 149, denies to the teachers the function of interpreting the O.T. scriptures and separates sharply the teachers from the prophets in Acts xiii. 1.

[70] *Beginnings*, 187. See a valuable article by Professor J. M. Creed, shortly to appear in the *Journal of Theological Studies*, showing 'that the *Didache* probably falls within the first three decades of the second century, and certainly cannot be much later.'

[71] *Didache*, xiii.

[72] *Didache*, xi.; see edition by Bigg and Maclean (1922), 34.

sense of brotherhood within the one people of God. But through these various travelling ministries new ideas travelled from place to place. Through them a new mode of communication was rendered possible and effective. The Catholic Epistles are the expression in literature of the Christian mission , which through the itinerants is expressed in persons and in life.[73]

(2) All these ministries were ministries of the Word of God; it is to this fact that they owe their pre-eminence.

> My son, night and day shalt thou remember him that speaketh to thee the word of God, and thou shalt honour him as the Lord, for in him by whom the Lordship is spoken of, there is present the Lord. And thou shalt seek daily the presence of the saints that thou mayest find rest in their words. *Didache*, iv. 1, 2.

Harnack has shown that these who speak the word of God comprise the three classes of Apostles, prophets, teachers.[74] The bishops and deacons, of whose ministry the writer of the *Didache* is a loyal supporter, derive their importance from the fact that they minister to the Church the ministry of prophets and teachers.[75] The minister who preaches the 'Lordship' is the representative of Jesus, and is so to be honoured. We are reminded both of the idea which we found central in the Christian Apostolate, and of the primitive Christian confession, Jesus is Lord. The test which St. Paul propounded for the prophets (I Cor. xiv. 3) is determinative of Christian preaching at the end of the century.

In the New Testament evidence the divisions between prophets, teachers, and evangelists are not sharply drawn.[76] But the fact that these are the ministries which are most prominent proves that the emphasis lies on the preaching and interpretation of the divine Word, which creates and sustains the Ecclesia.

---

[73] cf. Harnack, *Mission and Expansion*, i. 342.

[74] cf. Harnack, i. 334.

[75] xv. 1–2.

[76] Nor between Apostles and prophets, in the case of Barnabas (Acts xiii. 1), unless the 'ordination' in xiii. 3 be to the Apostolate. *Infra*, p. 203.

(3) If we may speak of these ministries, or of those of the bishops and deacons, which are coming into greater prominence at the end of the first century, as 'offices', they are offices entirely dependent on the divine life which governs the Ecclesia. They are gifts of the Spirit. They are not instituted by men but by God. This truth holds good even if they are elected by the local community or designated by the Apostles Barnabas and Paul.[77]

Was ordination necessary for any or all of these ministries? We do not even know whether ordination was practised for the chief of the offices which survived, that of presbyters. There are four passages in the New Testament in which the laying on of hands is connected with an act answering to ordination. In Acts vi. 6, the Twelve Apostles lay their hands on the Seven. In Acts xiii. 3, after a prophetic intimation had been received from the Spirit, that Barnabas and Saul have been called to a particular work, the representatives of the Church at Antioch lay their hands on them. Is this ordination to the Apostolate? St. Paul did not think so. He traced his credentials not to the mandate of a local community, but to his commission from the Risen Lord.[78] It is sometimes said that 'one "sign of an Apostle". . . is express appointment by Apostles, with invocation of the Holy Ghost'[79] But there is no evidence for this. If this passage is evidence for an ordination to the Apostolate, it is a lay ordination, by specially inspired prophets.[80] It is much more likely that the solemn rite was the sign of a commission from the Church for this particular

---

[77] *Didache*, xv. 1; Acts xiv. 23; see the discussion above (197) of Acts xx. 28. Lietzmann has neglected this in the sharp distinction which he still draws (*Beginnings*, 190) between 'charismatic' ministries, and the others which 'really arose out of the sociological needs of the individual churches'. The *Didache* has no real doctrine of the Spirit; the test is personal character (see H. B. Swete, *The Holy Spirit in the Ancient Church*, 21). In this respect the *Didache* is not a good commentary on St. Paul.

[78] Acts xxii. 10, 21; xxvi. 16–18; Gal. i. 1.

[79] T. A. Lacey, *Essays in Positive Theology*, 229.

[80] 'He was ordained irregularly', says Rackham, *Acts*, 193. 'A dangerous exception', says Canon Lacey.

missionary journey. The completion of their task is marked by the words in Acts xiv. 26: 'Thence they sailed to Antioch, from whence they had been committed to the grace of God for the work which they had fulfilled.'

Two passages in the Pastoral Epistles (I Tim. iv. 14; 2 Tim. i. 6) refer to a prophetic monition that Timothy should be set apart for his immediate task. The *charisma* or gift of God, was given with the laying on of hands, perhaps at Ephesus, for the work of an evangelist[81] rather than to any particular office. As the New Testament says so little about 'ordination' we may rest content with the conclusion of Hort:[82] 'It can hardly be likely that any essential principle was held to be involved in it. It was enough that an Ecclesia should in modern phrase be organized, or in the really clearer Apostolic phrase be treated as a body made up of members with a diversity of functions; and that all things should be done decently and in order.'

The phrase of Hort points us to the essential nature of the 'organization' of the Ecclesia. There is nothing in that Greco-Roman world comparable to this community, conscious of a universal mission, governed and indwelt by an inner Life, guided by the active divine Spirit to develop these ministries for the expression of its message to mankind. All the ministries are based on the principle of the universal ministry of all believers. The cup of cold water given to the thirsty, the visiting of the prisoners, the healing of the sick, the maintenance of the destitute at the expense of the community all are regarded as services rendered to Christ, or in the name of Christ.[83] The sharing of material goods was an expression of the inner sharing in the life of the Spirit, because such a sacramental fellowship united by allegiance to One whose passionate love always found form in outward act, could never

---

[81] Hort, *The Christian Ecclesia*, 181–7.
[82] ibid., 216.
[83] Matt. x. 42; Acts iii. 6; Matt. xxv. 31–46. Again the preservation of this 'Parable of the Great Surprise' is evidence of the existence of this conception of a universal ministry as a distinguishing mark of the community.

remain inward only. Such a wide conception of ministry naturally accounts for the rapid differentiation of function.[84] Those who were conscious of the guiding hand of God were quick to respond to the monitions which pointed to this man or to that as possessing a gift, a *charisma* from God, which could be used in the service of the Ecclesia. Thus the 'prophets' pointed to a Barnabas, a Saul, a Timothy, as possessing an individual capacity for some particular task, and which by the action of the community received external recognition.[85] The call from God was never merely individual, solitary, inward, but within a community which is indwelt by the Spirit. Do we possess any comparable picture of a community conscious of such an authoritative message, wherein the opportunity for the full expression of all the gifts granted to individuals was so freely given? 'Where the Spirit of the Lord is, there is liberty.' The individual allegiance to Jesus as Lord was no mere confidence in the salvation of the solitary soul, though it brought an expansion of the powers of the individual. It was adhesion to a message, and inclusion in a community. The Message brought with it a promise that life could be lived on a new and lofty level by the gift of new power. The Community, constituted by the Message, was God's instrument for the accomplishment of His final purpose. 'The early Christians felt themselves to be witnesses and participants in the mighty world-drama, which was moving onward to its climax before their very eyes.' 'In brief, the power of Jesus over their souls was now at last realized. This is the personal and moral basis of the overpowering enthusiasm which welled up among them and overflowed like a flood into the spiritual life of mankind.'[86] To compare this Ecclesia with any of the contemporary cults which, on a short and narrow view, seemed to be competing with it for the spiritual allegiance of mankind, seems irrelevant and ridiculous, when we consider the essential nature of the Ecclesia – its indwelling Spirit, its

---

[84] Anderson Scott, *The Fellowship of the Spirit*, 172.
[85] Acts xiii. 1–3; I Tim. iv. 14; cf. Walter Lock, *Pastoral Epistles* (*I.C.C.*, 1924), 53
[86] J. Weiss, *History of Primitive Christianity*, 35, 44.

allegiance to the Lord Jesus, its divine Word, its proud and yet humble confidence in its mission – in a word, its theology. Mithraism 'could and would have won plenty of adherents, but it could not have founded a holy Mithraic Church throughout the world. A man used Mithraism, but he did not belong to it body and soul.'[87] But a Christian belonged to the Church, body and soul, because in it he could live a new life, among a new people, in the power of a new divine gift. Among them, all his gifts could find employ. When all around was shifting and uncertain, it was 'the one cause on earth which would never betray whatever faith and love a man might give to it'. Whatever else might break up and disappear, there was one divinely wrought edifice, against which the gates of hell could not prevail.

---

[87] A. D. Nock, *Conversion*, 14.

Part Three

The Unity of the Apostolic Teaching

In the following part I hope to show that the idea of the Ecclesia which we have already found in the teaching and work of Jesus, and in the life of the Primitive Church, is also in its main outlines present in the Epistles of the New Testament and in the Johannine theology. But in this present volume no attempt will be made to give a complete survey of the New Testament doctrine of the nature of the Church. The stress will be on the unity rather than on the variety of the apostolic teaching. In the study of New Testament Theology, scholarship has been concerned for more than eighty years with the indispensable task of differentiating the various types of doctrine. To-day the need seems rather to demonstrate that in their views of the nature of the Ecclesia the apostolic writers are essentially at one.

Chapter Eleven

The Teaching of Paul

The view that Paul was the founder of the Christian Church was not uncommon a generation ago,[1] but in the light of our previous discussion it seems superfluous to refute it. The main outlines of the idea of the Ecclesia in the primitive *kerygma* reappear in the Pauline teaching with a new emphasis.

1. The Church is the New Israel

'As many as shall walk by this rule, peace be upon them, and mercy, and upon the Israel of God' (Gal. vi. 16). The rule for the Christian life which Paul has just enunciated is that of a new creation wherein Jew and Gentile are alike transformed. It would seem therefore that the benediction in this verse is pronounced on all those among his readers who walk by this rule, and not only on them, but on the whole Church of God. According to another interpretation, the phrase 'the Israel of God' refers to the faithful remnant in Israel who are as yet unenlightened but who are waiting for the Lord their God, and are marked out by Him for salvation.[2] But in this very epistle the Christians are the real sons of Abraham (iii. 7). In I Cor. x. 18 the phrase 'Israel after the

---

[1] See, e.g., Weinel, *St. Paul the Man and his Work* (E. tr. 1906), 208–37.
[2] G. S. Duncan, *Galatians*, 192; E. D. Burton, *Galatians*, 358. See the criticism of this view in Moffatt, *Grace in the New Testament*, 117.

flesh', implies an antithesis to the true Israel, which is drawn out more fully in Rom. ix . 6–8; 'it is not the children of the flesh that are children of God; but the children of the promise are reckoned for a seed'. It is therefore more likely that, even so early as the Epistle to the Galatians, Paul is definitely claiming by this phrase that true Christians, who follow the principle that God's creative Spirit has brought an entire transformation of former relationships, are the true Israel, the Catholic people of God.

Two other passages in Romans prove the complete continuity for the thought of Paul between the Israel of the Old Testament and the Christian Ecclesia. In the first (ix. 23–9) his thought is dominated by his grief that his brothers in Israel, his kinsmen according to the flesh, have no part in the salvation of the new age. The fact of their rejection of the divine message is as decisive for his mind as in the primitive *kerygma* of the Church of Jerusalem (Acts iii. 23). He quotes a passage from Hosea which in its original context refers only to Israel, rejected for its sins and destined to be restored, and interprets it as meaning that the Gentiles will be included in the people of God. With this he couples a passage in Isaiah, affirming that only a minority of the historical Israel is to be saved. His argument rests on the assumption that the complete fulfilment of the promises of God through the prophets is found only in the Christian Ecclesia.

In the second passage (Rom. xi. 17–24) he sees the true people of God as a single olive-tree. Some natural branches have been cut away, and shoots of wild olive have been grafted on to the original tree, to 'share the rich growth of the olive-stem' (Moffatt). The natural branches are the unbelieving Jews; the wild olive branches are the Gentiles, who are now organically united to the one continuous life of the people of God.[3] The allegory is based on three historical facts, three convictions common to Paul and to the earlier apostles; first, the fact that the old Israel through its leaders rejected and crucified the Messiah, and is steadily rejecting His messengers; second, the fact that Gentiles are being admitted into the Ecclesia, and therefore to a share of the promises made

---

[3]   See the exposition of Professor C. H. Dodd, *Romans*, 179–80.

to Israel; third, the fact that both Jews and Gentiles in the Ecclesia are looking forward to the consummation of those promises in the glorious future.

2. The Church is the Home of the Holy Spirit

That all Christians have received the Spirit is a postulate of the whole doctrine of redemption in the Pauline Epistles. 'The love of God has been shed abroad in our hearts through the Holy Spirit which was given unto us' (Rom. v. 5). 'You are not in the flesh, but in the Spirit, if so be that the Spirit of God dwelleth in you. But if any man has not the Spirit of Christ, he is none of his' (Rom. viii. 9). 'We have the first-fruits of the Spirit' (Rom. viii. 23). The attempts to discover a radical distinction, between this conception of the Spirit and that of the primitive community in Jerusalem, have broken down.[4] We are justified in concluding that the idea of the Spirit in the Church 'was no innovation of Paul, but represents a part of the tradition he had received'.[5]

3. The Church is Constituted Through its Allegiance

The first creed of the Ecclesia, 'Jesus is Lord', is common to Paul and to the primitive preaching. 'If thou shalt confess with thy mouth Jesus as Lord, and shalt believe in thy heart that God raised him from the dead, thou shalt be saved' (Rom. x. 9). So too in Philippians (ii. 10) the universal worship which will be accorded to Yahweh in the last days, according to the prophecy of Second Isaiah (xlv. 23) will be in the name of Jesus as Lord.[6]

---

[4] *Supra*, 146–59; compare the argument against Bousset in *The Idea of Perfection*, 46–7.

[5] C. H. Dodd, *Apostolic Preaching*, 51.

[6] See also I Cor. viii. 5–6; xii. 3; xvi. 22; Eph. v. 26, where the phrase, 'with the word', translated by Moffatt, 'as she utters her confession', probably refers to the creed, 'Jesus is Lord', uttered in baptism, which is 'in the name of Jesus'.

But the thought of Paul penetrates to the inner meaning of this allegiance. The formula 'in Christ' is his characteristic expression not only for individual Christians but for the principle which constitutes the community.

In a series of works, all of them instinct with mingled devotion and learning, Adolf Deissmann has brought home to the world of scholars the deep inner significance of this formula for the thought of Paul. But consecrated as he was in his later years to the task of overcoming the barriers which separate Christians from one another and uniting them in œcumenical fellowship, Deissmann interprets the phrase 'in Christ' with reference to the individual. Thus he defines it as 'the most intimate possible fellowship of the Christian with the living spiritual Christ'.[7] Not one word of this needs to be changed, but much must be added. And when Deissmann adds that 'to speak of Hellenistic influence is surely justifiable here',[8] he is in reality doing an injustice to the uniqueness of the religious thought of Paul. Hellenistic mysticism was in the main individualist. But the phrase 'in Christ' is used as defining the community.

> I was still unknown by face to the churches of Judaea which were in Christ. GAL. i. 22.
> Of him are ye in Christ Jesus. I COR. i. 30.
> In Christ Jesus I begat you through the gospel. I COR. iv. 15.
> We, who are many, are one body in Christ, and severally members one of another. ROM. xii. 5.
> . . . To the saints and faithful brethren in Christ at Colossae. COL. i. 2.
> Admonishing every man and teaching every man in all wisdom, that we may present every man perfect in Christ. COL. i. 28.

These passages do not contradict any other passages where a reference may lie to the communion of the individual believer with Christ. But they do prove that, for Paul, communion with Christ was not a mere individual possession or private privilege. It was

---

[7] *Paul* (E. tr. 1926), 140.
[8] Op. cit., 147.

inseparable from the thought of membership in the Ecclesia. Indeed it was the characteristic and constitutive mark of the Ecclesia. It seems reasonable to bear this principle in mind in the discussion of the meaning of the formula elsewhere.[9] Thus in Philippians ii. I where the first phrase probably means, 'if there be any ground of appeal in our union with Christ', the appeal is directed to the attainment of harmony in the Church. The intimate personal relationship with Christ should in its very nature have immediate social consequences,[10] because Christ has done what He has done. The ultimate purpose of God is that all should be united in the same great allegiance, proclaiming that Jesus is Lord.

The roots of this phrase 'in Christ' we have already discovered in the action of Jesus, who, as the Messiah, gathered His followers as the nucleus of the true Israel, and declared their solidarity with Himself. After His death and resurrection they saw clearly that the New Age had dawned. All things were to be made new. So in harmony with the belief of the primitive community in Jerusalem, Paul declares that the new creation is proceeding. 'There is a new creation whenever a man comes to be in Christ; what is old has gone, the new has come. It is all the doing of the God who has reconciled me to Himself through Christ and has permitted me to be a minister of His reconciliaion' (Cor. v. 17–18). There is thus a close connexion between the three concepts of the new creation, the formation of the new community 'in Christ', and the preaching of the Word. It is in the light of these three concepts that the Pauline description of the Church as the Body of Christ can be elucidated.[11]

4. The Word is Constitutive of the Ecclesia

This conviction also is common to Paul and the primitive community. 'Thanks be to God, He makes my life a constant pageant

---

[9] The chief recent discussion is Werner Schmauch, *In Christus* (1935), 68–102.

[10] Phil. ii. 5; see Moffatt's translation.

[11] No attempt has been made in the present essay to discuss the rich realities behind the Pauline metaphors which describe the Church.

of triumph in Christ' (2 Cor. ii. 14, Moffatt). The reference is to
success in preaching the gospel (ii. 12), in speaking the word in
Christ, before the very presence of God (ii. 17). It is the gospel
that effects salvation.[12] It is a revelation of God in action, and
cannot be separated either from the historical salvation which it
declares, or from the action of the Spirit in the very moment in
which it is proclaimed. 'Our gospel came to you not with mere
words but also with power and with the Holy Spirit and with full
conviction on our part' (I Thess. i. 5).[13] There is no difference
between Paul and the earlier Apostles in the content of the gospel
proclaimed. Just as in Acts the preaching of the Word is in the
power of the Spirit, and itself is a mighty power, so in Paul.[14] It is
only by reception of this divine message that the new communities
gathered by the work of Paul can be reckoned with 'the churches
of God in Christ Jesus throughout Judaea'.[15] 'In Christ Jesus I
begat you through the gospel.'[16] The Gospel, or Word, is the
mystery which has been concealed from ages and generations of
old, and has now been disclosed to the saints of God. To serve
that Word is the supreme apostolic function.[17] The Ecclesia shares
in the proclamation at the Lord's Supper.[18]

5. The Universal Mission of the Ecclesia

Whatever early differences there may have been between Paul and
the Twelve on the mode of admission of the Gentiles to the

---

[12] I Cor. xv. 2; Rom. i. 16.

[13] For a full description of the content of the word in Paul, see Friedrich,
art. εὐαγγέλιον, in *Theol. Wörterbuch*, ii. 726–33.

[14] Acts ii. 41; iv. 4, 29, 31; vi. 7; viii. 4, 14, 25; xi. 1; xii. 24 and many
other references. I Cor. i. 18; ii. 4. The same usage is found in the Synoptic
Gospels.

[15] I Thess. ii. 13; cf. Col. i. 5.

[16] I Cor. iv. 15.

[17] Col. i. 25–9.

[18] I Cor. xi. 26; see 170–2 above for an explanation of the singular
absence of reference to the Death of Christ in connexion with 'the
breaking of the bread'.

Church, all our sources bear witness that after the Council of Jerusalem the apostles were one in accepting the universal mission as the evident purpose of God.

The mission of the Ecclesia is declared to be the reconciliation of all things to God through Christ, who has made peace through the blood of His Cross.[19] While this conception of the task is explicit and clearly defined in the Captivity epistles, it is implicit in the earlier letters, and in all the missionary activity of Paul. But the vision of this all-inclusive ideal does not blind his eyes to the immediate practical duties which that ideal implies. The distinctively ethical sections of his epistles are vitally connected with the missionary message. The members of the Church are called upon to care for the poor, to show sympathy with the suffering, and restore those overtaken in a fault. Paul is eager to present the saints at Colossae perfect in Christ. Only thus can the Church be God's instrument, entirely adequate for the purpose for which He intended it. The life of holiness is the necessary expression of the message. This same principle we have seen governing the life of the primitive community.

In the light of this agreement in the essential elements of the idea of the Ecclesia, we turn to examine a modern view that there was a wide divergence between Paul's conception of the Church and that of the Jerusalem community. The influence of the brilliant essay of Karl Holl shows that the ghost of the Tübingen theory is still haunting German theology.[20] Thus Lietzmann says:[21] 'The life-story of Paul shows that early Christianity was characterized by a great contrast. On the one side was the Jewish-Christian Church at Jerusalem conscious of its roots in Judaism, and true to the Law in a way that constantly threatened to approximate it to Pharisaic narrowness. On the other side was the decided turning away from Jewish ritual in accordance with the preaching of the Antiochene Hellenists and of Paul.' There

---

[19] Col. i. 20; cf. Eph. i. 9–10.
[20] Karl Holl, *Der Kirchen begriff des Paulus in seinem Verhältnis zu dem der Urgemeinde*, in his *Gesammelte Aufsätze* (1927), ii. 44–67; cf. Lietzmann, *Beginnings* 142–3, 188–9.
[21] Op. cit., 199.

can be no doubt of the existence of this contrast. But English scholars cannot feel the same certainty that the opponents of Paul were always Judaizing Christians,[22] or that they were authorized by James.

Karl Holl traces, the contrast in divergent theories of the Ecclesia. He sees agreement between Paul and the primitive community, first, in the conception of the Church as an organized institution, a true body politic, with members fulfilling different functions, which traces its order to the will of God (I Cor. xiv. 33); second in the conception of the apostles as God's gift to the Church for its orderly administration (I Cor. xii. 28); third, in the conception of the primacy of the Church of Jerusalem, as the basis and centre of missionary expansion (Rom. xv. 19).

But the divergences, according to Holl, are many and serious. First, Paul sets the living Christ in the foreground as the centre of all authority. It is not on Peter but on Christ that the Church is built (I Cor. iii. 11). Lietzmann adds in support of this supposed contrast the passage in I Cor. x. 4, 'the rock was Christ' as containing a veiled polemic against the view that Peter was the rock. So the Apostles, instead of being the authoritative leaders of the Church, are God's fellow-workers, servants, workmen, ambassadors.[23] This, according to Holl, is a minimizing of their personal position. The stress which Paul lays on the Church as the temple of God, filled with the Spirit, leads him to regard the Apostles as subordinate to the Ecclesia.[24] The local church becomes an embodiment of the whole Ecclesia. The special claim of Jerusalem to be pre-eminently the Holy City, the Church of the saints is overthrown. In Corinth and Rome the Christians may be saints (I Cor. i. 2; Rom. i. 7).

Against this view we must place the whole of the argument of the preceding chapter. Once the Gentiles are admitted into the New Israel, they become 'saints' or 'holy', because they too belong to the people of God, and are worshipping Him as revealed in the Chris-

---

[22] e.g. in Philippians i. 15–18.

[23] I Cor. iii. 5; iv. 1; 2 Cor. v. 20, vi. 4.

[24] I Cor. iii. 16–22.

tian redemption.[25] The evidence of the Acts lays stress on the ministry of the Apostles, their service of the Word, rather than on any hierarchical privileges.[26] But Holl begins with a false antithesis, which admittedly governs the whole course of his argument. He assumes a polemic of Paul, especially in I Corinthians, against the privileged position of Peter as the Rock on which the Church is built. But there is hardly any trace of this polemical motive. Paul is combating the fact of party-feeling, not the position of Peter. Even in Galatians, where a controversial motive is dominant, the question at issue is the observance of the Jewish law, and not the nature of the Church or the authority of Peter. Holl's view repeats the old error of the Tübingen theory. Peter was certainly the original leader of the Church, but in the great controversy over the admission of Gentiles, he is on the Hellenistic, and not the Hebrew side.[27] As Holl himself acknowledged, if it is a question of divergence between Paul and the Church of Jerusalem, the papacy at Jerusalem belongs not to Peter but to James. Further, it may be asked whether any one in the Jerusalem Church, who believed that God had exalted Christ to the right hand of God would have denied that the living Christ was the Head of the Church to whom all authority had been given in heaven and on earth? Partisans of Peter and of Paul could join hands in this conviction. In the Corinthian Epistles, Paul is emphasizing all that creates and unites the Ecclesia; his motive is deeper than any desire to score a victory over a supposed theory of the Church current at Jerusalem. So far as the evidence of these letters goes, such a controversial desire has not entered into his mind.

---

[25] The part of Holl's argument which claims that 'saints' is a special designation for the members of the Jerusalem Church has been refuted by the discussions of the word ἅγιος by Procksch, in *Theol. Wuorterbuch*, i. 107, and Asting, *Die Religion der Heiligkeit* (1930), 153–9.

[26] *Supra*, 181–91.

[27] Lake, *Beginnings*, i. 312; Burkitt, *Christian Beginnings* (1924), 57. If Streeter's view is accepted that Matthew is the Gospel of the Church of Antioch, the preservation of the saying in Matt. xvi. 18, 'On this rock I will build my Church', is due to the conviction in Antioch that the rules of Peter for the admission of Gentiles were better than the conservatism of James. See *The Four Gospels*, 515.

Chapter Twelve

The First Epistle of Peter

In this Epistle, addressed to the Christians in a wide area of Asia Minor, the word 'Ecclesia' is never used. Nevertheless, it is possible to draw a clear and coherent outline of the idea of the Ecclesia which dominates the writer's mind.[1]

1. The New Israel

In the first place, the opening sentence indicates that the Christians addressed are the true heirs of the old Israel. They are the sojourners of the Dispersion; they have succeeded to the place of the Jewish Diaspora, but they are no longer exiles from Jerusalem, but from Heaven. The thought of the Epistle is set in an eschatological framework; the salvation which they are awaiting is the final deliverance (i. 5, 8). Meantime all the titles of privilege can be applied to them which were applied to Israel of old. They are the 'flock of God' (v. 2), the house of God (iv. 17), the 'elect race', a royal priesthood, a holy nation, a people for God's own possession (ii. 9–10). In time past they were no people, but now are they the people of God. The theory that these Asiatic Churches were composed only of Jewish Christians does not bear close examina-

---

[1] Any writer of this theme must acknowledge a deep debt to the great work of Theophil Spörri (Tutor at the Methodist Theological College in Frankfurt), *Der Gemeindegedanke im ersten Petrusbrief* (1925).

tion.[2] They were once in darkness, doing as Gentiles choose to do, leading lives full of Gentile vices and idolatry (ii. 9; iv. 3). Their former companions are astonished that they will not plunge into the same flood of profligacy (iv. 4). There may have been Jewish Christians among these Churches, but in any case no distinction is made. The Ecclesia of God is a universal community both by reason of its claim and its union of Jews and Gentiles in the one body. Not without reason is this letter placed by the early Church among the 'Catholic' Epistles.[3]

The place of the Christians in the new Israel is due to the call of God (ii. 9). Their life is to be holy because He who had called them is the Holy One (i. 15). They are called to suffering because Christ suffered (ii. 21). The title therefore which is given to them in virtue of their response to that call is the 'elect' or 'those who are chosen', which carries us back to the word which is given to the disciples by Jesus Himself.[4] The election is due to the love of God who is known by the Ecclesia as Father, and in all three passages where the word occurs, the application is to the community.[5] 'No anxious inquiry is to be made as to the election of the brethren, but all who through faith have become members of the Ecclesia are to be reckoned among the elect because they have been called.'[6]

2. The Distinctive Life of the Community is Life in the Spirit

The elect are what they are through the Spirit. It was through the preaching of the gospel in the power of the Spirit that they became Christians first (i. 12). By that divine action they were drawn out of the realm of darkness, and set apart as the consecrated people of God (i. 2). The weight of the word 'sanctification' on i. 2 lies

---

[2]   Hort, *First Peter* (1898), 7; Wand, *St. Peter and St. Jude* (1934), 32–3.
[3]   Spörri, 106.
[4]   *Supra*, p. 40; Matt. xxii. 14; Mark xiii. 20, 22, 27; Luke xviii. 7.
[5]   i. 1; ii. 9; v. 13. Spörri, 24, 25.
[6]   Calvin, *Commentary on First Peter*, i. 2; Spörri, 26.

rather on the 'hallowing' which the divine Spirit effects, than on
the ethical quality of the new life.[7] The Spirit has 'consecrated' the
elect so that now they are possessed and controlled by God, and
obey Jesus Christ. The following phrase 'the sprinkling of the
blood of Christ' recalls the ratification of the Covenant at Sinai
(Exodus xxiv. 7), where obedience is promised by the people, and
they are sprinkled with the blood, a token of the Covenant made
with Israel on the basis of their promise. Thus Peter's thought is
that the action of the Spirit, in setting the new Israel apart, is to
enable them to render their due obedience of faith to Jesus Christ;
and that the entire relationship with God depends on the sacrifi-
cial death of Jesus Christ.

There is probably another implied reference to the Spirit in the
phrase 'spiritual house', which is descriptive of the Ecclesia.

> You also, as living stones, are built up a spiritual house, to be a holy
> priesthood, to offer up spiritual sacrifices, acceptable to God through
> Jesus Christ. I Pet. ii. 5.

The majority of commentators interpret the word 'spiritual' in
both cases in a merely allegorical sense.[8] The support for this
meaning in the New Testament is found in I Cor. x. 3, 4, where
Paul allegorizes the manna and the water and the Rock, and
calls all three 'spiritual'. But even here there is no contrast
between material and spiritual. All three are spiritual as being
of supernatural origin,[9] and therefore the gift of God. But the
dominant sense of the word 'spiritual' in the New Testament is
'God-given', or 'partaking of the Spirit of God', the divine
Spirit.[10] It is probable, therefore, that in I Peter ii. 5, we should
also find a reference to the Spirit who has set the Ecclesia apart,
as the holy People of God to offer up sacrifices of thanksgiving

---

[7] So Hort, 21; Procksch, in *Theol. Wörterbuch*, i. 115.

[8] cf. Rev. xi. 8.

[9] So Plummer in *I.C.C.* ad loc.

[10] Bauer, *Wörterbuch*, 1088[b], so in Rom. i. 11; xv. 27; I Cor. ii. 13, 15;
xii. 1; Gal. vi. I; Col. i. 9; iii. 16.

in the Spirit.[11] The Spirit is the creative principle in the Ecclesia. 'Acts of self-oblation to God for the service of the community are described as performed in the invisible House, inasmuch as they take their meaning from its encompassing presence, and are manifestations of its reality, the acts which set forth its abiding state. . . . These acts are signs that His inspiring and uniting and ordering Spirit is indeed present.'[12]

The thought is parallel to the great passages on the Christian sacrifice in Romans xii. I and Eph. v. 1–2 and especially the latter, where the Ephesians are bidden to give themselves up for each other, as an offering and sacrifice to God for a sweet smelling savour. 'This offering is appealed to as the ruling principle of social duty' (Hort).

The same appeal is only implicit in I Peter ii. 5. But in a later passage (iv. 14) the sufferings of the Church if they are for the sake of Christ, are a sign that the Spirit of God, which in Isaiah (xi. 2) rests upon the Messiah, is resting on the Church as an abiding and inspiring possession. Already the Church is sharing in the glory of the coming salvation of God to which it is called. In the passage immediately preceding (iv. 10–11[a]), two of the spiritual gifts, the *charismata* which build up the community, are mentioned.

According as each has received a gift [*charisma*], ministering it among yourselves, as good stewards of the varied grace of God. If anyone preaches, let it be as uttering God's oracles. If anyone renders some service, let it be in the strength which God supplies.

Altogether, the fewness of the references to the Spirit proves that the concept was not so dominant in the writer's mind as in the thought of Paul. He does not doubt that it is through the power of God alone that Christians can fulfil the new moral demands. But the brotherly love which is the social bond of the community

[11] This interpretation goes back at least as far as Bernhard Weiss, *Der Petrinische Lehrbegriff* (1855), 131. cf. Hort, *First Peter*, 112; Spörri, 29–30.

[12] cf. Hort, op. cit., 112.

is expressly linked with the new birth, through the preaching of
the Word of God, and the Spirit is not mentioned (i. 22–3).[13] It is
difficult to avoid the conclusion that the early fervour had begun
to cool, and that the Church is already beginning to lose that
understanding of the work of the Spirit which was primary in the
earliest days.

3. The Allegiance to Jesus Christ

The chief passage is a declaration that Jesus, the Lord, is the living
stone, on which the Ecclesia is built (ii. 4–5). To enter the Church,
and to vow allegiance to Christ, are not two separate actions but
are indissolubly one. The reference to Baptism carries the same
meaning (iii. 21–2). The human side of the Sacrament is a prayer
for a clean conscience before God, in reliance on Jesus Christ who
rose from the dead and ascended to the right hand of God. He
came to life in the Spirit that He might bring us to God (iii. 18).
He still has a saving ministry for those that call on His name in
this Sacrament. He is the chief Shepherd of the flock (v. 2, 4) who
alone can gather the sheep who had gone astray.

4. The Preaching of the Word Creates the Ecclesia

The Word of God has a creative power in itself. It is the incorruptible seed to which the Churches in Asia owed their being (i.
23). They were begotten again, like the whole Church of God (i.
3), by the resurrection of Jesus Christ from the dead. So in the
Book of Enoch (lxii. 8), 'the congregation of the elect and holy
shall be sown'; the founding of the community is due to the
revelation of the Son of Man. In I Peter, the seed is not corruptible
but incorruptible. The Word of God abides for ever; 'Here there

---

[13]   The insertion of διὰ πνύματος in the Syrian text of i. 22 shows that
the omission was felt to be strange.

can be no idea of separate seeds, but the word may be chosen to express a seed which, though in one sense sown once for all, was also imparted by a continuous and perpetual sowing. . . . The new life of the Christians was being constantly renewed from its original source, a living stream from the living God.'[14]

Those who reject the Word, reject Christ, the Living Stone (ii. 8). If the Word is not obeyed, Christians may yet proclaim it by life, and so win the disobedient (iii. 1). But the end of the disobedient must be fearful (iv. 17). The Gospel is clearly regarded as creating, renewing, and defining the Ecclesia.

The content of the primitive *kerygma* reappears in this Epistle.

(i) First of all, the prophecies have been fulfilled in the Messianic salvation which has now been preached to the Asiatic Churches. The prophets of the old dispensation had sought and searched diligently. The Spirit of Christ in them pointed forward to the sufferings of Christ and the glories that should follow them (i. 9–12).

(ii) Jesus died to redeem His people (i. 18–19), to deliver them out of the realm of darkness (ii. 9), the present evil age. His sufferings were foretold in Isaiah (i. Pet. ii. 24; cf. i. 19).

(iii) He rose from the dead. It is the resurrection which is the centre of the Christian preaching (i. 3, 21; iii. 21).

(iv) He is exalted at the right hand of God, angels and authorities and powers being made subject unto him (iii. 22).

(v) Judgement is imminent. It will begin at the house of God (iv. 17). Gentiles, too, will give account to him who is prepared to judge the living and the dead (iv. 5).

It is striking that, in the main, these five articles appear consecutively in the thought of this Epistle.[15]

The only articles which are missing from this list are the statements that Jesus was born of the seed of David, and that He

---

[14] Hort, *First Peter*, 91.

[15] The reader who compares this list with that of Professor Dodd, *The Apostolic Preaching*, 28, will notice the striking similarity, a further proof, if proof were needed, of the value of Professor Dodd's reconstruction.

was buried. But the preaching to the spirits in prison is perhaps this writer's expansion of the latter article.

5. The Mission of the Ecclesia

The Ecclesia is called to proclaim the glory of God. This mission is declared as the goal of the various ministries of the Church (iv. 11), and we do wrong to the writer's devotion if we regard his doxology as merely formal or perfunctory. The word 'doxa', glory, deserves, and has recently received, the closest attention of students of the New Testament.[16] In I Peter we may distinguish two meanings. On the one hand, the aim of the Church is to give glory to God, by its life and ministries to proclaim the transcendent love and majesty of the Father (iv. 11). On the other hand, the goal of goal of the Church is to share in the glory which God gives to the faithful at the final manifestation of Jesus Christ (i. 7; v. 1). 'The God of all grace, who called you to share his eternal glory through Christ, after you have suffered for a short time, will himself make you perfect, firm, and strong' (v. 10 Weymouth).

We may interpret the task of the Church, according to I Peter, as worship, in the widest sense of the word. The proclamation of the Word is worship, because the Resurrection of Christ from the dead is a signal example of the glory given to Him by God (i. 11, 21). The sufferings of the Church are worship, a cause of rejoicing, a sign that the Spirit of Glory already rests upon believers, and is not merely a future hope (iv. 12–14). The prayers of the Church, the brotherly love which unites its members, the spiritual gifts which are given to them, the ordinary services of love, all are worship, because the aim of the Church is not selfglorificatio, but the glory of God. This proclamation of God's glory is directed to those that are without (iii. 1). Every Christian, who reverences Christ as Lord in his own heart, should be ready with a reply to any one who calls him to account for the hope he cherishes (iii.

---

[16] J. Schneider, *Doxa* (1932); Kittel's article in *Theol. Wörterbuch*, ii. 236–57. Compare previous studies by von Gall, and Israel Abrahams.

15). The greatest possible stress is laid on the outward expression in life of the inward call which comes from the Holy God (i. 15 18; ii. 12; iii. 12 16).[17] The Gentiles may slander Christians as bad characters; the proper reply of Christians is in life. Their aim must be so to live that the charges will break down, and that their accusers also will glorify God (ii. 12). The resemblances of this conception of the mission of the Ecclesia to that of the Pauline Epistles has often been pointed out. Both rest on the word of Jesus: 'Let your light so shine before men, that they may see your good works, and glorify your Father which is in heaven.'

Of the ministries of the Ecclesia there is little to be said. There is less emphasis than in the Pauline Epistles on the authority of the Apostle, but this may only be due to the fact that Paul's Apostleship was often questioned by opponents. If the letter is a pastoral letter sent out by Peter from Rome in the seventh decade of the first century, the first line of it is sufficient to stamp it with unquestioned moral authority. Peter is an apostle of Jesus Christ, a messenger whose one claim is that he has a message from His Lord, and is a witness of the sufferings of Christ (v. 1). 'The Apostle is as He who sent him.' The writer is as clear in his own mind as Paul that the one stone on which the Church is built is Christ (ii. 4–5).

There are several interesting points in the allusion to the Presbyters, or Elders (v. 1–5). In joining himself with them, the writer seems to be using the word in its original sense of 'older man' .The contrast between two groups in the Church, 'the older men' and 'the younger men', is present to his mind (v.5). On the other hand, it is clear that the word *presbyteroi*, elders, denotes a definite office of pastoral oversight, probably with a definite stipend (v. 2). But Peter lays all the stress upon the principle of the universal ministry in the Ecclesia. All have to serve one another (v. 5). The elders are especially cautioned not to 'lord it over' their charges. The same word is found in the injunction of Jesus to the disciples: 'Ye know that those who are deemed rulers among the Gentiles lord it over them. . . . But it is not so with you' (Mark x. 42–3[a]). Peter's ideal of office corresponds with that of his Lord.

---

[17] Spörri, 65–73.

Chapter Thirteen

The Epistle to the Hebrews

The word 'Ecclesia' is only used twice in the Epistle. The first occurrence is in a quotation from Psalm xxii, and is set by the author of the Epistle on the lips of Jesus:

> I will declare thy name unto my brethren,
> In the midst of the Ecclesia will I sing thy praise.
> And again, I will put my trust in him.
> And again, Behold, I and the children which God hath given me.
> HEB. ii. 12–13.

The second quotation is from Isaiah viii. 17. The human trust of Jesus in His Father is a token of His sympathy with His human brothers. The third quotation is from the LXX of Isaiah viii. 18. The whole passage is a characteristic description of the author's conception of the Christian community. It is the gift of God to the Messiah. It is the company of the true children of God, and is thought of as gathered for worship before God. The governing idea is given in the preceding verse (ii. 11). 'He who sanctifies, and those who are sanctified have all one origin', in their Father, God. Jesus, as in xiii. 12, has the divine prerogative of consecrating God's people as His very own.

The second occurrence is in Heb. xii. 22–3: 'You have come to Mount Zion, and to the city of the living God, the heavenly Jerusalem, to countless hosts of angels, to the festal gathering and Ecclesia of the first born whose names are recorded in heaven, and to God the judge of all, and to the spirits of righteous men made perfect.' It is doubtful whether, with Moffatt, we can regard the Ecclesia here as referring to human citizens linked with the festal assembly of angels in the heavenly city.[1] It may be that the two phrases both refer to the angels. In any case the author pictures his readers as mingling with the angels and the spirits of just men made perfect, the 'solemn troops and sweet societies' of the redeemed.

1. The Ecclesia on earth, thus joined to the heavenly company, is the inheritor and fulfilment of the promises made to the old Israel. Those who have been called are under a new covenant, that they may receive the promise of the eternal inheritance (ix. 15). The Sabbath rest into which believers are now entering (iv. 3) was promised to Israel, but they could not enter in because of unbelief (iii. 19). The whole argument of the Epistle rests on the assumption that there is only one religion, that of the New Covenant. The old Covenant was but a prelude, a foreshadowing of the final revelation through the Son. The Christian Ecclesia alone is the true Israel of God.[2]

2. Christian believers have been made partakers of the Holy Ghost and have tasted the powers of the age to come (vi. 4–5). God has confirmed the testimony of those who first heard the Lord, not only by signs and wonders and various miraculous powers but by distributing the gift of the Holy Spirit, according to His purpose (ii. 4). There is no divergence here from the view of the primitive community. The doctrine of the Spirit does not call for full treatment in this Epistle, and it may have held a more prominent place in the author's thought than we are allowed to see. But he does definitely place the gift of the Holy Spirit as a characteristic mark of the Ecclesia.

3. The formal confession of allegiance to Christ which the Ecclesia makes (iii. 1; iv. 14) is interpreted by the author in his

---

[1] See Moffatt, *Hebrews* (*I.C.C.*, 1924), 216–17; and against this H. T. Andrews in *Abingdon Commentary* (1929), 1323–4.

[2] For a fuller exposition see E. F. Scott, *The Epistle to Hebrews* (1922), 85–101.

own fashion. Jesus is the envoy (or 'apostle') of God; He is the High Priest in the sense which the author is concerned to expound throughout the Epistle. He is greater than Moses, who was but a servant in the household of God; for Jesus is both the founder of the household, and the Son of God (iii. 2–6). 'We are this household', says the writer. His doctrine of the nature of the Ecclesia is placed in the forefront of his argument (ii. 10–iii. 6).

4. The doctrine of the Word of God as constituting the community is found in the fourth chapter. The true Israel, the Ecclesia which God has called through Christ and has set apart for Himself, may look forward to the Sabbath-rest. But the whole stress of the argument rests on the word *To-day*. Owing to disobedience Israel of old had failed to enter into that rest. But the Church of God may enter into the heavenly realm of peace with God, and enter now, 'To-day!' if it listens to the voice of God. The Word of God is sounding now, and is charged with both promise and doom. It is the revelation of God's purpose in Christ. 'The Word of God is a living thing, active and sharper than any two-edged sword' (iv. 12). This is more than a mere poetical personification of preaching. The Word of God is God Himself speaking from heaven (xii. 25), speaking through the great Sacrifice of Christ, the supreme event in which history becomes fully real (x. 1, 20). By His dying, Jesus has consecrated a new and living way through the veil which separated the world of shadows from the world of abiding realities. To-day the Ecclesia may tread that way, and enter into that realm of rest.

The content of the Word is still that of the primitive *kerygma*, though the message is re-interpreted in the light of the Platonic doctrine of the two worlds.[3] The promises of God through the prophets have been fulfilled in the Son. Through His perfect act of obedience in His dying, He has brought us into communion with God. The Resurrection of Christ is only mentioned at the end of the Epistle, when he asks his readers to rest with him on the cherished elements in the primitive preaching (xiii. 20). But the exaltation to the right hand of God is declared in the opening

---

[3] See the exposition I have tried to give in *The Idea of Perfection*, 75–91.

verses (i. 3). The return of Christ for judgement, and for the salvation of His people is prominent throughout (iv. 13; ix. 27–8; x. 25–31, 37; xii. 25).

5. At first sight the mission of the Ecclesia is not prominent. The aim of the writer is to rescue those who are in danger of falling away from the living God, of drifting from the gospel. This work is part of the mission of the Church. But the whole conception of the Christian religion displayed in this magnificent argument implies the universal mission of the Ecclesia. Christianity is the final religion. Therefore it is meant for all mankind. The partial revelation which had been made to the prophets has now been both fulfilled and transcended in a revelation of absolute worth through God's own Son. The writer devotes himself to the establishment of one result of the new revelation. It is that in Christ we have now obtained a new, direct, and perpetual access to the heavenly realm. The Cross of Christ is the altar of the Ecclesia; the perfect sacrifice made there is the basis and guarantee of the perfect worship which now at last can be offered to God.

Of those who are the ministers of this work of commending the perfect worship to mankind we hear little. The author writes for those who ought to be 'teachers' and who are still 'ministering' to the Church (v. 12; vi. 10)[4] The writer himself is a teacher. The 'leaders' or 'rulers' of the community are pastors (xiii. 17).[5] Of their predecessors it is said that they spoke the word of God (xiii. 7); they may have been apostles, or prophets, or both.

---

[4] The word used is 'saints', vi. 10.

[5] For these ἡγούμενοι, see I Clem. i. 3; xxi. 6.

Chapter Fourteen

The Apocalypse

1. The universal Ecclesia is twice described as kings and priests. The word 'kingdom' (*Basileia*) is used of the community only here in the New Testament, but the meaning does not essentially contradict the invariable usage in the Gospels. Christians are a kingdom because they exercise rule.

> Thou wast slain, and didst purchase unto God with thy blood men of every tribe, and tongue, and people, and nation, and madest them to be unto our God a kingdom and priests; and they reign upon the earth. v. 9–10.
>
> He made us to be a kingdom, to be priests unto his God and Father. i. 6.

The rule is delegated to His Ecclesia by Christ.[1] 'They shall reign for ever and ever' (xxii. 5), but the quality of their kingship is other than that of the earthly dominions. They rule because they are slaves of God (xxii. 3);[2] they render the service of worship to God and the Lamb before the throne.

This conception of the rule of the saints over the world goes back to the Book of Daniel, where a kingdom[3] is assigned to the

---

[1] See K. L. Schmidt, *Theol. Wörterbuch*, i. 591–2.

[2] δοῦλοι (xxii. 3) is the presupposition of βασιλεύσουσιν (xxii. 5).

[3] For R.V. 'kingdom' the translation 'sovereignty' should be substituted, J. A. Montgomery, *Daniel* (*I.C.C.*, 1927), 305, R. H. Charles, *The Book of Daniel* (1929), 187, or 'empire', H. H. Rowley, *Darius the Mede and the Four World Empires* (1935).

'Son of Man' (vii. 14, 22, 27). The 'Son of Man' represents the people of the saints of the Most High; the kingdom is their own rule over all the dominions under the whole heaven. The appropriation of this prophecy for the Ecclesia by the Apocalyptist, at a time of danger from Imperial Rome, is strangely moving. We Christians, despised, harried, persecuted, are a community of princes and priests, 'with a great history and a greater hope. Our connexion with Christ makes us truly imperial'.[4]

> On all the kings of earth
>   With pity we look down:
> And claim, in virtue of our birth,
>   A never fading crown.[5]

Throughout the Apocalypse the Ecclesia is the true Israel. The Jews are those who say they are Jews but are not (ii. 9; iii. 9). The Christians are the 'saints', the consecrated people of God. (v. 8; xiii. 7, 10; xiv. 12; xvii. 6; xxii. 21).

2. There are surprisingly few references to the Spirit. The popular views which were current in the earliest days of the Church reappear.'We could never have guessed, had it not been for this book, how tenaciously the primitive ideas held their ground among the mass of ordinary Christians.'[6] The presence of the Spirit in the Church is attested by the words in xxii. 17: 'The Spirit and the Bride say, Come.' The Spirit inspires the invocations of the Lord in the assemblies for worship. In the Spirit the Apocalyptist delivers the message which is to rally the Churches. He is a Prophet, and the function of the prophets is to bear the word of God which the Spirit inspires.

The seven Spirits who are before the throne are the symbol, perhaps, of the fullness of the divine energy.[7] With the Father and

---

[4]   Moffatt, in *Expositor's Greek Testament* (1910), 339.
[5]   Charles Wesley, in a hymn with many allusions to the Apocalypse.
[6]   E. F. Scott, *The Spirit in the New Testament* (1923), 212.
[7]   cf. Lohmeyer, *Die Offenbarung des Johannes* (1927), 45: 'ein Zeichen göttlicher Totalität'. See the full discussion in Büchsel, *Der Geist Gottes*, 481–3.

the Son they are mentioned as the source of the grace and peace invoked upon the Church.

3. The sense of allegiance to Christ is expressed in the language of adoration which, in the Old Testament and in the New, is only given to God, a living sign of the unique bond between Christ and God in the Apocalypse.[8] The Word of God is also King of Kings and Lord of Lords, whose many diadems are a token of His supreme dominion. The destinies of the Churches are in His hands.[9] The uniqueness of the relationship of the Ecclesia to the Lord is conveyed in a single word. It is His Bride.[10] The cry of the primitive Church to its Lord, Maranatha, is echoed in the closing verses of the book. 'The Spirit and the Bride say, Come.'

4. The word 'gospel' is only used in a strange and startling passage (xiv. 6–9). There is no hint of the good news of Christ, only a stern demand for reverence towards God, and an announcement of the imminence of judgement.[11] The characteristic phrase for the message which constitutes the Ecclesia is 'the Word of God and the Testimony of Jesus.'[12] The gospel is the revelation of God's purpose, the utterance of His mind and heart, which Jesus declares and attests. John bears his own witness to it in life; that is why he was banished.[13] But word and testimony were entrusted to every Christian. The phrase 'those who hold the testimony of Jesus' is not merely a description of Christian prophets (xix. 10); it is equivalent to the title 'saints' (xiv. 12, *hagioi*), which elsewhere is used in the New Testament for members of the Ecclesia. To hold fast the testimony which Jesus gave to the purpose of God is to remain a steadfast member of the Church.

The Apocalypse is set in the framework of the primitive *kerygma*.[14] In the first chapter most of the articles reappear. The present fulfilment (i. 19) of the ancient prophecies is declared.

---

[8]   Lohmeyer, 10; cf. Rev. i. 5–6; v. 13; vii. 10.

[9]   i. 16, 20.

[10]   Rev. xxii. 17.

[11]   Friedrich in *Theol. Wörterbuch*, ii. 733.

[12]   Rev. i. 2; i. 9; xx. 4; cf. vi. 9; xii. 11.

[13]   So Hort, *The Apocalypse* (1908), 8.

[14]   See Chapter 8.

John announces the things which are, as well as the things which shall come to pass hereafter. Jesus has already attested by His life and death the purpose of God (i. 2, 5, 18). He is the first-born from the dead, who is alive for evermore (i. 5, 18). He is exalted in that He is the ruler of the kings of the earth (i. 5; cf. Ps. lxxxix. 27), and holds the keys of death and of Hades (i. 18). He is to come again, and every eye shall see Him (i. 7). In the final chapter (xxii. 16) Jesus speaks in His human personal name. 'I am Jesus. It is my angel whom I have sent, to bear this testimony to the churches. I am the root and offspring of David.' Thus another article in the primitive preaching[15] appears as authenticating the message of the book.

5. The mission of the Ecclesia is universal. One undivided Church has been gathered out of every tribe and tongue and people and nation. All who hold the testimony of Jesus belong to it, irrespective of race. The new song (v. 9–13) in which the new Israel on earth is joining, is sung to the Lamb by ten thousand times ten thousand and thousands of thousands. This remarkable passage, 'unique in early Christian literature', as Moffatt calls it, demonstrates alike the cosmic nature of the work of Christ, the scope of the Christian mission, and the final attitude of adoration.

The value of the witness of the Apocalypse to the idea of the Ecclesia which we have already traced in the teaching of the Pauline Epistles, First Peter, and Hebrews, is the more impressive in that this book, more than any other in the canon of the New Testament, represents the popular views of the first century Church. The writer is apparently untouched by the lofty theology of Paul. He does not move in the realm of ideas which were soon to issue in a work of rare genius from some one of commanding influence in the very Church of Ephesus which is the chief of the seven churches to which he wrote. Nevertheless, his outline of the idea of the Ecclesia agrees with theirs. He adds the testimony which he knows will be accepted by the ordinary man.

---

[15] See the table of the articles in the primitive *kerygma* in C. H. Dodd, *The Apostolic Preaching*, 28.

Chapter Fifteen

The Fourth Gospel

The word Ecclesia is nowhere used in the Fourth Gospel. At first sight it has seemed to many readers that there is no stress whatever on the visible concrete community of Christians. Thus a leading exponent of New Testament Theology declares that the richly developed Pauline teaching on the Ecclesia has no parallel at all in John, 'neither the sentences which elucidate God's dealing with Israel, nor those which portray the newness of the Christian community where in Jews and Gentiles are united'.[1] Fortunately, it is unnecessary for me to refute this view. I need only refer to the chapter of Professor E. F. Scott on the ecclesiastical aims of the Fourth Gospel.[2] There it is demonstrated that an ulterior aim was the establishment of the nature of the true Church. Dr. Wilbert F. Howard rightly regards this as an invaluable and permanent contribution to the study of the Fourth Gospel.[3] I will only add a few notes to justify the main contention of this essay that the writers of the New Testament agree in their doctrine of the nature of the Church.

---

[1] Schlatter, *Die Theologie der Apostel*, 233; Heiler, in his great book on Catholicism (66–76), sees only an *ecclesia invisibilis*, not bound to space and time, in the Fourth Gospel.

[2] *The Fourth Gospel: its Purpose and Theology* (1906), 104–44.

[3] *The Fourth Gospel in Recent Criticism and Interpretation* (1931), 38, 240.

1. The New Israel

The unanimous conviction that the Church is the New Israel is indirectly reaffirmed in the choice of imagery for the expression of the Johannine doctrine. There is one passing reference to the Church as the Bride of Christ. This like the Pauline metaphor goes back to the imagery of the Old Testament prophets.[4] The allegories of the Shepherd (x. 1–16) and the Vine (xv. 1–8) imply that the Ecclesia is the flock of God and the vine of God, as Israel has always been.[5] In the Shepherd allegory more is said of the protective and redemptive work of the Shepherd than of the gathering of the flock. But the decisive fact of the gathering of Jewish disciples and Gentiles into the one flock (x. 16) is plainly there. The Jews proved that they did not belong to the true flock of Israel by their very rejection of Jesus as their shepherd (x. 26).

The Vine allegory finds a striking parallel in the thanksgiving over the cup in the *Didache* (ix. 2), 'for the holy Vine of David thy Servant, which thou didst make known to us through Jesus thy servant'. Here the vine seems to be a symbol for the wine of which it is the source, and so for the blood of Christ. But a passage in Clement of Alexandria[6] seems to allude to the *Didache* thanksgiving. 'This is He who poured over our wounded souls the wine, the blood of David's vine'; the vine here may be the Messiah Himself, our Lord. In the Testament of Levi (c. ii.) the Messiah is called a Vine or Vineyard, and in the Apocalypse of Baruch the 'principate' of the Messiah which is to be revealed in the last days, is likened to a fountain and a vine. It is possible, then, to interpret 'the vine of David', as the Messiah who is the descendant of David, and who gives us His blood in this cup, as

---

[4] Hosea i., ii.; Ezek. xvi. 20.

[5] For the Shepherd imagery, see Micah v. 4; Isaiah xl. 11; and many familiar Psalms. For the Vine, Isaiah v. I; Jeremiah ii. 21; Ezek. xv. 1–6; xix. 10–14; Ps. lxxx. 8–15; Hosea x. 1. In correction of Bernard's view (*I.C.C.*, ii. 478), it should be said that the emphasis in John xv. is that Christ Himself is the true source of the life of the Church.

[6] *Quis div. salv.* 29; cf. Bigg and Maclean, *Didache*, 26. Harnack, *Lehre d. zwölf Apostel* (1884), 29, is doubtful.

the vine gives us the wine. In any case it seems certain that the *Didache* does not here contain a reference to the Fourth Gospel, but is an independent and almost contemporary witness to the fact that the Vine imagery was current in the early Church, and was interpreted variously of the life given by Christ to His Church. This may find support in the famous fresco in the vestibule of the Cemetery of Domitilla, which is probably contemporary with the Fourth Gospel.[7] Here the vine with the birds may be an allegory of Christ and His Church.

2. The Gift of the Spirit as the Distinctive Mark of the Community

Jesus is described as 'He who baptizes with the Holy Spirit' (i. 33). God has given the Spirit to Him in its fullness (iii. 34). There are five passages where this gift is expounded: in the conversations with Nicodemus (iii. 5, 6, 8), and the Samaritan woman (iv. 23–4); in the proclamation at the Feast of Tabernacles (vii. 38–9); in the Farewell Discourse; and in a post-Resurrection saying. The difficulties of the final passage should only be interpreted in the light of the previous four. In the first the gift of the Spirit is associated with the new birth and with Baptism; in the second with the true worship which all believers must render to the Father. In the Cry at the Feast, it is promised to all believers. These three passages therefore envisage the Spirit as a gift to all in the Christian community. In the Farewell Discourse the Spirit of Truth is promised to the disciples to lead them into all truth. Truth here is the whole range of reality, moral truth, the meaning of the Christian message, the recollection of the words of Christ. But the truth will make them free (viii. 32–4). We cannot therefore confine the work of the Spirit to intellectual illumination. The Spirit gives

---

[7]   H. Leclercq, in his article on 'Domitille (Cimitière de)' in the *Dictionnaire d'Archéologie Chrétienne et de Liturgie*, 1430, dates it in the second half of the first century. A coloured reproduction of the fresco is given, 1432.

life (vi. 63) from the dead, and sets believers free from sin.[8] This is not the privilege of the Twelve alone. Every attempt at an exposition of the Farewell Discourse brings us back to the conclusion of Hort with reference to the Last Supper. 'The Twelve sat that evening as representatives of the Ecclesia at large: they were disciples more than they were Apostles.' So with special reference to the Fourth Gospel, Hort declares that 'it is equally clear that the little band of chosen ones, with whom these marvellous discourses were held, was destined to become no mere partial order of men, but a people of God, an Ecclesia like the ideal Israel.'[9]

Our discussion of the final passage must be centred on the question whether the power promised was intended for the Ecclesia, or for the eleven apostles alone.

> Jesus said to them again, Peace be unto you: as the Father hath sent me, even so send I you. And when he had said this, he breathed on them, and saith unto them, Receive ye the Holy Spirit: whose soever sins ye forgive, they are forgiven unto them; whose soever sins ye retain, they are retained. JOHN xx. 21–3.

In his interpretation of this passage Archbishop Bernard has departed from that of Hort and Westcott, though without wrestling with the arguments which led the great Cambridge scholars to their conclusion. He declares that the language of 'sending' could only have been addressed to the eleven apostles there for two reasons.[10]

(1) Such language has reference to them alone in xiii. 20: 'He that receiveth whomsoever I send receiveth me,' and xvii. 18: 'As thou didst send me into the world, even so sent I them into the world.' Bernard's argument for the narrower circle in xvii. 18 is based on Mark iii. 14.

(2) In the later chapters of John, οἱμαθηταί generally stands for the Eleven. Bernard supports this by a reference to I Cor. xv. 5.

---

[8] See the full exposition of Büchsel, *Der Geist Gottes*, 499–503.

[9] *The Christian Ecclesia*, 30, 31.

[10] I have collected his reasons from the Commentary, ii. 672, 676, 575.

The first argument begs the question. Bernard himself declares that others besides the Eleven were probably present when the words of John xx. 21 were spoken. He accepts the view that the occasion corresponds with that of Luke xxiv. 33–49. There is no trace of any distinct function of the Eleven in the Lukan narrative. All are called to bear witness (xxiv. 48). So in the Johannine narrative there is no evidence whatever that the Eleven are separated from the other disciples present. All receive the Holy Spirit (xx. 21) as the promise of the Spirit is given to all in Luke xxiv. 49. Again, according to the Lukan tradition, Jesus 'sends out' the Seventy as well as the Twelve. The appeal to Mark iii. 14 alone is misleading.

The second argument, to be valid, would need a thorough examination of the phrase 'the disciples' throughout the Gospel, but this is not given. If, as Bernard admits, other disciples were present when John xx. 21–3 was spoken, there are at least two occasions (John xx. 19, 20) when the phrase 'the disciples' refers to a wider group. In xx. 24 Thomas is called expressly 'one of the Twelve'. This proves that the writer could distinguish sharply between the Twelve and the general body of disciples if he wished. In xx. 30 'the disciples' almost certainly refers to the larger group. In xix. 38 Joseph of Arimathea is called a disciple. It seems, therefore, far more likely on the basis of this review, that the author deliberately uses the term 'the disciples', instead of 'the Twelve' or 'the Apostles' in the latter part of the Fourth Gospel, because he did not wish to separate them from the general body of disciples. He regards them 'as representatives of the Ecclesia at large', rather than as officials with a specially privileged position in the Church. In support of this view we may note that elsewhere he is at pains to expound the meaning of discipleship.

If ye abide in my word, then are ye truly my disciples viii. 31.

This is spoken to the many Jews who had believed. So in the Farewell Discourse love is the mark of discipleship, and it must find outward expression.

By this shall all men know that ye are my disciples, if ye have love one to another. xiii. 35.

   Herein is my Father glorified, that ye bear much fruit; and so shall ye be my disciples. Even as the Father hath loved me, I also have loved you: abide ye in my love. xv. 8–9.

We conclude then that the gift of the Spirit, in the 'Johannine version of Pentecost', was intended for all. The clue to the meaning of verse 22 is found by writers of varying ecclesiastical traditions[11] in Genesis ii. 7: 'God breathed into his nostrils the breath of life'. As the life of Adam was due to the breath of God, so the gift of spiritual life to the Ecclesia was imparted by the breath of Christ. There is a powerful imagination at work here as in the Prologue. As the Word was 'in the beginning' at the creation, so the Word incarnate is here at a new creation. The work of redemption is over, and He is creating new men to be His fellow-workers.

   What is the power given? The first clause is clearly forgiveness. The Church has power to open the kingdom of heaven to penitent sinners.

   But what is meant by retaining sins? When men reject Jesus as the Christ they die in their sins (viii. 24). To the Pharisees He says: 'If you were blind, you would have no sin. But now you say, We see, your sin remaineth' (ix. 41). This, then, is judgement. The retaining of sins means that the Church is empowered to pass the judgement which Jesus could pass. To those earliest disciples, as representative of the Ecclesia, is given 'the last and final word on the sins of frail humanity; the last and decisive word in removing the wrongs of our tangled world; the last and decisive power of judgement on the distinction between right and wrong. It is a dangerous gift, fraught with grave responsibility and only to be exercised by the Spirit of Christ working in and through His People.'[12]

---

[11] So, e.g., Bernard, Bauer, Strachan, Lagrange; Stauffer's full exposition in *Theol. Wörterbuch*, ii. 533. See Ezekiel xxcvii. 5–10, Wisdom xv. 11, where the same word, ἐμφυσάω, is used. Here only in N.T.

[12] R. H. Strachan, *The Fourth Evangelist* (1925), 319.

The foregoing exposition of the position of the 'disciples ' in the Fourth Gospel leads us to consider the growing tendency in the early Church to regard the Apostles, not only as authorities on the teaching of Jesus, but as 'types' for the whole Ecclesia. The habit of the writer of the Fourth Gospel, to give his profoundest teaching on the nature of the Church in the form of a discourse addressed to 'the disciples', is a conspicuous example of this tendency. But it is apparent elsewhere. Indeed, one most attractive solution suggested for the whole problem of the authority of the Twelve in the first century is that they are 'authorities for the teaching Church, types for the worshipping Church'.[13] Thus, when the Eucharist is described, we conclude that 'the Twelve sat that evening as representatives of the Church at large'. As the nucleus of the new community the function of the Twelve is to represent the true Israel, alike in penitence and in faith, in allegiance to their Lord and in fidelity to His Word.

3. The Idea of Messiahship

The Christology of the Fourth Gospel is essentially an interpretation of the idea of Messiahship in terms of Sonship. That Jesus was Messiah is the foundation on which the writer builds.[14] As King of Israel (i. 38–49), He gathers the disciples. As Shepherd He protects them and knows His own. He has other sheep, and will gather together into one the scattered children of God.[15] The confession (vi. 69) which makes the Twelve one united and faithful company is that He is the Holy (or consecrated) One of God – a Messianic title which carries a richer meaning in the

[13] See the exposition of this phrase of Kattenbusch by Linton, *Das Problem der Urkirche* (1932), 96–101, who supports this view with fresh evidence.

[14] I have already set out the evidence for this statement in *The Idea of Perfection*, 103–5. For a fuller interpretation of the dominant idea of Sonship, see W. F. Lofthouse, *The Father and the Son* (1934), especially 40–55.

[15] John x. 16, xi. 52.

context of the Johannine theology. He is consecrated by God (xvii. 11, x. 36), and His function is for the sake of the disciples to consecrate Himself that they too may be consecrated in truth (xvii. 19).

4. The Word of God Constitutes the Ecclesia

The Greek words for 'gospel', 'preaching the gospel' are not used by the Fourth Evangelist. He prefers the term 'the word'. Apart from the Prologue this is used seventeen times[16] for the revelation which Jesus brings, and once for the message which the disciples are to preach.[17] This word is conceived in the Hebraic way, as dynamic and creative. It constitutes the community of disciples; rejection of its dynamic power is a proof that Jews are no longer the seed of Abraham but children of the devil.[18] The word exercises judgement; it discriminates at the last day,[19] just as God judges, or the Son.[20] In the light of this usage we are to interpret the 'Logos doctrine' of the Prologue.[21] Jesus Himself is God's Word, His expressed purpose, His revelation. It is He who when He is received makes men to become children of God.

The 'word' which Jesus speaks in reference to the Eucharist points to the inner meaning of the rite. It is a feeding upon Christ, the living bread, and it proclaims that Jesus gives His flesh for the life of the world. It is indeed a 'hard word' (vi. 60, 52) and the Jews do not understand it. But those who by divine revelation (vi. 65) understand the spiritual meaning of the 'words' of Christ will find them spirit and life.

---

[16] iv. 41; v. 24, 38; viii. 31, 37; 43, 51, 52, 55; xii. 48; xiv. 23, 24; xv. 3, 20; xvii. 6, 14, 17.

[17] xvii. 20.

[18] viii. 31–2, 37, 39–47.

[19] xii. 48.

[20] viii. 50; v. 22.

[21] cf. C. J. Wright, *The Meaning and Message of the Fourth Gospel* (1933), 87–9.

5. The Mission of the Ecclesia

'The universalism of the Gospel is combined with a sharp-cut conception of the Church.'[22] I cannot see that the second 'neutralizes' the first, as Professor E. F. Scott thinks. The death of Jesus which has power to draw all men to Christ and gather into one the children of God that are scattered abroad, is an essential part of the divine word which, as we have seen, creates the Church and gives meaning to its central rite.[23] The function of the Church is to proclaim the divine word, and so win believers, 'that they may all be one, even as thou, Father, art in me, and I in thee, that they also may be in us: that the world may believe that thou didst send me' (xvii. 20–1). These and the verses which follow, in the High-Priestly prayer of our Lord, express the goal of the Ecclesia, its perfected unity for the sake of the winning of the world to faith:

> And the glory which thou hast given me I have given unto them; that they may be one, even as we are one; that they may be perfected into one, that the world may know that thou didst send me, and lovedst them, even as thou lovedst me. xvii. 22–3.

On this passage three observations may be made. First, the emphasis is on the words 'believe' (xvii. 21) and 'know' (xvii. 23). The 'world' which in many passages in the Fourth Gospel is regarded as hostile is here regarded as the object of God's purpose of salvation. God so loved the world that He sent His Son. His purpose is that the world should believe that He sent His Son. The word 'believe', for the author of the Fourth Gospel, implies full trust in the Christian revelation, and 'marks a moral attitude to Christ.'[24] The word 'know', which is parallel to 'believe' in this passage, is closely connected in this chapter and elsewhere with the relationship of 'love', and carries with it the idea of doing the

---

[22] E. F. Scott, *The Fourth Gospel*, 117; cf. 114.

[23] xii. 32; xi. 49–52; vi. 51.

[24] W. F. Howard, op. cit., 239.

will of God.[25] Thus the full conversion of the 'world' to Christ is envisaged as the purpose of God.

Second, the basis of the knowledge which the world is to receive is the word of God, the historical revelation in Jesus Christ. To 'know' is impossible where the word is not heard,[26] that is where faith is refused to Christ. It is the reception of this Word which constitutes the Church, and makes it into a clearly defined society. The sharp-cut conception of the Ecclesia is due to the very nature of the Christian revelation. He who accepts it belongs to the Church; he who rejects it remains outside. But the universalism of the Gospel is also due to the nature of the Word. It is God's revelation for all mankind. It becomes incarnate in Christ. In the adoption of the Logos concept in the Prologue, the universalism which 'Paul had fought for is accepted by John in its widest compass, and determines his whole theology'[27] Christ is the Light of the world, the Saviour of the world, the expression of the love of God which embraces the world. He is the Lamb of God which taketh away the sin of the world.

It seems, therefore, unjustifiable to claim that the universalism of the gospel, which is due to the essential nature of the Word, can be neutralized by the exclusiveness of the Church which is also directly due to the same principle. Both are the result of the final revelation wherein Jesus has declared the purpose of God. The Church exists, not as a closed company of the predestined, but to make God's purpose known to the world, and therefore to extend its own boundaries. Already, according to the author, it is gathering into its fold Samaritans and Greeks. So Jesus prays for the generation of believers who will believe through the word of the disciples.[28] The Church is conceived as catholic, in virtue of its divine gospel and its immediate task.

---

[25] vii 17; cf. viii. 31–2. See Bultmann, in *Theol. Wörterbuch*, i. 711–13.

[26] viii. 43; cf. v. 24, vi. 60 with 64, 69; xii. 46–8; xvii. 8. See Bultmann, 713.

[27] E. F. Scott, 112.

[28] iv. 40–2; xii. 20–32; xvii. 20. cf. Gaugler, *Die Bedeutung der Kirche in den johanneischen Schriften* (Bern, 1925), 71–2.

In the third place, the unity of the Church is based on a personal relationship between God and His Son, and therefore on the principle of divine love.[29] Its mission is to manifest this unity, whereby the reconciliation of Jew and Gentile has already been effected, so that the rest of the 'world' may believe. The binding principle of divine love is shown in the sacramental act of the washing of the feet of the disciples. Love is not only a heavenly reality, a future bliss; it is essentially expressed in act and in the present world, in the humblest services rendered by members of the community to one another. 'It is the principle of the realm of Christ which is being built in the cosmic crisis of the present age.'[30]

Less emphasis is laid on the fact of reconciliation of Jew and Gentile than is found in the captivity epistles of Paul. But this is only because by the time of the Fourth Gospel, the reconciliation of both in one Body is already an accomplished fact. The account given above of the mission of the Church according to the Fourth Gospel is essentially the same as that in the Pauline statement and in the Apocalypse.[31] All mankind is to find its unity in the divinely given message of reconciliation. The message is of a divine purpose expressed in the creation of the world, for all things were made through Christ, the Logos, 'and without him was not anything made that hath been made'. So in Paul it was God's good purpose to sum up or gather together all things in Christ, whether things in the heavens or things upon the earth. In the Apocalypse the goal of all created things is to join in the chant of praise to the Lamb upon the throne. The Church may therefore proceed in confidence to its appointed task to proclaim in word, and manifest in life, the revealed purpose of God. The ultimate forces of the universe are on its side.

---

[29] xvii. 21–2.
[30] cf. Stauffer, art. ἀγάπη, *Theol. Wörterbuch*, i. 53–4.
[31] Col. i. 20; Eph. i. 9–10; Rev. v. 9–13.

Part Four

Conclusion

The unanimity of the various types of teaching in the New Testament with regard to the nature of the Church is extraordinarily impressive. We have seen how writers so diverse as Paul, the authors of First Peter, Hebrews, the Apocalypse, and the Fourth Gospel, all agree on the characteristic marks of the Ecclesia. They are not describing an invisible Church. They are thinking all the time of one society on earth which is grouped in various local communities. They are well aware of the disparity between their ideals for the Church, and the actual state of the primitive Christian communities. Indeed, they only write because they are all called to some kind of pastoral responsibility, and because the Word of God lays hold of them with a divine constraint to discharge their debt to the communities which they love. Nevertheless, they all know what the Ecclesia on earth is called to be in the purpose of God.

1. It is God's own creation. It is not described as a certain number of individuals who have formed themselves into an association for a common purpose. Neither is it described as a number of local communities which have found themselves in being and suddenly decided to coalesce in one world-wide organization. The Ecclesia of God is the People of God, with a continu-

ous life which goes back through the history of Israel, through Prophets and martyrs of old, to the call of God to Abraham; it is traced back farther still to the purpose of God before the world began. The origin of the Ecclesia lies in the will of God. All that Israel had from God the Church has through Christ. A new era had been inaugurated by the Spirit as a result of the revelation of God in the whole work of Christ, in His earthly life, in His suffering on the Cross, in His resurrection from the dead. All who accepted this revelation through Christ as a divine message entered immediately into the New Israel, the one universal Ecclesia of God, which is manifest on the earth, inheritors of a glorious past, and destined to a still more glorious future in the heavenly city, the New Jerusalem which is the home of the saints.

This then is the first unanimous testimony of the New Testament writers. The Ecclesia is constituted not by anything that man has done or should do, but by what God has done.

2. In the second place, the Word of God which called the Church into being has been verified in human experience. The testimonies of the five writers whom we have cited concur in the one conviction that their descriptions have been already vindicated in the life of the Ecclesia. Thus Christians are already acting in the proud consciousness that they are the New Israel. Gentiles as well as Jews are appropriating the promises made by God through the prophets and seers of the past. Already the divinely given principle of fellowship in the Holy Spirit is being translated into the concrete life of the new community. The allegiance of Christians to Jesus as Lord and Christ has already been sealed by life and by death. The message of the Cross is being worked out as a new way of life. The process of claiming for Christ every activity of the Christian man, and redeeming every department of the corporate life of the world, has already begun in these early days. The universal mission of the reconciliation of all men to God through Christ, and therefore to one another, is already accepted by these five writers and the communities for which they speak. Already before any New Testament book has been written on the papyrus roll, the mission has won notable victories. We thus can join to the proclamation of the Word the testimony of human

experience. They set their seal to it that God is true, that the purpose of God for His Ecclesia has already, in part at least, been verified in their own case.[1] The Church, they know, has been constituted through the work of the Incarnate Word of God, by the sharing in the Spirit, the preaching of the Word, and the administration of the Sacraments.[2]

3. Thirdly, the principle of authority in the New Testament Church is closely – connected with the Word. The Apostles' teaching has authority because they were the original eye-witnesses and ministers of the Word,[3] because they were witnesses of the Resurrection,[4] because a chosen few among those who were sent forth to preach had enjoyed the incommunicable privilege of close personal intercourse with our Lord in His earthly life. Thus the principle of authority in the Ecclesia is firmly based on the divine revelation. In the Pauline writings we find that all the varied ministries are regarded as the divine gift to the Church, and are regarded as an integral part of its organic life. There is one emphasis in I Cor. xii and Romans xii, and another emphasis in Ephesians iv. In the first case the Church as the Body of Christ is the recipient of the fullness of the divine gift of the Spirit, and within the body various members are given particular functions. In Eph. iv., on the other hand, the ministries of apostle, prophet, evangelist, and teacher, are given by the glorified Lord to the Church for the building up of the Body of Christ. The emphasis here is on the gift of the ministry to the Church. But the two views are complementary. In I Corinthians and Romans the ministry is not created by the Church but by the Spirit whose divers gifts (*charismata*) mark out this man and that

---

[1] This conception of 'the appeal to experience' is, I think, essentially in harmony with that set out by A. R. Vidler, in the recent small but valuable book, *The Gospel of God and the Authority of the Church* (1937, by W. L. Knox and A. R. Vidler), 108–37. The one paragraph which I think misleading is on p. 130.

[2] cf. N. Micklem, *What is the Faith* (1936), 210.

[3] cf. Luke i. 1; Acts i. 22; ii. 42.

[4] *Supra*, pp. 172–3.

for special functions. In Ephesians, also, the one Body is the home of the One Spirit, and the gifts are possessed by the Church as a whole.[5]

Thus the authority of the ministry is regarded as given by Christ, the Head of the Church; the ministers exercise powers and functions which are inherent in the Church. But no one ministry is singled out as alone constituting the Ecclesia. When Paul describes the Church as built on the foundation of apostles and (Christian) prophets, he is clearly assigning the divine creation of the Church to the Word which apostles and prophets alike proclaimed. This is no mere theological principle, but an historical fact. The Ecclesia came into being through the preaching of the Word.

We may, therefore, hold with confidence to the view that, in the New Testament, order, important as it is to the organic life of the Ecclesia, is never equated with faith. The authority of the New Testament cannot be claimed for the view which would make Word and Sacrament contingent upon the office, rather than the office contingent on the Word.

It can hardly be denied that in the Epistles of Ignatius we see the emergence of another doctrine of the Ecclesia, which simply cannot be equated with the doctrine of the New Testament. 'Certainly nothing could exceed the majesty with which in St. Ignatius' thought the episcopal office is surrounded.'[6] If the presbyters are like the Apostles, the bishop is like God. 'The bishop is the centre of each individual Church, as Jesus Christ is the centre of the universal Church.'[7] There is no parallel claim in the New Testament for any office. No doubt the main interest of Ignatius is in the unity of the Church, and his conception of the ministry is not in the strictest sense of the word sacerdotal.[8]

---

[5] I am deeply indebted to Professor C. H. Dodd for the thought of this paragraph.

[6] K. D. Mackenzie, now Bishop of Brechin, *The Case for Episcopacy* (1929), 41.

[7] Lightfoot on *Smyrn.*, viii. The language of Ignatius is called 'hierarchical hyperbolism' by Father Sergius Bulgakoff, in *The Ministry and the Sacraments* (1937 ed., Dunkerley and Headlam), 113.

[8] Lightfoot, *The Christian Ministry*, 108.

Nevertheless, according to Ignatius, the Bishop has absolute power of disposal over the whole life of the members of the community.[9] The early judgement of Lightfoot, which he reaffirmed before he died, may still stand. 'It need hardly be remarked how subversive of the true spirit of Christianity, in the negation of individual freedom, and the consequent suppression of direct responsibility to God in Christ, is the crushing despotism with which this language, if taken literally, would invest the episcopal office.'[10]

It is open to any one to argue that the new view of the authority of the Ecclesia as concentrated in the Presbyters and Bishop, but especially in the Bishop, is a natural and legitimate development, or on the other hand to say, with Sohm, that this is a change not merely in the constitution of the Ecclesia, but in its faith.[11] The question cannot be debated here. But the doctrine is new. There is not a trace of the transmission of the power to rule despotically in the Christian literature of the first century.[12]

The principle of authority which may be gathered from the New Testament teaching, is as we have seen, of another order. It is founded on revelation and verified in the experience of the Church. But the question still remains why we should ourselves attach greater authority to that view of the Ecclesia and its ministry which we find in the New Testament than to any later view, whether of Ignatius, or Cyprian, or Thomas Aquinas himself. Is not the Church, the home of the Holy Spirit, a family with a developing life? Should not this unique life become richer as time goes on? Can we not therefore trace in the emergence even of the Ignatian theory another token of that rich life of the early Church, coming to flower, as it were, in a monarchical episcopacy?

The danger of the metaphor of growth in describing a society is apparent here. The emergence of the episcopal office may have

---

[9] Proof given by Gerke, in *The Ministry and the Sacraments* (1937), 363.

[10] Op. cit., 87–8.

[11] *Outlines of Church History* (E. tr. 1909), 39.

[12] cf. Anderson Scott, *Romanism and the Gospel* (1937), 219.

been due to other reasons than the guidance of the Spirit. Further, the question to-day is whether that development in the second century, by which episcopacy became universal, is to be regarded as a divine provision binding all parts of the universal Ecclesia for all time. The development of the Creed, and the gradual formation of the Canon, do not afford genuine parallels. The Creed may be traced in its main outline in the primitive *kerygma*. If the first-century Church had no accepted body of New Testament writings, they had already what was better, the actual eye-witnesses, the apostles and teachers who wrote the New Testament books, or whose testimony was the court of appeal for the writers. But monarchical episcopacy does not appear in the first-century evidence, even if something like it may possibly be traced in the ascendancy of James at Jerusalem.

Few would maintain to-day that the form of organization taken by the Apostolic Church should be determinative for the Church for all time. But the idea of the Ecclesia in the New Testament belongs to the realm of faith as well as to that of order. Is that idea to control the subsequent developments or to be controlled and revised by them? The communions which acknowledge 'the Divine revelation recorded in Holy Scripture as the supreme rule of faith and practice'[13] can have no doubt as to the answer. 'The Apostolic tradition should be the criterion of the subsequent tradition. This is not a mere Protestant provincialism.'[14] We should not simply bracket Holy Scripture and tradition as equally authoritative for the present life of the Church. Here I may quote, in support of the view put forward, an excellent paragraph from the recently published report on *Doctrine in the Church of England*.

Christians, as creatures of time and history, are not exempt from the necessity of giving definite shape to this life which they share in common; and they do so in forms which are at once correlated to

---

[13] So the Methodist Church; in its *Deed of Union*, paragraph 32. cf. the report, *Doctrine in the Church of England* (1938), 27–33, with the corollary on p. 113.

[14] From an unpublished paper read recently in Cambridge by Professor J. M. Creed.

their own past history and to present needs. Examples of such forms which have actually been developed are the formulation of the faith, the articulation of the ministry, and the liturgical structure of worship. Some such forms are essential for the perpetuation of the Christian society in the process of history, though at the same time no one particular system of such forms is to be taken as being of necessity constitutive of the fundamental idea of the Church. That idea, as has already been stated above, hinges essentially upon the unity of mankind as redeemed in Christ, and as in Him finding fellowship with the Father, and therefore also with one another.[15]

To-day there is stirring in the minds of men a strong discontent with the present broken communion of the Ecclesia, and a fresh hope of a clearer expression, in outward act and form, of its essential unity in Christ. That unity has not to be created by men. It is already there, and it is the gift of God. May it not be the next step towards the fulfilment of the cherished hope, for the great Christian communities which share in the Faith and Order Movement to make a venture in fellowship on the basis of the New Testament idea of the Ecclesia, to acknowledge one another gladly and frankly as within the one Ecclesia of God on earth, to refrain from any condemnation of the ministries and sacraments which are regarded by any modern Church as God's gift, and to join repeatedly, and as fully as may be, in united worship? The time is short; we are treading the path of understanding late in the day, and the shadows over Christendom lengthen ominously. But in the mercy of God we may not be too late. Already we are one in Christ. 'Since the Gospel brings victory over sin and death, God

---

[15] P. 106. The statement on p. 111 seems ambiguous and needs further explanation. 'The Church has been called apostolic primarily in that it preserves the essential tradition of the apostolic preaching and teaching, and maintains as a safeguard of that tradition a duly appointed order of ministers who derive their commission in historical succession from the original apostolate. The Church may also be called apostolic as being charged with the mission to bear witness to Christ and to declare His Gospel before the world.' But if this second sense of the word 'apostolic' is not primary, the conception of the Word of God as understood in the New Testament is not really honoured.

has knit together the whole family of the Church in heaven and on earth in the communion of saints, united in the fellowship of service, of prayer and of praise; and the Church on earth looks forward to the vision of God, the perfect consummation of its present fellowship in the life of heaven.'[16]

> Grant us, O Lord, to rejoice in beholding the bliss of Thy Jerusalem, and to be carried in her bosom with perpetual gladness; that as she is the home of the multitude of the Saints, we also may be counted worthy to have our portion within her; and that Thine Only-begotten Son, the Prince and Saviour of all, may in this world graciously relieve His afflicted, and hereafter in His kingdom be the everlasting Comfort of His redeemed.

---

[16] *The Nature of the Christian Church according to the Teaching of the Methodists*, 40, Affirmation 7.

Index of Subjects

[References to the prinicpal discussions of a subject are given in italic.]

Index of Proper Names

Index of New Testament References